Praise for *The War on Cops*

"Heather Mac Donald is an unsung hero in the transformation of New York into the safest large city in the United States. Her essays helped to lay out the rationale that gave me and my police commissioners guidance during the largest continuous reduction in crime ever accomplished in our city and nation. This book is a necessary read for anyone wondering what is happening in 'the capital of the world.'"

—The Honorable Rudolph Giuliani,
former mayor of New York City

"*The War on Cops* is an important and timely book. Mac Donald's clear-eyed analysis separates fact from fiction and provides keen insights into the politics at play and the consequences for law-enforcement officers and the communities they are sworn to protect."

—Ray Kelly, former commissioner
of the New York City Police Department

"If you have heard the rhetoric on all sides of the issues involving the police, and would like some facts to put that rhetoric to the test, there is no better source than *The War on Cops*. Whether you want facts about the explosive events in Ferguson, Missouri, or in Baltimore, or you want to know why murder rates in New York City fell sharply in the 1990s, this is the place to find solid information. If you want to understand the role of race in all this, that, too, is documented with data. This is a book that can save lives."

—Thomas Sowell, the Rose and Milton Friedman
Senior Fellow on Public Policy
at the Hoover Institution, Stanford University

"Heather Mac Donald has made an indispensable contribution to our public debates with her incisive and critical reporting on the thorny issues of race, crime, and policing in America's big cities. Time and again, I have found myself turning to her writings for guidance. While I do not always agree with what I find, I often do. Moreover, I am invariably edified.

All serious students of urban America today should read this book and reckon with its arguments."

"*The War on Cops* offers a perspective that supporters of law enforcement have long been waiting for. It is informed by street-level reporting, knowledge of real-world policing, and empirical research. Unlike many in academia and journalism, Mac Donald understands that assertive policing protects law-abiding poor—and often minority—citizens trapped in ghettos where violence and crime are unfortunately making a comeback."

THE WAR ON COPS

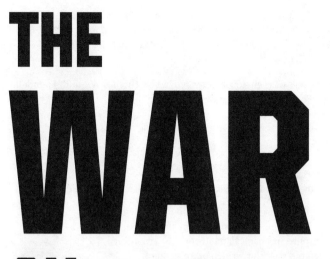

HOW THE NEW ATTACK ON LAW AND ORDER
MAKES EVERYONE LESS SAFE

HEATHER
MAC DONALD

ENCOUNTER BOOKS
New York • London

Versions of these chapters originally appeared in the following publications: *City Journal*, chap. 1, 2, 5–7, 15–22; The Marshall Project, chap. 13; *National Review*, chap. 3, 8; *New York Daily News*, chap. 16; *InsideSources*, chap. 12; *Wall Street Journal*, chap. 9–11, 16; *Weekly Standard*, chap. 4, 14.

Support for this book was generously provided by the Thomas W. Smith Foundation, the Arthur N. Rupe Foundation, and Randy P. Kendrick.

First American edition published in 2016 by Encounter Books, an activity of Encounter for Culture and Education, Inc., a nonprofit, tax exempt corporation.
Encounter Books website address: www.encounterbooks.com

Manufactured in the United States and printed on acid-free paper. The paper used in this publication meets the minimum requirements of ANSI/NISO Z39.48-1992 (R 1997) (*Permanence of Paper*).

First paperback edition published in 2017.
Paperback edition ISBN: 978-1-59403-968-3

THE LIBRARY OF CONGRESS HAS CATALOGUED
THE HARDCOVER EDITION AS FOLLOWS:
Names: Mac Donald, Heather, author.
Title: The war on cops : how the new attack on law and order makes everyone less safe / by Heather Mac Donald.
Description: New York : Encounter Books, [2016] | Includes bibliographical references and index.
Identifiers: LCCN 2016002500 (print) | LCCN 2016010780 (ebook) | ISBN 9781594038754 (hardcover : alk. paper) | ISBN 9781594038761 (Ebook)
Subjects: LCSH: Police—United States. | Police-community relations—United States. | Crime prevention—United States.
Classification: LCC HV8139 .M34 2016 (print) | LCC HV8139 (ebook) | DDC 363.20973—dc23
LC record available at http://lccn.loc.gov/2016002500

Interior page design and page composition by: BooksByBruce.com

CONTENTS

PART THREE
The Truth About Crime
119

PART FOUR
Incarceration and Its Critics
149

PREFACE TO THE PAPERBACK EDITION

Days after *The War on Cops* was first published in June 2016, five police officers in Dallas were assassinated by a killer inspired by Black Lives Matter ideology. Less than two weeks later, another three cops in Baton Rouge were murdered out of the same anti-cop hatred. This violence had no effect on the rhetoric coming out of the White House. At the memorial service for the slain Dallas officers, President Barack Obama returned to his familiar theme that policing was lethally biased against blacks. Black parents were right to fear that their child could be killed by a cop whenever he "walks out the door," the president said.

Chicago presented a test case for the president's claim. The city was in the midst of an epidemic of drive-by shootings, with one person shot every two hours. By the end of 2016, over 4,300 people would be shot, almost all of them black. Two dozen children under the age of twelve would be struck, including a three-year-old boy who is now paralyzed for life, and a ten-year-old boy whose pancreas, intestines, kidney, and spleen were torn apart. None of those child victims was shot by the police. In fact, the Chicago police shot only 0.5 percent of the shooting victims in the city in 2015, and virtually all of the twenty-one people shot by the police were armed and dangerous. Yet Chicago members of Black Lives Matter still chant: "CPD, KKK, how many children did you kill today?"

As 2016 wore on, the anti-cop movement and its high-placed political and media enablers remained impervious to all facts that contradicted their "policing is racist" narrative. They were also indifferent to the mounting loss of black lives. Officers in minority neighborhoods were backing off of proactive policing, under the constant refrain that such policing was racist. As a consequence, violence accelerated. I have called this combination of depolicing and rising crime the Ferguson Effect, after the fatal police shooting in Ferguson, Missouri, that sparked the Black Lives Matter movement. Chicago again exemplified the new reality on the streets. "I haven't seen this kind of hatred towards the police in my nineteen years on the force," a Chicago cop told me. "It's basically an undoable job now." Pedestrian stops and drug arrests in the Windy City dropped over 80 percent in 2016, homicides rose nearly 60 percent, and violence reached a level not seen in at least two decades. Carjackings, robberies, and shootings on the expressways are now spreading from the high-crime periphery into the city center.

Activists and criminologists have denied that violent crime is rising in many American cities and have scoffed at the idea that any such increase could be connected with depolicing. The data that have come out since *The War on Cops* was published last year, however, have only confirmed the Ferguson Effect. The FBI's final tally for reported homicides nationally in 2015 showed close to a 12 percent increase, the largest one-year homicide spike in almost half a century. Homicides rose by double digits across all size categories of cities, except for those under ten thousand in population, where homicides rose 7 percent. Cities with large black populations had the greatest homicide increases: 54 percent in Washington, D.C., 72 percent in Milwaukee, and 90 percent in Cleveland. An additional nine hundred black males were murdered in 2015 compared with 2014, bringing the black homicide toll in 2015 to over seven thousand—which is two thousand more than the number of white and Hispanic homicide victims combined.

Preliminary estimates show a 14 percent homicide increase in 2016 in the thirty largest U.S. cities and an 8 percent increase nationwide. The vast majority of officers polled by the Pew Research Center in summer 2016 said that officers in their department had become less likely to stop and question suspicious individuals and were less willing to use lawful force. Just how much less willing was demonstrated in Chicago in October 2016, when a black suspect beat a female police officer unconscious by banging her head repeatedly into the pavement and ripping out handfuls of her hair. She had refrained from using her gun for fear of being called a racist, she later said.

While the deadly violence was growing in 2016, four studies came out from the academy and from independent research groups rebutting the Black Lives Matter narrative. There was no bias against blacks in police shootings, the studies found; if anything, blacks were less likely to be shot than whites. Yet the Obama administration continued its pursuit of phantom police racism into its final week, when the Justice Department put the Baltimore police under federal control. That federal takeover was set in motion by the death of drug dealer Freddie Gray in 2015 following an arrest. In mid-2016, a black Maryland judge acquitted three of the six officers involved in the Freddie Gray incident of all criminal charges against them, leading the state's attorney, Marilyn Mosby, to drop the remaining three prosecutions. The Obama Justice Department, however, still maintained that Baltimore policing was discriminatory, thanks to the DOJ's usual practice of ignoring the fact that the vast majority of criminal victimization occurs in minority neighborhoods. The Washington attorneys deemed public-order enforcement in the city to be racially oppressive, and proceeded to virtually ban it in the Baltimore consent decree.

Arrests in Baltimore, especially drug arrests, have already dropped 45 percent since 2015; they will drop further under the new prohibitions. The per capita homicide rate in Baltimore in the first five months of 2017 was at the highest level in the city's history. In March 2017, a gang member retaliating for an earlier drive-by shooting threw two Molotov cocktails into a house, burning two teenagers to death and injuring two children and four other residents. Law-abiding residents of Baltimore's high-crime neighborhoods have been begging the police to restore order; under the strictures of the consent decree, their pleas will just have to wait.

A public backlash against the Black Lives Matter narrative helped fuel the improbable ascent of Donald Trump to the White House. In an inauspicious omen for the Hillary Clinton campaign, a Gallup poll taken in October 2016 found that support for the police—among minorities and whites alike—had surged to a high not seen since 1967, after falling to a twenty-two-year low in 2015. Alarm over the targeting of police officers contributed to that change in attitude: gun murders of officers rose 53 percent in 2016. Hillary Clinton, in an early Democratic presidential debate, had said it was "reality" that cops see black lives as cheap, and she continued to accuse the police of systemic racism throughout the campaign. Trump, by contrast, denounced the "false narrative" about the police and promised to restore law and order to American cities. He decried the growing loss of black life, and was promptly labeled a racist for doing so. During the campaign, President Obama dismissed Trump's warning about the rising urban death rate. Apparently, black lives don't matter so much when they are taken by a criminal.

The most important thing that a president can do now to restore law and order is to change the narrative about policing. The Justice Department should publicly recognize that policing today is data-driven: officers are deployed to where crime is highest. Under the new administration, the department is already subjecting the consent-decree process to a much-needed review. It should also declare that the federal government will no longer deem police bigoted for responding to community demands for order.

The campaign against the cops is a battle in a larger culture war, in which one camp seeks to redefine the American experience as the continual oppression of an ever-growing number of victim groups. Social norms, the legitimacy of authority, the rule of law—all are denigrated as the machinery of oppression, and the police are tarred as the most conspicuous embodiment of American injustice. In this climate, it was hardly surprising that *The War on Cops* would draw heat for subjecting the charges against the police to rational analysis, with some critics pronouncing the author a "fascist" and a "white supremacist." The attacks on the book have not refuted its factual argument, nor have the critics acknowledged the extra challenges that cops now confront as they strive to bring safety to all Americans, regardless of race.

INTRODUCTION

The Policing Revolution, Crime, and the Anti-Law-Enforcement Movement

As the most anti-law-enforcement administration in memory draws to a close, crime is shooting up in cities across the United States. Homicides in the country's 50 largest cities rose nearly 17 percent in 2015, the greatest surge in fatal violence in a quarter-century, reports the *Washington Post*. Milwaukee was experiencing its deadliest year in a decade. Homicides in Baltimore were at their highest per capita rate ever by mid-November—50 killings per 100,000 residents. "Crime is the worst I've ever seen it," said St. Louis alderman Joe Vaccaro at a City Hall hearing in May 2015. President Obama himself conceded that "gun violence and homicides have spiked—and in some cases they've spiked significantly."

The crime surge was especially troubling in that it reversed a two-decade-long decline, during which American cities vanquished a 1960s-era notion that had made urban life miserable for so many. Breaking the law, the thinking went, was but a symptom of social failure and governmental neglect, or even an understandable expression of protest. Until poverty and racism were eliminated, routine behaviors such as walking down a street, strolling through a park, or operating a store would necessarily remain fraught with fear and the possibility of violence. Under the influence of this "root causes" conceit, acres of city space were ceded to thieves and thugs, to hustlers and graffiti "artists." Disorder and decay became the urban norm.

A combination of forces eventually reversed this state of affairs. Starting in the late 1970s, legislators demanded that convicted criminals

1

serve more of their sentences; habitual felons were finally locked up for lengthy prison stays. And police leaders challenged the "root causes" concept with a countervailing idea: the police could actually prevent crime and, in so doing, would make civilized urban life possible again. This sea change in policing philosophy originated in New York in 1994 under Mayor Rudolph Giuliani, a former U.S. attorney who had campaigned on the promise to free the city from its growing squalor and anarchy. Giuliani's first police commissioner, William J. Bratton, was a champion of Broken Windows policing, which holds that allowing a neighborhood to become overrun by graffiti, litter, public drunkenness, and other forms of disorder breeds more crime by signaling that social control in the area has collapsed. Bratton had already shown the effectiveness of Broken Windows enforcement in New York's subways as transit police chief in the early 1990s; now he would have an entire city upon which to test the concept.

Bratton's deputy commissioners began rigorously analyzing crime data on a daily basis and ruthlessly holding precinct commanders accountable for the safety of their precincts. And they asked officers to stop and question individuals engaged in suspicious behavior—whether hanging out on a known drug corner at 1 AM or casing a jewelry store on a commercial strip plagued by burglaries.

Crime in New York City dropped 12 percent in Bratton's first year in office and 16 percent the next year, while crime rates in the rest of the country were virtually flat. The New York crime rout became national news, spurring other police departments to adopt similar data-intensive, proactive tactics. Over the next two decades, crime would fall 50 percent nationwide, revitalizing cities across the country. The biggest beneficiaries of that crime decline were the law-abiding residents of minority neighborhoods. Senior citizens could go out to shop without fear of getting mugged. Businesses moved in to formerly desolate areas. Children no longer had to sleep in bathtubs to avoid getting hit by stray bullets. And tens of thousands of individuals were spared premature death by homicide.

Now, that triumph over chaos and lawlessness is in jeopardy. Fueling the rise in crime in places like Baltimore and Milwaukee is a multipronged attack on law enforcement. Since late summer 2014, a protest movement known as Black Lives Matter has convulsed the nation. Triggered by a series of highly publicized deaths of black males at the hands of the police, the Black Lives Matter movement holds that police officers are the greatest threat facing young black men today. That belief has spawned riots, "die-ins," and the assassination of police officers. The movement's targets include Broken Windows policing and the practice of stopping and questioning suspicious individuals, both of which are said to harass blacks.

At the same time, a long-standing academic discourse about "mass incarceration" went mainstream. According to this theory, the American penal system practices "systematic imprisonment of whole groups." The nation's prison rate is allegedly a product of discrimination, and drug laws are purportedly a means of re-enslaving black Americans. President Obama repeatedly charged that the criminal-justice system treats blacks differently from whites.

In New York City, a trilogy of lawsuits challenged the NYPD's stop, question, and frisk tactics as racist; a federal judge ruled in favor of the plaintiffs by ignoring the incidence of crime in minority neighborhoods. A previously obscure politician, Bill de Blasio, ascended to City Hall two decades after Mayor Giuliani by campaigning against the NYPD and pledging to drop the city's appeal of the stop, question, and frisk decision.

As 2015 progressed, few law-enforcement practices escaped attack for allegedly imposing unjust burdens on blacks. But it was the virulent anti-cop rhetoric that was most consequential. Officers working in inner cities routinely found themselves surrounded by hostile, jeering crowds when they tried to make an arrest or conduct an investigation. Cops feared becoming the latest YouTube pariah when a viral cell-phone video showed them using force against a suspect who had been resisting arrest.

In response, the police began to disengage from proactive policing. Rather than getting out of their squad cars to question an individual who appeared to be hiding a gun, officers increasingly just drove on by, waiting for the next robbery or shooting to come over the police radio. Criminal summons and misdemeanor arrests for public-order offenses plummeted.

If the Black Lives Matter movement were correct, this falloff in discretionary policing should have been a boon to black lives. Instead, a bloodbath ensued, and its victims were virtually all black. When the cops back off, blacks pay the greatest price. That truth would have come as no surprise to the legions of inner-city residents who fervently support the police and whose voices are almost never heard in the media.

The Black Lives Matter narrative about racist law enforcement occurred in a vacuum; carefully excluded was any acknowledgment of inner-city crime and social breakdown. It was as if officers arbitrarily deployed more heavily in certain neighborhoods out of a sheer desire to oppress. In reality, the police were in those areas because—despite the record-breaking crime drop of the 1990s and 2000s—a culture of drive-by shootings and gang warfare persisted, largely due to the breakdown of the black family. That reality was assiduously kept offstage, leaving the focus exclusively on the alleged bias of the police.

This book challenges the premises of the growing crusade against law enforcement. In Part One, I rebut the founding myths of the Black Lives Matter movement—including the lie that a pacific Michael Brown was gunned down in cold blood by Officer Darren Wilson in Ferguson, Missouri, in August 2014. I document the hotly contested "Ferguson effect," a trend that I first spotted nationally, wherein officers desist from discretionary policing and criminals thus become emboldened. In Part Two, I outline the development of the misguided legal push to force the NYPD to give up its stop, question, and frisk tactic. In Part Three, I analyze criminogenic environments in Chicago and Philadelphia and put to rest the excuse that crime—black crime especially—is the result of poverty and inequality. Finally, in Part Four, I expose the deceptions of the mass-incarceration conceit and show that the disproportionate representation of blacks in prison is actually the result of violence, not racism.

However much the recent crime increase threatens the vitality of America's cities—and thousands of lives—it is not, in itself, the greatest danger in today's war on cops. The greatest danger lies, rather, in the delegitimation of law and order itself. Riots are returning to the urban landscape. Police officers are regularly pelted with bricks and water bottles during the course of their duties. Black criminals who have been told that the police are racist are more likely to resist arrest, requiring the arresting officer to use force and risk an even more violent encounter. If the present lies about law enforcement continue, civilized urban life may once again break down.

PART ONE

Burning Cities and the Ferguson Effect

The August 2014 police shooting of Michael Brown in Ferguson, Missouri, spawned a narrative as stubborn as it was false: Ferguson police officer Darren Wilson had allegedly shot the 18-year-old "gentle giant" in cold blood while the latter was pleading for his life, hands raised in surrender. After Brown's death, rioters torched and looted Ferguson businesses. The facts were that Brown, a budding criminal who weighed nearly 300 pounds, had punched Wilson in the face, tried to grab Wilson's gun, and charged at him, leading Wilson to fire in self-defense.

In the months that followed, the lie that Brown had died in a racially motivated police execution was amplified by the media, college presidents, and the left-wing political class. The newly formed Black Lives Matter movement promoted the notion that black American males were being hunted down and killed with impunity by renegade white police officers. Eric Garner, who had died after a forceful police takedown on Staten Island, New York, was added to the list of martyrs to racist police brutality.

Riots broke out in Ferguson for a second time in November 2014 when a grand jury declined to indict Wilson for Brown's death. Black

Lives Matter protests grew ever more virulent as a second myth took hold: that the American criminal-justice system is rigged against blacks. In December 2014, Ismaaiyl Abdullah Brinsley assassinated Officers Wenjian Liu and Rafael Ramos of the New York Police Department in retaliation for the deaths of Garner and Brown. Police actions in minority neighborhoods became increasingly tense; suspects and bystanders routinely challenged officers' lawful authority.

Slandered in the media and targeted on the streets, officers reverted to a model of purely reactive policing that had been out of vogue since the early 1990s. The inevitable result? Violent crime surged in city after city, as criminals began reasserting themselves—a phenomenon that I and others controversially described as the "Ferguson effect." President Barack Obama's FBI director, James Comey, confirmed the Ferguson effect in a speech at the University of Chicago Law School in October 2015. The rise in homicides and shootings in the nation's 50 largest cities was likely due to the "chill wind blowing through American law enforcement over the last year," he said, a wind that "is surely changing behavior." Sadly, the president himself contributed directly to that chill wind against the nation's police forces.

1

Obama's Ferguson Sellout

On November 24, 2014, President Obama betrayed the nation. Even as he went on national television to respond to the grand-jury decision not to indict Officer Darren Wilson for fatally shooting 18-year-old Michael Brown in Ferguson, Missouri, the looting and arson that had followed Brown's shooting in August were being reprised, destroying businesses and livelihoods over the next several hours. Obama had one job and one job only in his address that day: to defend the workings of the criminal-justice system and the rule of law. Instead, he turned his talk into a primer on police racism and criminal-justice bias. In so doing, he perverted his role as the leader of all Americans and as the country's most visible symbol of the primacy of the law.

Obama gestured wanly toward the need to respect the grand jury's decision and to protest peacefully. "We are a nation built on the rule of law. And so we need to accept that this decision was the grand jury's to make," he said. But his tone of voice and body language unmistakably conveyed his disagreement, if not disgust, with that decision. "There are Americans who are deeply disappointed, even angry. It's an understandable reaction," he said.

Understandable, so long as one ignores the evidence presented to the grand jury. The testimony of a half-dozen black observers at the scene had demolished the early incendiary reports that Wilson attacked Brown in cold blood and shot Brown in the back when his hands were up. Those early witnesses who had claimed gratuitous brutality on Wilson's part contradicted themselves and were, in turn, contradicted by the physical evidence and by other witnesses, who corroborated Wilson's testimony that Brown had attacked him and had tried to grab his gun. (Minutes before, the hefty Brown had thuggishly robbed a diminutive shopkeeper of a box of cigarillos; Wilson had received a report of that robbery and a description of Brown before stopping him.) Obama should have briefly reiterated the grounds for not indicting Wilson and applauded the decision as the product of a scrupulously thorough and fair process. He should have praised the jurors for their service and courage in following the evidence where it led them. And he should have concluded by noting that there is no fairer criminal-justice system in the world than the one we have in the United States.

Instead, Obama reprimanded local police officers in advance for an expected overreaction to the protests: "I also appeal to the law-enforcement officials in Ferguson and the region to show care and restraint in managing peaceful protests that may occur. . . . They need to work with the community, not against the community, to distinguish the handful of people who may use the grand jury's decision as an excuse for violence . . . from the vast majority who just want their voices heard around legitimate issues in terms of how communities and law enforcement interact."

Such skepticism about the ability of the police to maintain the peace appropriately was unwarranted at the time and even more so in retrospect; the forces of law and order didn't fire a single shot. Nor did they inflict injury, despite having been fired at themselves. Missouri's governor, Jay Nixon, was under attack for days for having authorized a potential mobilization of the National Guard—as if the August rioting didn't more than justify such a precaution. Any small-business owner facing another wave of violence would have been desperate for such protection and more. Though Nixon didn't actually call up the Guard, his prophylactic declaration of a state of emergency proved prescient.

Obama left no doubt that he believed the narrative of the mainstream media and race activists about Ferguson. That narrative held that the shooting of Brown was a symbol of nationwide police misbehavior and that the August riots were an "understandable" reaction to widespread societal injustice. "The situation in Ferguson speaks to broader challenges that we still face as a nation. The fact is, in too many parts of this country, a deep distrust exists between law enforcement and communities of color." This distrust was justified, in Obama's view. He reinvoked the "diversity" bromide about the racial composition of police forces, implying that white officers cannot fairly police black communities. Yet some of the most criticized law-enforcement bodies in recent years have, in fact, been majority black.

"We have made enormous progress in race relations," Obama conceded. "But what is also true is that there are still problems, and communities of color aren't just making these problems up. . . . The law too often feels like it's being applied in a discriminatory fashion. . . . [T]hese are real issues. And we have to lift them up and not deny them or try to tamp them down."

To claim that the laws are applied in a discriminatory fashion was a calumny, unsupported by evidence. For the president of the United States to put his imprimatur on such propaganda was bad enough; to do so following a verdict in so incendiary a case was grossly irresponsible. But such partiality followed the pattern of this administration in Ferguson and elsewhere, with Attorney General Eric Holder prematurely declaring the Ferguson police force in need of wholesale change and President Obama invoking Ferguson at the United Nations as a manifestation of America's ethnic strife.

The wanton destruction that followed the grand jury's decision was overdetermined. For weeks, the press had been salivating at the potential for black violence. The *New York Times* ran several stories a day, most on the front page, about such a prospect. Media coverage of racial tension portrayed black violence as customary, and riots as virtually a black entitlement.

The press dusted off hoary tropes about police stops and racism, echoing the anti-law-enforcement agitation and the crusade against "racial profiling" of the 1990s. The *New York Times* selected various features of Ferguson almost at random and declared them racist, simply by virtue of their being associated with the city where Michael Brown was killed (a theme that Chapter 2 examines further). A similar conceit emerged regarding the grand-jury investigation: innocent or admirable aspects of the prosecutor's management of the case, such as the quantity of evidence presented, were blasted as the product of a flawed or deliberately tainted process—so desperate were the activists to discredit the grand jury's decision.

This kind of misinformation about the criminal-justice system and the police can only increase hatred of the police. That hatred, in turn, will heighten the chances of more Michael Browns attacking officers and getting shot themselves. Police officers in the tensest areas may hold off from assertive policing. Such de-policing will leave thousands of law-abiding minority residents who fervently support the police ever more vulnerable to thugs.

Obama couldn't have stopped the violence in Ferguson with his address to the nation. But in casting his lot with those who speciously impugn our criminal-justice system, he increased the likelihood of more such violence in the future.

2

Ferguson's Unasked Questions

Press reports on the Ferguson "unrest," as the media prefer to call such violence, quickly began to reveal an operative formula: select some aspect of the city's political or civic culture; declare it racist by virtue of its association with Ferguson; disregard alternative explanations for the phenomenon; blame it for the riots. Bonus move: generalize to other cities with similar "problems." By this process, the media could easily reach predetermined conclusions.

For example: Ferguson's population is two-thirds black, but five of its six city council members are white, as is its mayor. Conclusion: this racial composition must be the product of racism. Never mind that blacks barely turn out to vote and that they field practically no candidates. Never mind that the mayor ran for a second term unopposed. Is there a record of Ferguson's supposed white power structure suppressing the black vote? None has been alleged. Did the rioters even know who their mayor and city council representatives were? The press didn't bother to ask. It only saw an example of what was imagined to be a disturbingly widespread problem. In a front-page story complete with a sophisticated scatter-graph visual aid, the *New York Times* summed up the problem: "Mostly Black Cities, Mostly White City Halls."

Another example: Ferguson issues fines for traffic violations, and 20 percent of its municipal budget comes from such receipts. If people with outstanding fines or summonses don't appear in court, a warrant for their arrest is issued. Conclusion: this is a racist system. The city is deliberately financing its operations on the backs of the black poor. The only reason that blacks are subject to fines and warrants, according to the media, is that they are being hounded by a racist police force. "A mostly white police force has targeted blacks for a disproportionate number of stops and searches," declared *Time* (September 1). What was the evidence for such "targeting"? *Time* provided none. Might blacks be getting traffic fines for the same reason that whites get traffic fines—because they broke the law? The possibility was not considered.

The most frequently summonsed traffic offense is driving without insurance, according to an "exposé" of Ferguson's traffic-fine system by the *New York Times*. Perhaps the paper's editors would be blasé about being hit by an uninsured driver, but most drivers would be grateful that the insurance requirement is being enforced. Might poor blacks have a higher rate of driving without insurance than other drivers? Not relevant to know, apparently.

The next highest categories of driving infraction are blasting loud music out your car and driving with tinted windows. If you attend police-and-community meetings in poor areas, you will regularly hear complaints about cars with deafening sound systems. Should the police ignore such complaints? Are they ignoring similar complaints in white areas because they want to give whites a pass? Do Ferguson's white and black drivers blast loud music from their cars at the same rate? We never learn. Tinted windows pose a possibly lethal threat to the police during traffic stops, since they prevent officers from assessing the situation inside the car before approaching. Ignoring this infraction puts officers' lives at risk. Should the police nevertheless do so? Such is the implication, if doing so would mean fewer fines for black motorists. The *New York Times* quotes a victim of the "racist" Ferguson traffic-enforcement system who was fined for driving without a license. Why was his license suspended? Was he driving drunk? Did he hit someone? We will never know. What is the crime rate in the black areas of Ferguson? That is also something that the mainstream press is not interested in finding out.

The most ubiquitous "Ferguson is racist" meme was that the city's police force is too white. Four of Ferguson's 53 officers are black. This imbalance, it was suggested, must be the result of racism and must itself cause racist enforcement activity. How many qualified black applicants have been rejected after applying to join the Ferguson police force? Not an interesting question, evidently.

The "too-white police force" meme, which the *New York Times* generalized into another front-page article ("Mostly White Forces in Mostly Black Towns," September 10), complete with another impressive set of graphs, is of particular interest in light of the federal government's investigation of New York City's sprawling Rikers Island jail complex. In August 2014, the U.S. attorney for the Southern District of New York issued a report denouncing the "deep-seated culture of violence" among Rikers corrections officers toward adolescent inmates. He accused guards of handcuffing juvenile inmates to gurneys and beating them. Rikers had been bedeviled by such claims of officer abuse of inmates for years, but the resulting problem for the "abusive white cops" meme is that the Rikers officer force is about two-thirds black. (New York's population is 23 percent black, but no one has complained about the racial imbalance among Rikers guards.)

Also in August, the Detroit Police Department emerged from 11 years of federal oversight for alleged abuse of civilians, including a pattern of unjustified shootings. The Detroit force, too, is about two-thirds black. In 2012, after a two-year investigation for a pattern of civil rights violations, the U.S. Justice Department imposed on the New Orleans Police Department an exceptionally expansive consent decree—a nominally consensual agreement overseen by a court—to try to rein in the alleged unconstitutional behavior of its officers, the majority of whom are black.

Now perhaps these civil rights allegations against these majority black forces are trumped up. But if so, perhaps similar allegations against majority white forces are, too. Or maybe the race of officers has little to do with whether they can police fairly.

As the grand jury was deliberating over whether to charge Darren Wilson with murder for shooting Michael Brown, cops were being shot at in and around Ferguson. Authorities hastily discounted any connection with the ongoing protests. Death threats against police officers multiplied. Even after the grand jury found insufficient grounds to indict Officer Wilson, the media kept flogging a story that was driven by facile, and ultimately dangerous, preconceptions.

3

Finding Meaning in Ferguson

Shortly after President Obama's speech on the grand-jury decision, the *New York Times* officially pronounced on the "meaning of the Ferguson riots." A more perfect example of what the late Daniel Patrick Moynihan called "defining deviancy down" would be hard to find. The *Times*' editorial encapsulated the elite narrative around the shooting of Michael Brown and the mayhem that twice followed it.

The *Times* could not bring itself to say one word of condemnation against the savages who self-indulgently destroyed the livelihoods of struggling entrepreneurs and their employees in Ferguson, Missouri. The real culprit behind the riots, in the *Times*' view, was not the actual arsonists and looters; it was Robert McCulloch, the county prosecutor who presented the shooting of Brown by Officer Darren Wilson to a St. Louis County grand jury. After hearing three months of testimony, the grand jury decided not to bring criminal charges against Wilson. The *Times* recited a now-familiar litany of McCulloch's alleged improprieties, turning the virtues of this grand jury—such as its methodical thoroughness—into flaws. If the jurors had indicted Wilson, none of the riot apologists would have complained about the length of the process or the range of evidence presented.

To be sure, most grand-jury proceedings are pro forma and brief because the evidence of the defendant's guilt is so overwhelming. Here, however, McCulloch faced a dilemma. His own review of the case would have shown the unlikelihood of a conviction. Physical evidence discredited the initial inflammatory claims about Wilson attacking Brown and shooting him in the back, and Missouri law accords wide deference to police officers who use deadly force against a dangerous suspect. Not initiating any formal criminal inquiry against Wilson was politically untenable, however, especially since the eyewitness accounts that corroborated Wilson's version of events would have remained unknown. (Not surprisingly, the six black witnesses who supported Wilson's story did not go to the press or social media, unlike the witnesses who spread the early lies about Wilson's behavior.) So McCulloch used the grand-jury proceeding as a way to get the entire dossier about the case into the public domain by bringing a broad range of evidence before the grand jury and then releasing it to the public after the proceeding ended—a legal arrangement.

In its editorial, the *Times* is silent about that evidence. Blood and DNA traces demonstrated that Brown had initiated the altercation by attacking Wilson while the officer was inside his car. Brown then tried to grab Wilson's gun—presumably, to shoot him. Such an assault on a law-enforcement officer is nearly as corrosive to the rule of law and a stable society as rioting. But to the mainstream media, it is apparently simply normal behavior not worth mentioning when a black teenager attacks a cop, just as it was apparently normal and beneath notice that Brown had strong-armed a box of cigarillos from a shopkeeper moments before Wilson accosted him for walking in the middle of the street. Amazingly, anyone who brought up that earlier, videotaped felony was accused of besmirching Brown's character, even though the robbery was highly relevant to the encounter that followed (and showed that Brown did not have much character to besmirch in the first place, something his sealed juvenile records would likely have confirmed).

Even if we ignore the exculpatory evidence, it is absurd to blame the riots, as the *Times* does, on McCulloch's management of the grand jury or the way he announced the verdict. There would have been rioting if the grand-jury proceeding had lasted only a day so long as it failed to indict Wilson for murder. It is unlikely that the rioters even listened to, much less carefully parsed, McCulloch's post-verdict press conference, which the *Times* finds biased. No evidence suggests that the grand jury's decision not to indict resulted from unprofessional behavior on McCulloch's part or from prejudice that somehow infected the proceedings.

The *Times* then goes into blazing hyperbole about the reign of terror inflicted "daily" on blacks by the police in Ferguson and nationally. The *Times* coyly cites "news accounts"—i.e., its own—claiming that the police in Ferguson "systematically target poor and minority citizens for street and traffic stops—partly to generate fines." The *Times* has no evidence of such systematic targeting, proof of which would require determining the rate at which blacks and whites violate traffic and other laws and then comparing those rates with their stop rates. Studies elsewhere have shown that blacks speed at higher rates than whites. Blacks likely also have lower rates of car registration and vehicle upkeep, for economic reasons. Moreover, if authorities are using traffic fines to generate revenue, they would presumably "target" the people most likely to be able to pay those fines, not the poorest residents of an area.

Even more fantastically, the *Times* claims that "the killing of young black men by police is a common feature of African-American life and a source of dread for black parents from coast to coast." A "common feature"? This is pure hysteria, likely penned by *Times* columnist Charles Blow. The public could perhaps be forgiven for believing that "the killing of young black men by police is a common feature of African-American life," given the media frenzy that follows every such police killing, rare as they are, compared with the silence that greets the daily homicides committed by blacks against other blacks.

The *Washington Post* found press documentation of 258 black victims of fatal police shootings in 2015, most of whom were seriously attacking the officer. In 2014, the most recent year for which such data are available, there were 6,095 black homicide victims in the United States, which means that the police could eliminate all of their own fatal shootings without having a significant impact on the black homicide death rate. The killers of those black homicide victims are overwhelmingly other blacks—who are responsible for a death risk ten times that of whites in urban areas.

The *Times* trotted out the misleading statistic published by ProPublica in October 2014 that young black males are 21 times more likely to be shot dead by police than are young white males—a calculation that overlooks the fact that young black men commit homicide at nearly ten times the rate of young white and Hispanic males combined.‡ That astronomically higher homicide-commission rate means that police officers are going to be sent to fight crime disproportionately in black neighborhoods, where they will more likely encounter armed shooting suspects. If the black crime rate were the same as the white crime rate, the victims of police shootings would most certainly also be equal among the races. Asians are minorities, which, according to the *Times'* ideology, should make them the target of police brutality. But they barely show up in police-shooting data because their crime rates are so low.

For the period 2005–09, a significant portion of victims in the ProPublica study—62 percent—were resisting arrest or assaulting an officer, as Michael Brown did. The cop-hatred that activists and press organs like the *Times* do their best to foment significantly increases the chances of such aggressive and dangerous behavior.

The *Times* serves up a good example of anti-cop propaganda when it confidently states that "many police officers see black men as expendable figures on the urban landscape, not quite human beings." That would be news to the thousands of police officers who are the *only* people willing to put their lives on the line to protect innocent blacks from predation. Until editors and reporters from the *Times* start patrolling dark stairwells in housing projects and running toward gang gunfire, their superior concern for black men will lack credibility.

Without question, there are plenty of officers who treat civilians rudely and who desperately need retraining in professional courtesy. Officers have a duty to respect the public, even if having trash thrown at you from roofs or being cursed at and blocked in your pursuit of suspects does not conduce to a cheerful attitude on the streets. But the police are not on those streets out of malice. It is black crime—and the need of law-abiding black residents to be protected from it—that drives police presence and activity in black neighborhoods.

The Ferguson episode has starkly revealed several key, and sometimes contradictory, elements of the elite liberal mind-set. The elites are in deep denial about black underclass behavior. Ezra Klein, for example, was

---

‡ ProPublica, moreover, chose for its analysis a three-year period whose ratio of black to white deaths was twice as high as the historical norm, as noted by Peter Moskos, a professor at John Jay College of Criminal Justice.

dumbfounded that Michael Brown would have refused to move from the middle of the street or cursed at or attacked an officer. (Klein has clearly not spent much time in central Brooklyn.) Liberal elites seem to believe that black crime is no higher than white crime, and therefore they assume that law-enforcement activity, if unbiased, would be equally distributed between white and black neighborhoods. At the same time, they have so lowered their expectations for black behavior that they accept criminality as normal. Stealing from a store clerk or assaulting an officer is now considered beneath mention. Black rioting is deemed understandable when, as in Ferguson, the police are "justifiably seen as an alien, occupying force that is synonymous with state-sponsored abuse," in the words of the *New York Times*.

Plenty of blacks reject such condescension and excuse-making. A corporate executive in Atlanta observed to me after the riots: "Michael Brown may have been shot by the cop, but he was killed by parents and a community that produced such a thug." The blight in Ferguson may well be "incurable," the executive wrote me in an email, but at the very least, "we should mount a campaign to hire ALL of the White cops out of the city/county and see how THEM cow chips come to smell." Such views almost never find their way into the mainstream media.

The *Times'* most influential readers often know even less about policing and crime than its editorialists, and they use the paper as an authoritative source of information about such matters. This transmission belt of ignorance ineluctably spreads into policy as well as culture. We have entered an era of intense antipolice activism, led by the federal government in conjunction with agitators like Al Sharpton. The Justice Department has imposed a costly and unnecessary consent decree on the Ferguson Police Department and ratcheted up pressure on other departments to equalize their law-enforcement activity between black and white neighborhoods, regardless of crime disparities. President Obama has disseminated the dangerous lie that the criminal-justice system treats whites differently from blacks. The Ferguson authorities have rewarded the rioters by promising new programs and incentives to diversify the town's allegedly too-white police force. Such anti-law-enforcement activism puts the public-safety triumph of the last two decades at risk. The unprecedented crime decline over that period was the product of data-driven, proactive policing and stricter incarceration practices, themselves under attack as well. Officers facing the risk of specious "racial profiling" charges are likely to back off from proactive policing—a reality that will be examined in later chapters.

The nation hurriedly turned away from the orgy of hatred, destruction, and entitlement that incinerated Ferguson, even as protesters, wedded to the myth of an innocent teenager's unprovoked martyrdom, continued to indulge in sporadic violence across the country. But before the riots are shelved under the "too uncomfortable to confront" category, it is well to remember that such mass destruction threatens civilization itself by exposing the rule of law as powerless to check hate-driven anarchy. And the only people responsible for such an inferno are the perpetrators themselves.

4

Justice Is Blind

Eight months after the shooting of Michael Brown, the Justice Department released its official report on the incident, in March 2015. The report shredded the incendiary story that had fueled the riots in Ferguson, Missouri—that a teenaged "gentle giant" was gunned down by a trigger-happy cop who feared black people—and made it clear why the department would not be bringing civil rights charges against Officer Darren Wilson. Among those who were clearly not happy with this outcome was Eric Holder, the attorney general.

Holder had already commissioned a second report on the allegedly racist Ferguson police force to counter his own agency's expected demolition of the martyr narrative. But for good measure, a few days before the Brown report was to be released, Holder provided the press with another mechanism for sidelining its findings. Holder wanted to lower the standard of proof in civil rights cases, he told *Politico*. The subtext of this announcement: the decision not to pursue civil rights charges against Wilson was forced on the Justice Department by an overly stringent evidentiary standard; under a more realistic standard, Wilson would have been prosecuted.

Voilà! The media had their angle. "The Justice Department announced on Wednesday that its investigation did not support federal civil rights charges against Darren Wilson," the *New York Times* acknowledged morosely in an editorial, before immediately turning to the good news: "Still, the department found overwhelming evidence of entrenched racism in Ferguson's police force." The *Times'* understatement of the findings on the Brown shooting was echoed in the *Huffington Post,* which said that the Justice Department had decided "not to file federal charges against Wilson for fatally shooting Brown last July."

The investigation "did not support" the charges? The DOJ decided "not to file charges"? This phrasing massively misrepresents the content of the report on the shooting. It was not a question of evidence "not supporting" high-threshold civil rights charges; it was a question of evidence *eviscerating* virtually every aspect of the pro-Brown, anti-Wilson narrative. Under no imaginable standard of proof could Wilson be found guilty of civil rights violations—or, for that matter, murder. As the report states: "Multiple credible witnesses corroborate virtually every material aspect of Wilson's account and are consistent with the physical evidence." Those "material aspects" include Wilson's testimony that Brown punched and grabbed him while Wilson was in his SUV, that Brown tried to seize his gun, and that Brown charged at Wilson after Wilson had exited his car.

Wilson had first seen Brown walking in the middle of Canfield Drive with another young man. Wilson saw boxes of cigarillos in Brown's hands and suspected that Brown was the thief who was reported to have robbed a convenience store and roughed up its owner a few minutes earlier. Wilson asked Brown to move to the sidewalk. Brown responded: "F— what you have to say." Wilson called for backup and then tried to block Brown from proceeding. At that point, Brown reached into Wilson's car and started pounding him and grabbing for his gun. Wilson fired, and Brown ran off. Wilson gave chase on foot. Brown then turned and charged toward Wilson. At no point did Wilson fire at Brown when Brown's back was turned or when he was on the ground.

As for the now-iconic "Hands up, don't shoot" claim, the DOJ report is withering: "There are no credible witness accounts that state that Brown was clearly attempting to surrender when Wilson shot him. As detailed throughout this report, those witnesses who say so have given accounts that could not be relied upon in a prosecution because they are irreconcilable with the physical evidence, inconsistent with the credible accounts of other eyewitnesses, inconsistent with the witness's own prior statements, or in some instances, because the witnesses have acknowledged that their initial accounts were untrue."

In other words, no prosecutor with any understanding of his professional duties would think of going forward with this case, since there is *no* evidence to support it. This is not a standard-of-proof issue; it is an absence-of-any-case-whatsoever issue.

The report also explains why Brown's body lay on the ground for four hours after he was killed, before being taken away by an ambulance—another plank in the "Black Lives Matter" indictment of the allegedly racist treatment of Brown. The reason for the delay is that detectives' efforts to process the crime scene were continuously interrupted by protesters who were encroaching on their work, chanting, "Kill these motherf—ers" and "Kill the police." What sounded like automatic gunfire was reported in the area, resulting in further suspension of activity until more backup arrived.

The initial news stories on the Brown killing contained several key elements of Wilson's self-defense, which the Justice report would vindicate, but they were immediately purged from the dominant narrative. They resurfaced periodically: a caller to a local radio show in mid-August, for example, reiterated the essential facts; in October, the *St. Louis Post-Dispatch* reported that the autopsy and several witnesses corroborated Wilson's account of the encounter. (A San Francisco pathologist who had seconded the autopsy conclusions for the *Post-Dispatch* story recanted a day later, after coming under attack for her initial assessment.) None of this had the slightest effect on the anti-Wilson juggernaut.

Eyewitnesses who corroborated Wilson's account were intimidated away from cooperating with the police. The Canfield Green neighborhood, where the shooting occurred, was plastered with SNITCHES GET STITCHES signs. A 74-year-old black male who believed that the shooting was justified had told a friend two days after the incident that he "would have f—ing shot that boy, too." He refused to give formal statements to county or federal authorities, however. He would rather go to jail than testify before the grand jury, he said, so enormous was the community pressure to support a "hands up" surrender narrative. A 53-year-old black male called a police tip line after seeing Brown's companion lie about the incident on national television. He, too, stated that the shooting was justified, but told authorities that he would deny everything if his phone call were traced. He was served with a grand-jury subpoena but refused to honor it. A 27-year-old biracial male said that it appeared to him that Wilson's life was in jeopardy, describing Brown as a "threat" moving at a "full charge." At the scene, as angry crowds were gathering and collecting false narratives about the shooting, two black women asked him to recount what he had seen into their cell phones. When he told them that they would not like what he had to say, they called him a "white motherf—er" and other racial slurs. A 31-year-old black female initially told investigators that she had seen Wilson fire shots into Brown's back as he lay dead in the street. When challenged with the autopsy findings that revealed no shots to the back, she confessed to making up her story. "You've gotta live the life to know it," she said. In fact, she then admitted, it looked like Wilson's life was in danger as Brown was charging him. When authorities tried to serve her with a subpoena, however, she blocked her door with a couch.

In short, a reign of terror against witnesses had served to sustain a false narrative. The exposure of the hoax should have demolished the antipolice movement, since its core conceit—that police officers are the biggest threat facing young black men today—was launched off a phony story. The idea that local district attorneys are incapable of prosecuting shootings by cops derived from the claim that the grand jury's failure to indict Officer Wilson represented a grotesque miscarriage of justice. It turns out that the only reason that the prosecutor, Robert McCulloch, took the case to the grand jury at all was political (as explained in Chapter 3). Under circumstances that were not so politically charged, the case would have been thrown out from the start. Yet there is now a dangerous campaign to create special prosecutors dedicated solely to indicting cops for using deadly force.

Meanwhile, true believers either rejected the Brown report entirely or adopted the "it could just as well have been true" apologetics that followed the discrediting of the gang-rape hoaxes at Duke University and the University of Virginia. Benjamin Crump, attorney for Brown's parents, complained on *Face the Nation* that the Justice Department was "sanitizing all these shootings of people of color who are unarmed." Crump invoked Holder's own complaints regarding the purportedly excessive standard of proof as grounds for dismissing the report. Democratic strategist Donna Brazile told the *New York Times*: "'Hands up, don't shoot' has become a larger symbol of the desire to prove one's innocence. In many ways, it will always resonate as a symbol of an unarmed dead teenager lying for hours on the street." Never mind that that symbol never happened. Racist cops gunning down innocent black men in cold blood is simply too good a story to retract. "Hands up, don't shoot" has lived on among diehard cop-haters.

• • •

The mainstream media quickly turned their full attention to the second Justice Department report, on Ferguson's police department, consigning the Brown examination to oblivion. The two reports were produced by different sections of the Justice Department's Civil Rights Division, and it shows. The report on Michael Brown, written by the Criminal Section in conjunction with the FBI and the U.S. attorney's office for the Eastern District of Missouri, displays a striking understanding of police work. It respects long-standing legal presumptions protecting police discretion from unjustified second-guessing. The report on the Ferguson Police Department came out of the Special Litigation Section, known for its hostility to the police and staffed almost exclusively by graduates of left-wing advocacy groups, as Hans von Spakovsky noted in *The National Interest*. No wonder it strains so hard to cobble together a case of systemic intentional discrimination out of data that show only that law enforcement has a disparate impact on blacks.

The most disturbing section of that second report consists of anecdotes about unconstitutional stops and arrests made by Ferguson police officers. These accounts portray rude, aggressive cops who abuse their authority and trash-talk to suspects. In a November 2013 incident, for example, an officer allegedly approaches five black young people listening to music in their car. He claims to have smelled marijuana and places them under arrest for gathering for the purpose of engaging in illegal activity. The officer allegedly finds no marijuana in the car but detains and charges them anyway, taking some teens home to their parents and delivering others to jail. In a summer 2012 stop, an officer accosts a man sitting in a car with illegally tinted windows. The officer groundlessly accuses the driver of being a pedophile—the car is next to a children's park—tells him not to use his cell phone, and orders him out of his car for a pat-down without reason to believe that he is armed. The driver refuses to allow the officer to search his car. The officer then points his gun at the suspect's head and arrests him for making a false declaration because the suspect initially gave his name as "Mike" rather than "Michael" and provided an address that differed from the one on his driver's license, among other charges.

If these incidents and others are true exactly as alleged, they suggest a police agency deplorably ignorant of the Fourth Amendment and grossly deficient in courtesy and respect. But are they true? And if so, do they represent normal procedure in the department? After the implosion of the Michael Brown martyr myth, accepting one-sided accounts of inter-actions between officers and civilians seems risky. In New York City, as a point of comparison, the Civilian Complaint Review Board, which hears complaints about the New York Police Department, substantiated only 7 percent of the complaints that it received in 2014. If the Justice Department's Special Litigation Section sought to corroborate its anec-dotes or get the department's version of the incidents, it is not letting on. Nor is it clear that these questionable arrests, even if reported accurately, represent standard procedure in the department, rather than aberrations. The report routinely uses the words "frequently" and "common" as sub-stitutes for an actual showing of established practice. One of the targets of an allegedly unconstitutional arrest is white, suggesting that the police are equal-opportunity offenders when they allegedly offend.

The report is more persuasive in describing the department's shoddy record-keeping and the lax oversight of beat cops. The failure to super-vise officers' use of force results in excessive resort to Tasers. Equally problematic is Ferguson's practice of issuing a quasi-warrant known as a "wanted" without the requisite probable cause to believe that the target has committed a crime. (Many other departments abuse "wanteds," too.) The municipal court, like the police department, is error-prone in its records and notice systems.

Had the Justice Department blasted Ferguson's management and training failures and left it at that, it would have been on solid footing. But the imperative to racialize the problems was overwhelming, espe-cially given Holder's previous statements against Ferguson and the sub-sequent discrediting of the Brown story. So the department trots out the usual statistical analyses with which to bootstrap a charge of "intentional discrimination" against blacks. And these statistical analyses are irredeemably deficient.

The Justice attorneys use population data as the benchmark for police activity, rather than rates of lawbreaking. The most frequently quoted statistic from the report is that blacks constitute 67 percent of Ferguson residents but made up 85 percent of all vehicle stops between 2012 and 2014. Whites made up 15 percent of all traffic stops during that period, but 29 percent of the population. Such figures are meaningless unless we know, just for starters, what the rate of traffic violations is among black and white drivers. Though most criminologists are terrified of studying that matter, the research that has been done, in New Jersey and North Carolina, found that black drivers speed disproportionately. On the New Jersey Turnpike, for example, black drivers studied in 2001 sped at twice the rate of white drivers (with speeding defined as traveling at 15 mph or more above the posted limit) and traveled at the most reckless levels of speed even more disproportionately. Moreover, low-income car owners are less likely to update their vehicle registration and maintain required equipment. Are black drivers in Ferguson more likely to be poor? The *New York Times* itself says that "economic chasms" separate black and white neighborhoods there.

A proper traffic-stop study would also determine the demographics of the population on the roadways, which often differ radically from the surrounding residential areas and which change over the course of a day and week. The Special Litigation Section attempted none of this.

The report also seized on the fact that blacks made up 93 percent of arrests by Ferguson police officers. It is unclear whether "arrests" here refers to arrests following a traffic stop or arrests for all types of crime throughout the entire city. Assuming the latter, this figure, too, is meaningless without knowing the black and white crime rates. Blacks made up 60.5 percent of all murder arrests in Missouri in 2012 and 58 percent of all robbery arrests, though they are less than 12 percent of the state's population. Such vast disparities are found in every city and state in the country; there is no reason to think that Ferguson is any different. (The voicemail box of the Ferguson Police Department's press office was full and not accepting messages when I tried to find out.) New York City is typical: blacks are only 23 percent of the population but commit over

75 percent of all shootings in the city, as reported by the victims of and witnesses to those shootings; whites commit under 2 percent of all shootings, according to victims and witnesses, though they are 33 percent of the city's population. Blacks commit 70 percent of all robberies; whites, 4 percent. The black-white crime disparity in New York would be even greater without New York's large Hispanic population. Black and Hispanic shootings together account for 98 percent of all illegal gunfire. Ferguson has only a 1 percent Hispanic population, so the contrast between the white and black shares of crime is starker there.

Holder's attorneys find damning the fact that 11 percent of black drivers were searched after a traffic stop from 2012 to 2014, but only 5 percent of white drivers were. Yet as the report itself notes, blacks are more likely to have outstanding warrants against them and are more likely to be arrested for an outstanding warrant. Given the higher rate of outstanding warrants, it is predictable that black drivers would be searched more often. Whites are slightly more likely to have contraband found on them after a search: 30 percent of searches of whites, but only 24 percent of searches of blacks, yielded contraband. The report says that this disparity exists "even after controlling for the type of search conducted, whether a search incident to arrest, a consent search, or a search predicated on reasonable suspicion," but the report does not reveal how much of a disparity persisted in each type of search: automatic searches incident to an arrest should not be used to measure alleged police bias. The analysis also does not take into account differences in driver behavior following a stop that could increase an officer's inclination to search. This minimal disparity in the contraband hit rate is the only piece of evidence in the report that could support a finding of disparate treatment, and it's negligible evidence at that.

The press has also highlighted the following data as further proof of Ferguson police racism: blacks make up 95 percent of Manner of Walking in Roadway charges; 94 percent of Failure to Comply charges; 92 percent of Resisting Arrest charges; 92 percent of Peace Disturbance charges; and 89 percent of Failure to Obey charges. Ironically, Ferguson's most famous resident displayed behavior that would plausibly fall under four of these five categories. A black couple driving on Canfield Drive minutes before the shooting had to swerve around Michael Brown and his friend, walking in the middle of the street, in order to avoid hitting them. "Why don't they just get on the sidewalk?" the wife exclaimed. Another bystander told the FBI that when Wilson asked Brown to move out of the street, Brown refused and responded to the effect: "F— the police." It is dubious that the black and white residents of Ferguson engage in such low-level lawlessness at identical rates, given widely documented differences in felony offending and the complaints about lawless street behavior that routinely emanate from inner-city communities. But even if the rates were identical, if officers are dispatched on 911 calls more frequently to Ferguson's "disconnected" apartment complexes (DOJ's term), they will witness more public-order offenses in that area of the city.

The Justice Department's evidence for "intentional discrimination" is even thinner than its statistical analyses. The agency criticizes city officials who used the term "personal responsibility" to explain law-enforcement disparities among "certain segments" of the community. The phrase is code for "negative stereotypes about African Americans," the federal lawyers believe. In reality, denouncing any invocation of "personal responsibility" as racist is itself code for liberal blindness to underclass culture.

DOJ's alleged smoking gun is half a dozen racist jokes emailed by two police supervisors and a court clerk. While juvenile and offensive, the emails are far from establishing that the police department's law-enforcement protocols are intentionally discriminatory.

Justice's final salvo against Ferguson is the charge that its officials view traffic and misdemeanor enforcement as a revenue generator for the city (a claim that the New York Times also asserted in its editorial on the grand-jury decision). A revisionist history of the riots, hastily cobbled together after the collapse of the Brown execution myth, holds that they were triggered by compounding traffic fines as much as by the shooting. But if Ferguson uses traffic violations for revenue, so do the majority of municipalities across the country. DOJ does not come close to showing that the reason that the city wants to raise money from enforcement is to discriminate against blacks.

To be sure, Ferguson's system of fees and warrants for failure to pay those fees or to show up in court—like identical systems throughout the country—needs reform to avoid any possibility of punishing people for being poor. Making community service more available for offenders who cannot afford their fines is a good idea. But if those offenders ditch their community assignments, the court system will be back to the same dilemma of how to induce their compliance. Hapless Ferguson officials used the taboo term "personal responsibility" to try to explain to their Washington investigators why some people face an escalating series of fines for repeated failures to attend their court hearings. DOJ attorneys were scandalized yet again. But this explanation is not unique to "racist" Ferguson. The black mayor of a neighboring town defended similar fees and enforcement methods under his own government. "Everyone is saying, 'Oh, no, that's cities just taking advantage of the poor,'" he told the *New York Times*. "When did the poor get the right to commit crimes?"

For the last 20 years, America's elites have talked feverishly about police racism in order to avoid talking about black crime. The Justice Department's second Ferguson report is just the latest example of that furious attempt to change the subject.

On March 11, 2015—only hours before two police officers were shot at protests in Ferguson, either targeted directly or the unintended casualties of a gang dispute—a six-year-old boy named Marcus Johnson was killed by a stray bullet in a St. Louis park. There have been no protests against his killer; Al Sharpton has not shown up to demand a federal investigation. Marcus is just one of the 6,000 black homicide victims a year (more than all white and Hispanic homicide victims combined) who receive virtually no attention because their killers are other black civilians.

Black males between the ages of 14 and 17 die from shootings at more than six times the rate of white and Hispanic male teens combined, thanks to a ten times higher rate of homicide committed by black teens. Until the black family is reconstituted, the best protection that the law-abiding residents of urban neighborhoods have is the police. They are the government agency most committed to the proposition that "black lives matter." The relentless effort to demonize the police for enforcing the law can only leave poor communities more vulnerable to anarchy.

5

De-Policing New York

One of the most effective remedies against urban anarchy over the past two decades is under attack. Proactive policing—also called Broken Windows policing—calls for the enforcement of low-level misdemeanor laws regulating public order. Manhattan Institute fellow George Kelling and Harvard professor James Q. Wilson first articulated the Broken Windows theory in 1982 as a means of quelling public fear of crime and restoring order to fraying communities. William Bratton embraced the thinking in his first tour as commissioner of the New York Police Department in the 1990s, with great benefit to public safety. Subsequently, police commanders across the country also adopted it. But in the summer of 2014, longtime critics of the NYPD seized on the death of Eric Garner while in police custody to call for an end to proactive policing.

Officers approached the 43-year-old Garner on July 17 in a high-crime area near the Staten Island Ferry Terminal and accused him of illegally selling untaxed cigarettes—the kind of misdemeanor that Broken Windows policing aims to curb. Garner had already been arrested more than 30 times, mostly for selling loose cigarettes but also for marijuana possession and other offenses. As captured in a cell-phone video, the 350-pound man loudly objected to the charge and broke free when an officer tried to handcuff him. The officer then put his arm around Garner's neck and pulled him to the ground. Garner repeatedly stated that he couldn't breathe, and then went eerily stiff and quiet. After a seemingly interminable time on the ground without assistance, Garner was finally put on a stretcher to be taken to an emergency room. He died of cardiac arrest before arriving at the hospital. Garner suffered from severe asthma and diabetes, among other ailments, which contributed to his heart attack.

Anger over Garner's death is understandable. No one should die for selling untaxed cigarettes or even for resisting arrest, though the officers certainly did not intend to kill Garner, and a takedown may be justified when a suspect resists. Protests initially centered on the officer's seeming use of a choke-hold, which is banned by NYPD policy. But critics of the NYPD expanded the campaign against the police to include misdemeanor enforcement itself. This is pure opportunism. There is no connection between the theory and practice of quality-of-life enforcement, on the one hand, and Garner's death, on the other. It was Garner's resistance to arrest that triggered the events leading to his death, however dispropor-tionate that outcome, not the policing of illegal cigarette sales. Suspects resist arrest for all sorts of crimes. The only way to prevent the remote possibility of death following an attempted arrest, beyond eliminating the use of choke-holds (if that is indeed what caused Garner's heart attack), is to make no arrests at all, even for felonies.

Having eviscerated the legitimate practice of pedestrian stops, the anti-cop brigades set their sights on Broken Windows policing. Leading the charge is Alex Vitale, a Brooklyn College sociologist. Members of the New York City Council and a preposterously named protest group called "New Yorkers Against Bratton" are close on his heels. Naturally, Vitale plays the race card, following other anti–Broken Windows academics (such as Bernard Harcourt, now at Columbia Law School). According to Vitale, the NYPD disproportionately and unjustifiably targets minority neighborhoods for misdemeanor enforcement, resulting in the "over-policing" of "communities of color."

Vitale should spend more time in poor neighborhoods. No stronger proponents of public-order policing exist than law-abiding residents of high-crime areas. Go to any police-and-community meeting in Brooklyn, the Bronx, or Harlem, and you will hear pleas such as the following: Teens are congregating on my stoop; can you please arrest them? SUVs are driving down the street at night with their stereos blaring; can't you do something? People have been barbecuing on the pedestrian islands of Broadway; that's illegal! The targets of these complaints may be black and Hispanic, but the people making the complaints, themselves black and Hispanic, don't care. They just want orderly streets.

In May 2014, a public meeting in East Harlem discussed at length how the police could break up an entrenched cluster of vagrants and shelter residents on Lexington Avenue and 125th Street; the unsightly gathering was a daily source of street fights and drug dealing. A representative from the office of Melissa Mark-Viverito, the city council speaker, complained that the benches on Lexington, though designed by the Metropolitan Transit Authority to be uncomfortable for long-term sitting or lying down, were not uncomfortable enough to discourage the squalid encampment. (Even the most left-wing politician can change her tune when disorder is in her own backyard.) In another complaint that defies the critics of Broken Windows policing, an emissary from Strive, a left-leaning job-placement program, asked the commander of the 25th Precinct to evict a female squatter who was selling drugs from her illegally occupied apartment. "Drugs are still the driving force of everything in our community," he said. All these complaints embody a truth ignored by criminologists and street-level agitators: the fierce yearning of the law-abiding poor to enjoy the same civility and order in their neighborhoods as the residents of Park Avenue take for granted in their own.

Vitale charges that the crime of selling untaxed cigarettes is enforced almost exclusively in communities of color. No surprise: that's where the trade overwhelmingly occurs. I am regularly solicited for loosies on 125th Street; I have never been approached for such a sale south of 96th Street. Vitale claims that "in many courts around the boroughs," a random spot-check performed by the Police Reform Organizing Project, a group he advises, found that 100 percent of those appearing for minor violations were people of color. Such a statistic only shows that the police are going where the crime and disorder are. All crime commission, whether felony or misdemeanor, is racially disproportionate.

The cop-critics also dispute the efficacy of quality-of-life policing. "There just isn't any evidence that arresting squeegee men and aggressive panhandlers in midtown Manhattan helps reduce robberies and shootings in the outer boroughs," Vitale says. That argument is a straw man: no proponent of misdemeanor enforcement has ever attempted to prove such a geographically attenuated causal link. But Michael

Jacobson of the City University of New York and James Austin of the JFA Institute, both liberal-to-left organizations, have shown that New York City's misdemeanor enforcement led to a drop in felony arrests and felony incarcerations by getting potential felony offenders off the streets for low-level violations. And the core concept of Broken Windows policing—that low-level disorder breeds more crime by sending the message that public norms and law enforcement have broken down—has been confirmed. Moreover, ending midtown Manhattan's low-level lawlessness in the 1990s sparked the urban renaissance there, reviving the tourist and hospitality industries and producing thousands of jobs for outer-borough New Yorkers. To the extent that one believes that criminality is an economic problem, not a cultural one, New York's public-safety-induced economic revival was the best antipoverty and anticrime program that the city has ever offered.

Vitale also argues that New York's crime drop is no different from elsewhere: "There is very little support for the idea that Broken Windows policing in and of itself is responsible for the crime drop. The crime drop is a national and international phenomenon, and it's been happening in cities that never had Broken Windows policing," he says. More straw men. No one has ever claimed that Broken Windows efforts were uniquely responsible for the crime drop. But they were part of a related set of strategies that catapulted New York far ahead of the competition. New York's crime drop far exceeded the national norm in degree and duration. It's hard to find a police chief anywhere in the country who doesn't advocate Broken Windows policing, because commanders see with their own eyes its value in lowering crime and disorder.

Even if quality-of-life enforcement had no effect whatsoever on felony crime, it would still be a moral imperative, for it responds to the demands for order that police commanders in poor neighborhoods hear from their constituents every day. If the NYPD were to cut back on misdemeanor enforcement, it would be spurning the very New Yorkers whom Vitale and the city council purport to represent. Scarily, however, Vitale sits on the New York State Advisory Committee to the U.S. Civil Rights Commission. Expect to see his views amplified in a national forum.

The biggest threat facing minority New Yorkers now is not "over-policing," and certainly not brutal policing. The NYPD has one of the lowest rates of officer shootings and killings in the country; it is recognized internationally for its professionalism and training standards. Deaths such as Eric Garner's are an aberration, which the department does everything it can to avoid. The biggest threat facing minority New Yorkers today is de-policing. After years of ungrounded criticism from the press and activists, after highly publicized litigation and the passage of ill-considered laws—such as the one making officers financially liable for alleged "racial profiling"—NYPD officers have radically scaled back their discretionary activity. Pedestrian stops have dropped 80 percent citywide and almost 100 percent in some areas. The department is grappling with how to induce officers to use their lawful authority again to stop crime before it happens. Garner's death was a heartbreaking tragedy, but the unjustified backlash against misdemeanor enforcement is likely to result in more tragedy for New Yorkers.

6

The Big Lie of the Anti-Cop Left Turns Lethal

In the summer of 2014, as we have seen, a lie overtook significant parts of the country and grew into a kind of mass hysteria. That lie holds that the police pose a mortal threat to black Americans—indeed, that the police are the greatest threat facing black Americans today. Several subsidiary untruths buttress that central myth: that the criminal-justice system is biased against blacks; that there is no such thing as a black underclass; and that crime rates are comparable between blacks and whites, so that disproportionate police action in minority neighborhoods cannot be explained without reference to racism. The poisonous effect of these lies manifested itself in the cold-blooded assassination of two NYPD officers in December that year.

The highest reaches of American society promulgated those untruths and participated in the mass hysteria. President Barack Obama, speaking after a grand jury decided not to indict the police officer who fatally shot Michael Brown, declared that blacks were right to believe that the criminal-justice system was often stacked against them. Obama repeated that message as he traveled around the country subsequently. Eric Holder escalated a long-running theme of his tenure as U.S. attorney general: that the police routinely engaged in racial profiling and needed federal intervention to police properly.

University presidents rushed to show their fealty to the lie. Harvard's Drew Gilpin Faust announced that "injustice" toward black lives "still thrives so many years after we hoped we could at last overcome the troubled legacy of race in America. . . . Harvard and . . . the nation have embraced [an] imperative to refuse silence, to reject injustice." Smith College's president abjectly flagellated herself for saying that "all lives matter," instead of the current mantra, "black lives matter." Her ignorant mistake, she confessed, drew attention away from "institutional violence against Black people."

The *New York Times* ratcheted up its already-stratospheric level of anti-cop polemics. In an editorial justifying the Ferguson riots (as quoted in Chapter 3), the *Times* claimed that "the killing of young black men by police is a common feature of African-American life and a source of dread for black parents from coast to coast." In reality, however, police killings of blacks are an extremely rare feature of black life and a minute fraction of black homicide deaths. Blacks are killed by police at a lower rate than their threat to officers would predict. To cite more data on this point: in 2013, blacks made up 42 percent of all cop-killers whose race was known, even though blacks are only about 13 percent of the nation's population. Little over a quarter of all homicides by police involve black victims. Moreover, there is a huge, unacknowledged measure of support for the police in the inner city: "They're due respect because they put their lives every day on the line to protect and serve. I hope they don't back off from policing," a woman told me on the Staten Island street where Eric Garner was killed. (This was two nights before Officers Wenjian Liu and Rafael Ramos were assassinated in Brooklyn.)

Among all the posturers, none was so preening as New York's mayor, Bill de Blasio. In advance of a trip to Washington for a White House summit on policing, he told the press that a "scourge" of killings by police was "based not just on decades, but centuries of racism." De Blasio embroidered on that theme several days later, after a Staten Island grand jury declined to indict an officer for homicide in Garner's death. (Recall that the 350-pound asthmatic Garner had resisted arrest for the crime of selling loose cigarettes; officers brought him to the ground, provoking a fatal heart attack.) "People are saying: 'Black lives matter,'" de Blasio announced after the grand jury concluded. "It should be self-evident, but our history requires us to say 'black lives matter.' It was not years of racism that brought us to this day, or decades of racism, but centuries of racism."

De Blasio added that he worries "every night" about the "dangers" his biracial son, Dante, might face from "officers who are paid to protect him."

The mayor's irresponsible rhetoric was a violation of his role as the city's leader and as its main exponent of the law. If he really believes that his son faces a significant risk from the police, he is ignorant of the realities of crime and policing in the city that he was elected to lead. There is no New York City institution more dedicated to the proposition that "black lives matter" than the New York Police Department; thousands of black men are alive today who would have been killed years ago had data-driven policing not brought down the homicide levels of the early 1990s. The Garner death was a tragic aberration in a record of unparalleled restraint. The NYPD fatally shot eight individuals in 2013, six of them black, all posing a risk to the police, compared with scores of blacks killed by black civilians. But facts do not matter when one is crusading to bring justice to a city beset by "centuries of racism."

New York police officers were rightly outraged at de Blasio's calumny. The head of the officers' union, Patrick Lynch, circulated a form allowing officers to request that the mayor not attend their funeral if they were killed in the line of duty—an understandable reaction to de Blasio's insult. De Blasio responded primly on *The View*: "It's divisive. It's inappropriate." The city's elites, from Cardinal Timothy Dolan on down, reprimanded the union. The New York police commissioner called the union letter "a step too far."

Meanwhile, protests and riots against the police were gathering force across the country, all of them steeped in anti-cop vitriol and the ubiquitous lie that "black lives" don't "matter" to the police. "What do we want? Dead cops," chanted participants in a New York anti-cop protest. Two public defenders from the Bronx participated in a rap video extolling cop-killings. Few people in positions of authority objected to this dangerous hatred. The desire to show allegiance with allegedly oppressed blacks was too great. The thrill of righteousness was palpable among the media as they lovingly chronicled every protest and among politicians and thought leaders who expressed solidarity with the cause. At another march across the Brooklyn Bridge, a group of people tried to throw trash cans onto the heads of officers on the level below them; police attempts to arrest the assailants were fought off by other marchers.

The elite's desperation to participate in what they hopefully viewed as their own modern-day civil rights crusade was patent in the sanctification of Michael Brown, the would-be cop-killer. He was turned into a civil rights martyr. His violence toward Wilson, and toward the convenience-store owner he had strong-armed, was wiped from the record. Protesters at anti-cop rallies across the country chanted "hands up, don't shoot," allegedly Brown's final words before Wilson shot him. Never mind that the source of that alleged final utterance, Brown's companion Dorian Johnson, was a proven liar. There is no reason to believe his claim regarding Brown's final words.

Protesters' willingness to overlook anti-cop homicidal intent surfaced again in St. Louis in November. A teen criminal who had shot at the police was killed by an officer in self-defense; he, too, joined the roster of heroic black victims of police racism. This sanctification of black aspiring cop-killers would prove prophetic. It's profoundly irresponsible to stoke hatred of the police, especially when the fuel used for doing so is a set of lies. Hatred of the police among blacks stems in part from police brutality during this country's shameful era of Jim Crow laws and widespread discrimination. But it is naïve not to recognize that criminal members of the black underclass despise the police because law enforcement interferes with their way of life. The elites are oblivious both to the extent of lawlessness in the black inner city and to its effect on attitudes toward the cops. Any expression of contempt for the police, in their view, must be a sincere expression of aggrievement.

Cop-killer Ismaaiyl Brinsley, who assassinated NYPD officers Wenjian Liu and Rafael Ramos on December 20, 2014, exemplified everything the elites have refused to recognize as the antipolice crusade marches on: he was a gun-toting criminal who was an eager consumer of the current frenzy of cop-hatred. (Not that he paid close enough attention to the actual details of alleged police malfeasance to spell Eric Garner's name correctly.) His homicidal postings on Instagram—"I'm Putting Wings on Pigs Today. They Take 1 of Ours . . . Let's Take 2 of Theirs"—were indistinguishable from the hatred bouncing around the Internet and the protests that few bothered to condemn. That vitriol continued after the assassination. Social media filled up with gloating at the officers' deaths and praise for Brinsley: "That nigga that shot the cops is a legend," read a typical message. A student leader and a representative of the African and Afro-American Studies department at Brandeis University tweeted that she had "no sympathy for the NYPD officers who were murdered today."

The only good that could have come out of this wrenching attack on civilization would have been the delegitimation of the lie-based protest movement. That did not happen. The *New York Times*, instead, denounced as "inflammatory" the statement from the head of the officers' union that there was "blood on the hands [that] starts on the steps of City Hall"—while the *Times* itself has promoted the inflammatory idea that police officers routinely kill blacks without cause. The elites' investment in black victimology was too great to hope for an injection of truth into the dangerously counterfactual discourse about race, crime, and policing.

7

Baltimore in Flames

The false narrative about race and policing was well rehearsed and ready to be deployed in April 2015 when Baltimore erupted in riots after a black man died of injuries sustained in police custody. The apologetics began almost as soon as the fires were lit on April 27, heralding a night of violence and looting that would leave dozens of police officers injured and 19 buildings torched, including a $16 million senior center providing affordable housing and drugstores providing crucial medications for elderly customers. Society "refuses to help [young blacks] in a serious fashion. . . . We're only there when they riot," Michael Eric Dyson declared on MSNBC. Mika Brzezinski observed on *Morning Joe*: "This was an extremely, desperately poor city. This was bound to happen." We were seeing an "uprising of young people against the police," the result of a "combination of anger and disparity," said Wes Moore, a professional talking head. Neill Franklin, a former Baltimore police officer and member of Law Enforcement Against Prohibition, blamed the drug laws.

In other words, the looters and arsonists were pushed to the breaking point by racism, poverty, and police brutality, the last exemplified by the death of Freddie Gray. A 25-year-old drug dealer with a lengthy arrest record, Gray had taken off running after making eye contact with an officer on bike patrol in a high-crime area on April 12; police reportedly claimed that he was involved in illegal activity. After a chase, he surrendered and was cuffed, searched, and arrested for possession of an illegal knife. According to the Baltimore prosecutor, he asked for an asthma inhaler but was not given one; he was not secured by a seatbelt while being transported in the police van, and though the officer driving the van repeatedly checked up on Gray, the officer did not provide requested medical assistance. It was during this time, according to the prosecutor, that he suffered his ultimately fatal spine injury.

Protests began on April 18, the day before Gray died in the hospital, turning violent a week later and especially on April 27. As the media narrative framed it, the rioters' means may have been regrettable but they were engaged in a profound cri de coeur against the social injustice in which we all play a part.

Bunk. What happened in Baltimore was simply a larger and better-covered version of the flash mobs that have beset American cities in recent years, with black youths gathering via social media to steal from stores and assault whites. In May 2012, for example, students from Mervo High School in Northeast Baltimore crammed into a 7-Eleven store that was offering free Slurpees as a promotion. The teens grabbed all the merchandise they could get their hands on—$6,000 worth in total—and fled from the store. The manager tried to close the door to prevent the thieves from escaping and was viciously beaten. On St. Patrick's Day that same year, a flash mob converged on Baltimore's Inner Harbor. The *Baltimore Sun* reported that by the time the rampage ended, "one youth had been stabbed, a tourist had been robbed, beaten and stripped of his clothes, and others had been forced to take refuge inside a hotel lobby to escape an angry mob." In April 2014, a bicyclist in Baltimore was attacked by a group of black teens who knocked him off his bike and pummeled him.

Philadelphia, Los Angeles, Minneapolis, and Washington, D.C., among other cities, have all grappled with similar violence. None of it deserves a righteous political gloss. Nor does the violence in Baltimore, which began with an invitation sent out over social media to convene at a local mall and "purge" it.

Perhaps if the media had not shrunk from reporting on the flash-mob phenomenon and the related "knockout game"—in which black teenagers try to knock out unsuspecting bystanders with a single sucker punch—we might have made a modicum of progress in addressing, or at least acknowledging, the real cause of black violence: the breakdown of the family. A widely circulated video from the mayhem shows a furious mother whacking her hoodie-encased son to prevent him from joining the mob. This tiger mom may well have the capacity to rein in her would-be vandal son. But the odds are against her. Try as they might, single mothers are generally overmatched in raising males. Boys need their fathers. But over 72 percent of black children are born to single-mother households today, three times the black illegitimacy rate when Daniel Patrick Moynihan wrote his prescient analysis of black family breakdown in 1965.

Baltimore councilman Brandon Scott came closest to the truth in a city news conference when he angrily called on adults to "get out there and stand up for your neighborhood" as the mayhem was unfolding. "Adults have to step up and be adults and control our future," Scott declared. True enough. But primary responsibility lies with children's own two parents. *Pace* Michael Eric Dyson, "we" have spent trillions of dollars since the 1960s trying to help black youth. A social worker and a government check are no substitute for a father and a mother, however.

The same day that the teenage mob looted the 7-Eleven in 2012, eight people were shot in Baltimore in just 24 hours, a toll typical of Baltimore's astronomical crime rate. Magnitudes more black men are killed by other black men in Baltimore and other American cities than by the police, yet those killings are ignored because they don't fit into the favored narrative of a white, racist America lethally oppressing blacks. Police misconduct is deplorable and must be eradicated wherever it exists. But until the black crime rate comes down, police presence is going to be higher in black neighborhoods, increasing the chances that when police tactics go awry, they will have a black victim.

Baltimore's response to the rioting was shamefully hesitant. The police stood by during the start of the arson, even as looters severed a fire hose brought in to try to save a burning CVS store. Apparently, the ludicrous meme that the press promulgated after the August 2014 riots in Ferguson, Missouri—that the violence was provoked by a military-style police presence, rather than by the rioters themselves—had taken hold and inhibited police agencies from fulfilling their core duty to protect life and property. It is not clear whether the police diffidence was ordered by Mayor Stephanie Rawlings-Blake or by Police Commissioner Anthony Batts.‡ But any future outbreak of mob violence should be greeted with the force that it deserves.

---

‡ A Police Executive Research Forum report issued in November 2015 confirmed that officers had been told both before and during the violence to take a "soft approach," including not making arrests and not wearing helmets, but the report does not clarify the ultimate source of the order.

8

The Riot Show!

What if they held a race riot and the news media stayed away? At the very least, we would be spared the nauseating spectacle of sycophantic reporters fawning on opportunistic thieves, as happened yet again during the outbreak of antipolice violence in Baltimore in April 2015. We wouldn't see talking heads blaming the mayhem on "desperate poverty" or on "disparity," or characterizing it as an "uprising" born of understandable anger. More important, the vandals would lose a bounty as valuable as their purloined booty: notoriety and legitimacy.

The riots held in the name of Freddie Gray, the drug dealer who died of a spinal injury in police custody, followed a drearily familiar script. Upon the first outbreak of violence, a crush of reporters flock to the scene with barely suppressed cries of glee. Surrounded by sound trucks and camera crews, outfitted with cell phones and microphones, they breathlessly narrate each skirmish between police and looters for the viewing public, thrusting their microphones into the faces of spectators and thugs alike to get a "street" interpretation of the mayhem. The studio anchors melodramatically caution the reporters to "stay safe," even though the press at times may outnumber looters as well as the police. Meanwhile, the thieves get to indulge in the pleasures of anarchic annihilation while enjoying the desideratum of every reality-TV cast: a wide and devoted audience.

The performative quality of the live, televised race riot has created a new genre: riot porn, in which every act of thuggery is lasciviously filmed and parsed in real time for the benefit of at-home viewers. "Did you see that?" CNN reporter Miguel Marquez asked studio anchor Wolf Blitzer when vandals slashed a fire hose as businesses burned on April 27. "Wolf, if you just saw that, they just, while we were talking there, they just cut the hose with a knife . . . there are others who are thwarting the authorities at every turn." (Marquez is given to philosophizing on social justice as he walks alongside protesters during antipolice demonstrations.)

Wolf confirmed that he had, in fact, seen the close-up footage: "I just saw that guy, yeah, I just saw that guy cut the hose as well, [a guy] with a gas mask." Naturally, the TV audience also got to see the vicious sabotage. The street scene at these televised riots can be eerily static. People mill around listlessly like extras on a movie set. Within that sea of idleness, more energetic thugs, perched on the roofs of police cruisers, stomp out the cars' windshields or throw garbage cans through the rear windows. The smartphone camera has only magnified the specular nature of the anarchy, as passersby memorialize their own presence at the festival of lawlessness.

As in the race riots in Ferguson, Missouri, CNN topped all other television channels for relentless oversaturation, keeping a phalanx of reporters in West Baltimore around the clock to meditate portentously on the meaning of the riots long after the looting was finally suppressed. Among national print outlets, the *New York Times* had the most frenzied output, with four or five stories a day on policing and racism, topics that the *Times* had already been obsessively pursuing for the last nine months. Both organizations diminished their coverage of Baltimore only marginally in the days and weeks after the fires were extinguished.

Thanks in large measure to the media deluge, the ideological yield from this urban tantrum was considerable. Inevitably, academics and pundits conferred political legitimacy on the riots, deeming them, in the words of the online publication Vox, "a serious attempt at forcing change." Baltimore's mayor, Stephanie Rawlings-Blake, apologized for calling the rioters "thugs." President Obama and Hillary Clinton both affirmed the dangerous myth that the criminal-justice system is racist. Speaking at Lehman College in the Bronx a week after the Baltimore riots, President Obama opined that young black men experience "being treated differently by law enforcement—in stops and in arrests, and in charges and incarcerations. The statistics are clear, up and down the criminal-justice system. There's no dispute." Hillary Clinton played the same theme at Columbia University several days after the riots: "We have to come to terms with some hard truths about race and justice in America. There is something profoundly wrong when African-American men are still far more likely to be stopped and searched by police, charged with crimes, and sentenced to longer prison terms than are meted out to their white counterparts."

This claim of disparate treatment is simply untrue. For decades, liberal criminologists have tried to corroborate the Left's cherished belief that the criminal-justice system responds to similarly situated whites and blacks unequally. The effort always comes up short. "Racial differences in patterns of offending, not racial bias by police and other officials, are the principal reason that such greater proportions of blacks than whites are arrested, prosecuted, convicted and imprisoned," concluded Michael Tonry, a criminologist, in his book *Malign Neglect* (1995). A Justice Department survey of felony cases from the country's 75 largest urban areas, conducted in 1994, found that blacks had a lower chance of prosecution following a felony than whites, and were less likely to be found guilty at trial. Blacks were more likely to be sentenced to prison following a conviction, but that result reflected their past crimes and the gravity of their current offense (a subject examined in Chapter 19).

The rioting in Baltimore also gave fresh impetus to the liberal narrative about cities: that their viability depends on government spending. "There are consequences to indifference," Obama said at Lehman College. *New York Times* columnist Paul Krugman opined that the riots "have served at least one useful purpose: drawing attention to the grotesque inequalities that poison the lives of too many Americans." Krugman blamed stingy federal outlays for the "grotesque inequalities."

The idea that the federal and local governments have been "indifferent" to urban decay is ludicrous. Taxpayers have coughed up $22 trillion on more than 80 means-tested welfare programs (not including Social Security, Medicare, or grants for economic development) since the War on Poverty was launched in 1964, according to the Heritage Foundation. In the 1990s, Baltimore "invested" $130 million in public and nonprofit dollars to transform the West Baltimore neighborhood where Freddie Gray lived, to no effect, as *National Review*'s Ian Tuttle has documented.

This lack of effect is not surprising. Baltimore's crime rate has been among the nation's highest for decades. In 2013, the only cities with higher murder rates were Detroit, New Orleans, Newark, and St. Louis. Baltimore's violent-crime rate is over twice that of New York. That violence would have doomed any hope for economic revival in high-crime areas even without the destruction of 350 businesses by arson and looting. West Baltimore residents complained to the tenacious post-riot crowd of reporters that Baltimore's Inner Harbor area was spiffy and thriving, while their neighborhood was not. But potential business owners, if they have any other options, are not going to locate in a neighborhood where they fear for the safety of their employees and customers. Lowered crime is a precondition to economic revival, not its consequence. New York's economic renaissance began only when crime started plummeting in 1994, thanks to a policing revolution there.

The post-riot media narrative virtually ignored Baltimore's sky-high crime in favor of an all-consuming focus on allegedly racist policing practices. To its credit, the *Baltimore Sun* noted the shooting rampage that began after Freddie Gray was arrested on April 12 and escalated following the riots, as officers backed off from proactive enforcement. From April 28, the day after the most destructive riot, to May 7, there were 40 shootings, including ten on May 7. Fifteen people were murdered during that period, more than one a day. The total of 82 homicides from the beginning of 2015 through May 7 was 20 more than the number at the same point in 2014. All these deaths did nothing to dislodge the "Black Lives Matter" conceit that the biggest threat facing young black men today is the police, rather than other young black men. None of Baltimore's post-riot killings has triggered protests.

Baltimore police officers now face a street environment that is even more dangerous and hostile than usual. A total of 155 officers were injured, 43 seriously, during the riots. Every arrest now brings a crowd of bystanders pressing in, jeering, and spreading lies about the encounter. On May 4, 2015, officers received a call about a man with a gun at the corner of a torched CVS store. His movements, captured on a police camera, also suggested that he had a gun. The suspect, 23-year-old Robert Edward "Meech" Tucker, had previously been convicted on gun and drug charges. When the officers approached him, he took off running (just as Freddie

Gray did when he saw officers watching him). Tucker's gun fired. Tucker then dropped to the ground and began screaming and rolling around as if he had been shot. Bystanders claimed that they had seen the police shoot him. The crowd threw bricks, Clorox bottles, and water bottles at the officers; one man lunged at them but was held back by other pedestrians. In fact, no officer had discharged his gun or even taken aim at Tucker. Even though Tucker had not been shot, not even by his own gun, word in the street continued to maintain that the cops had shot him.

Such lying about interactions between officers and civilians is endemic in urban areas. But even after the country witnessed the evisceration of the Michael Brown "hands up" hoax by none other than the federal Department of Justice, the media and the authorities have continued to seek out allegations of officer misconduct and to treat them as the gospel truth. The *New York Times* quoted a drug dealer as an authority on the Baltimore police: "They trip you, choke you out, cuss you out, disrespect you." Maybe so. (The antipolice bar won judgments or settlements against the Baltimore Police Department in more than a hundred civil rights and brutality cases from 2011 to 2015, a fact that could reflect a pattern of abuse or a pattern of aggressive litigation and a supine city law department.) But it is also possible that the drug dealer was lying through his teeth. It never occurs to elite opinion-makers that the pervasiveness of crime in the inner city creates a large block of residents—not just criminals but their friends and families as well—who view and treat the police as antagonists.

The riots also led to rushed and likely excessive criminal charges against the six officers involved in the arrest and transport of Freddie Gray. (Four officers face homicide counts ranging from involuntary manslaughter to second-degree murder.) Upon announcing the charges mere hours after receiving Gray's autopsy and a day after receiving a police report on the arrest, Baltimore's prosecutor, Marilyn Mosby, declared that she had heard the "call for 'no justice, no peace.'" Positioning herself as the head of a crusade rather than as part of a legal system dedicated to prosecuting individual cases, not causes, Mosby continued in an Obama-esque vein: "Last but certainly not least, to the youth of the city: I will seek justice on your behalf. This is a moment. This is your moment. Let's ensure we have peaceful and productive rallies that will develop structural and systemic changes for generations to come. You're at the forefront of this cause, and as young people, our time is now."

Mosby had already displayed her penchant for the crassest of racial rabble-rousing following the grand-jury decision not to indict Officer Darren Wilson for the shooting death of Michael Brown. Mosby, reported St. Louis Public Radio, questioned the "motives" of Robert McCulloch, the St. Louis County district attorney who presented the Wilson case to the grand jury. On Baltimore TV, Mosby said, "In Ferguson, over 68 percent of the population is black and less than 6 percent votes." (She did not explain why that low turnout is the fault of anyone other than the nonvoters.) "So you have an individual who is in office and does not share your interests and values and is making decisions about your daily life. . . . We say bring in special prosecutions."

Mosby reversed herself regarding special prosecutors when the Baltimore Fraternal Order of Police called for one in the Freddie Gray case, expressing concerns that Mosby had several financial and familial conflicts of interest. "I can tell you that the people of Baltimore City elected me," Mosby said at a press conference after the six officers were indicted, "and there's no accountability with a special prosecutor." One could only hope that the criminal-justice system would backstop whatever accountability to the facts Mosby herself might feel.

While the second-degree-murder charge against the driver of the police van carries the direst individual consequences, Mosby's charge of "false imprisonment" against the arresting officers raises a risk of shutting down policing across Baltimore. Mosby alleged that the switchblade knife possessed by Gray was not illegal under Maryland law. The Baltimore police responded that it was prohibited under a city code. Even if Mosby's reading of the knife statutes is correct, her imposition of criminal liability for an officer's good-faith interpretive error is preposterous. The remedy for an arrest not supported by probable cause is to throw the case out at the station house or prosecutor's office, or in court.

If officers face prison terms for trying to keep the streets safe, they will stop making discretionary arrests. Baltimore's spike in gun violence suggests that such de-policing has already begun. Meanwhile, shortly after the riots, Mayor Rawlings-Blake requested that the U.S. Justice Department investigate the Baltimore police for systemic civil rights violations, and Attorney General Loretta Lynch agreed the next day. The result may be more handcuffing of the police in their efforts to protect lives in poor neighborhoods—a result encouraged by the media spin on the Baltimore riots.

A riot's unchecked destruction of livelihoods and property is certainly newsworthy, threatening, as it does, the very possibility of civilization. The breakdown of law and order is a policy concern of enormous note. But the 24-hour cable-news cycle, with its insatiable craving for live visual excitement, creates a codependency between reporters and rioters, while the politics of the mainstream media guarantees a "root causes" exculpation of the violence. Short of a filming blackout on the actual violence, riots should be covered in sorrow, shame, and dismay.

9

The New Nationwide Crime Wave

The most pressing question every morning in Baltimore is how many people were shot the previous night. By the end of May 2015, according to Baltimore police, the rate of gun violence for the year had climbed more than 60 percent over the same period in 2014, with 32 shootings over Memorial Day weekend alone. May 2015 was the most violent month the city had seen in 15 years.

Baltimore is just one indicator that the nation's two-decade-long crime decline may be over. Gun violence, in particular, is spiraling upward in cities across America. In Cleveland, homicides for 2015 increased by 90 percent over the previous year. Through the end of April 2015, shootings in St. Louis were up 39 percent, robberies 43 percent, and homicides 25 percent. Murders in Nashville rose 83 percent in 2015; Milwaukee closed out the year with a 72 percent increase in homicides. Shootings in Chicago had increased 24 percent and homicides 17 percent by May 2015; that surge continued into 2016, with more than 100 Chicagoans shot in the first ten days of the new year, a threefold increase from the same period in 2015. Washington, D.C., ended 2015 with a 54 percent increase in murders; Minneapolis was up 61 percent in homicides. This ongoing crime spike is a stark contrast to the 20-year trend of increasing public safety that continued into the middle of 2014, and cities with large black populations have been hit the hardest.

The most plausible explanation for the surge in lawlessness is the intense agitation against American police departments that began in the summer of 2014. The airwaves filled up with suggestions that the police are the biggest threat facing young black males today, in the wake of a handful of highly publicized deaths of unarmed black men, typically following resistance to arrest—most famously, Eric Garner on Staten Island, New York, in July 2014; Michael Brown in Ferguson, Missouri, in August 2014; and Freddie Gray in Baltimore in April 2015. In the midst of violent protests and riots, including attacks on the police, President Obama and Attorney General Eric Holder embraced the notion that law enforcement in black communities is infected by bias. The news media have pumped out a seemingly constant stream of stories about alleged police mistreatment of blacks, with the reports often buttressed by cell-phone videos that rarely capture the behavior that caused an officer to use force.

Almost any police shooting of a black person, no matter how threatening the behavior that provoked the shooting, now stirs up angry protests, like those that followed the death of Vonderrit Myers in October 2014. The 18-year-old Myers, awaiting trial on gun and resisting-arrest charges, had fired three shots at an officer at close range in St. Louis. Arrests in black communities have become even more fraught than usual.

Not only are police officers at risk of violent attack, but acquittals of officers for the use of deadly force against black suspects are now automatically characterized as a miscarriage of justice. Proposals aimed at producing more convictions of cops abound, but New York State seems especially enthusiastic about the idea. Governor Andrew Cuomo signed an executive order in July 2015 that takes police lethal-force cases away from local district attorneys and refers them to the state's attorney general for investigation and prosecution. The state attorney general's office now has an entire prosecutorial unit dedicated exclusively to prosecuting cops. The District Attorneys Association of the State of New York and local law enforcement unions objected to Cuomo's order as gravely flawed because it created a separate justice system for police officers, among other reasons.

The incessant drumbeat against the police has resulted in what Sam Dotson, police chief of St. Louis, called the "Ferguson effect." Cops are disengaging from discretionary enforcement activity, and the "criminal element is feeling empowered," Dotson reported in November 2014. By that point, arrests in the city and county of St. Louis had dropped a third since the shooting of Michael Brown in August. Not surprisingly, homicides in the city had surged 47 percent by early November and robberies in the county were up 82 percent.

Similar "Ferguson effects" are happening across the country as officers scale back on proactive policing under the onslaught of anti-cop rhetoric. Arrests in Baltimore, for instance, were down 56 percent in May 2015, compared with 2014.

"Any cop who uses his gun now has to worry about being indicted and losing his job and family," a New York City officer told me. "Everything has the potential to be recorded. A lot of cops feel that the climate for the next couple of years is going to be nonstop protests."

Police officers now second-guess themselves about the use of force. "Officers are trying to invent techniques on the spot for taking down resistant suspects that don't look as bad as the techniques taught in the academy," said Jim Dudley, former deputy police chief in San Francisco. Officers complain that civilians don't understand how hard it is to control someone resisting arrest.

A New York City cop told me that he was amazed to hear people scoffing that Officer Darren Wilson, who killed Michael Brown in Ferguson, looked only "a little red" after Brown assaulted him and tried to grab his weapon: "Does an officer need to be unconscious before he can use force? If someone is willing to fight you, he's also willing to take your gun and shoot you. You can't lose a fight with a guy who has already put his hands on you because if you do, you will likely end up dead."

The level of hostility toward the police has skyrocketed, observed Milwaukee police chief Edward A. Flynn: "I've never seen anything like it. I'm guessing it will take five years to recover." Officer morale has understandably plummeted as a consequence. Even if it were miraculously to rebound, there are policies being put into place that will make it harder for the police to keep crime down in the future. Those initiatives reflect the belief that any criminal-justice action that has a disparate impact on blacks is ipso facto racially motivated.

In New York, pedestrian stops—when the police question and sometimes frisk individuals engaged in suspicious behavior—have dropped nearly 95 percent from their high point in 2011, thanks to litigation charging that the NYPD's stop, question, and frisk practices were racially biased. A judge agreed. (Two of those cases will be discussed in Chapters

15 and 16.) Mayor Bill de Blasio, upon taking office in 2014, embraced the resulting judicial monitoring of the police department. It is no surprise that shootings increased in the city.

Politicians and activists in New York and other cities have taken aim at Broken Windows policing, which has shown remarkable success in reducing crime since the 1990s. The strategy (as noted earlier) targets low-level public-order offenses so as to diminish the air of lawlessness in rough neighborhoods and get criminals off the streets before they commit bigger crimes. Opponents of Broken Windows policing somehow fail to notice that law-abiding residents of poor communities are among the strongest advocates for enforcing laws against public drinking, trespassing, drug sales, and drug use, among other public-order laws.

As attorney general, Eric Holder pressed the cause of ending "mass incarceration" on racial grounds; elected officials across the political spectrum have jumped on board. In California, years of litigation (discussed in Chapter 21) had already been advancing a deincarceration agenda before a voter initiative in 2014, Proposition 47, retroactively downgraded a range of property and drug felonies to misdemeanors, including forcible theft of guns, purses, and laptops. As of late May 2015, more than 3,000 felons had already been released from California prisons, according to the Association of Deputy District Attorneys in Los Angeles County. Burglary, larceny, and car theft had surged in the county, the association reported. (Prop. 47 and its aftermath are examined in more detail in Chapter 22.)

"There are no real consequences for committing property crimes anymore," said Los Angeles police lieutenant Armando Munoz to *Downtown News* in May 2015, "and the criminals know this." The Milwaukee district attorney, John Chisholm, has diverted many property and drug criminals to rehabilitation programs in order to reduce the number of blacks in Wisconsin prisons; critics see the rise in Milwaukee crime as one result.

If these decriminalization and deincarceration policies backfire, the people most harmed will be their supposed beneficiaries: black Americans, since they are disproportionately victimized by crime. No government policy in the past quarter-century has done more for urban reclamation than proactive policing. Data-driven enforcement, in conjunction with stricter penalties for criminals and Broken Windows policing, has saved thousands of black lives, brought lawful commerce and jobs to once-drug-infested neighborhoods, and allowed millions to go about their daily lives without fear.

To be sure, any fatal police shooting of an innocent person is a horrifying tragedy, and police training must work incessantly to prevent such an outcome. But unless the demonization of law enforcement ends, the liberating gains in urban safety that began with a proactive policing strategy will be lost.

10

Explaining Away the New Crime Wave

In May 2015, I observed in the *Wall Street Journal* that violent crime was rising sharply in many cities. Having spoken with police officers and commanders, I hypothesized that a growing reluctance of cops to engage in proactive policing might help explain the spike in violent crime. Officers in urban areas were encountering unusually high levels of resistance and hostility when they tried to make an arrest. An unprecedented amount of antipolice agitation had sprung up around the proposition that bias infects policing in predominantly black communities—a message that was echoed throughout government and the media. Officers told me that they were increasingly hesitant to investigate suspicious behavior, given the prospect of ending up in a widely distributed video if an arrest goes awry, and possibly being indicted.

The relationship between decreased law enforcement and increased crime is what St. Louis police chief Sam Dotson called the "Ferguson effect." I noted that if it continues, the primary victims will be the millions of law-abiding residents of inner-city neighborhoods who rely on police to keep order.

A sharply critical response greeted the article from some quarters. In the *Guardian*, Professor Bernard Harcourt of Columbia Law School decried it as "crime fiction" intended to undermine "the country's newest civil rights movement," and as one among "a long line of conservative efforts to undermine racial equality." Charles Blow of the *New York Times* called me a "fear-mongering iron fist-er" who was using "racial pathology arguments" and "smearing the blood running in the street onto the hands holding the placards." My article, wrote Radley Balko in the *Washington Post*, was part of a "growing backlash against police reform," an attempt to "shame people who dare to speak up about police abuse."

The police came in for criticism as well. Officers who are not doing what Blow calls "normal police work" simply because of protests against police brutality are acting unprofessionally, it was said. Balko called it being "too afraid or spiteful to do their jobs."

Other writers challenged the focus on the multicity crime rise. Not every city was seeing a crime increase, some critics said—or at least, not an increase in every category of crime. And whatever the increases, crime was still much lower than it had been 20 years earlier. In any case, critics argued, it was premature to draw conclusions about the significance or the possible causes of the crime rises, since crime is predominantly a local phenomenon and naturally fluctuates over short periods.

These criticisms speak volumes about how activists, members of the media, and many academics understand crime and policing.

It is true that violent crime has not skyrocketed in every American city—but my article didn't say that it had. It has gone up in enough places, though, and at startling enough rates, to warrant close attention. Law-enforcement officials share that opinion. Police chiefs in New York and Los Angeles—the two cities paradoxically singled out by criminologist Franklin Zimring to dismiss the significance of the crime increases—have implemented extraordinary, manpower-intensive initiatives to quell gun violence. It is also true that a half-dozen months or so of rising crime are not going to wipe out the 20-year crime drop overnight. But as I noted, *if* that downward trend is now reversing itself, the reversal will happen in such increments as we are now seeing.

To be sure, crime does fluctuate over short periods, and usually in response to local conditions. Ordinarily, the longer the span of data that one has for assessing trends, the better. But in the present environment of nonstop animosity toward police nationally, with officers' self-professed reluctance to engage reflected in a documented drop in stops and summonses, it is not too early to flag what might be going on. The trend of increasing crime rests on firmer statistical evidence than does the claim that we are living through an epidemic of racist police killings.

Police are actually not backing off from what Charles Blow and others presumably think of as "normal police work": responding to 911 calls for emergency assistance. Officers continue to rush to crime scenes, sometimes getting shot at in the process. They are, however, refraining from precisely the kind of policing that many in the media, along with legions of activists, have been denouncing: pedestrian stops and enforcement of low-level, quality-of-life laws (known as Broken Windows policing).

"The reactive policing of the early 1990s was easy," Lou Turco, president of the Lieutenants Benevolent Association in New York City, told me in an interview. "You waited for a complainant to tell you that they've been a robbery victim. The hard thing is to get someone off the corner before there's a victim." It is this proactive policing, when there is no complainant, that can get you in trouble now, Turco says. "Every cop today is thinking: 'If this stop turns bad, I'm in the mix.'"

An officer in South Central Los Angeles described the views of his fellow cops: "Guys and gals in coffee shops are saying to each other: 'If you get out of your car, you're crazy, unless there's a radio call.'"

One would think that cop-critics would celebrate this drop in self-initiated police activity, which Radley Balko calls "dehumanizing." They can't have it both ways: denouncing the police for proactively enforcing the law, and then accusing them of a "dereliction of duty," in Charles Blow's words, when they quite understandably decrease such enforcement.

Many residents of high-crime areas don't look at proactive and public-order enforcement the way their alleged advocates do. In a May 2015 Quinnipiac poll of New York City voters, 61 percent of black respondents said that they wanted the police to actively enforce quality-of-life laws in their neighborhood, compared with 59 percent of white voters.

At a police-and-community meeting in the South Bronx on June 4, 2015, residents begged the officers to arrest the crowds of teens who hung out on local street corners and fought with one another. Shootings in that precinct through May 31 were 167 percent higher than at the same point in the previous year—but that wasn't serious enough to qualify for the NYPD's high-priority list because the trouble was even worse elsewhere in the city. "Oh, how lovely when we see the police!" an elderly woman exclaimed at the meeting. "They are my friends." That is not a voice that you are likely to encounter in the mainstream media.

Activists and many criminologists may continue to deny the importance of proactive policing, even as shootings increase, but its effectiveness was central to America's remarkable crime reduction of the past two decades. Of course, police departments must constantly reinforce the message of courtesy and respect for the public, and train officers to minimize the use of force. But when the police back off, crime eventually goes up. If anti-cop vituperation tapers off and police start to feel supported in their work, the recent crime increases may also taper off. If the media-saturated agitation continues, however, the new normal may be less policing and more crime.

11

America's Legal Order Begins to Fray

"I'm deliberately not getting involved in things I would have in the 1990s and 2000s," an emergency-services officer in New York City tells me. "I won't get out of my car for a reasonable-suspicion stop; I will if there's a violent felony committed in my presence." He is not alone in this reluctance to engage. This is what law enforcement has come to after two decades of the most remarkable crime drop in U.S. history.

The virulent antipolice campaign that began with a now-discredited narrative about a police shooting in Ferguson, Missouri, has made police officers think twice before undertaking precisely the type of enforcement that led to that twenty-year crime drop. The Black Lives Matter movement proclaims that the police are a lethal threat to blacks and that the criminal-justice system is pervaded by racial bias. The media amplify that message on an almost daily basis. Officers now worry about becoming the latest racist cop of the week, losing their job or being indicted if a good-faith encounter with a suspect goes awry or is merely distorted by an incomplete cell-phone video.

With police so discouraged, violent crime has surged in dozens of American cities, as we have seen. The alarming murder increase prompted an emergency meeting of the Major Cities Chiefs Association in August 2015. Homicides were up 76 percent in Milwaukee, 60 percent in St. Louis, and 56 percent in Baltimore for the year through mid-August, compared with the same period in 2014. Murder was up 47 percent in Minneapolis and 36 percent in Houston through mid-July.

But something even more fundamental than public safety may be at stake. There are signs that the legal order itself is breaking down in urban areas. "There's a total lack of respect out there for the police," says a female sergeant in New York. "The perps feel more empowered to carry guns because they know that we are running scared."

The lawful use of police power is being met by hostility and violence, which is often ignored by the press. In Cincinnati, a small riot broke out in late July 2015 when the police arrived at a drive-by shooting scene, where a four-year-old girl had been shot in the head and critically injured. Bystanders loudly cursed at officers who had started arresting suspects at the scene on outstanding warrants, according to a witness I spoke with.

During antipolice demonstrations in Ferguson, Missouri, in August 2015, 18-year-old Tyrone Harris opened fire at police officers, according to law-enforcement officials, and was shot and wounded by police in response. A crowd pelted the cops with frozen water bottles and rocks, wounding three officers, while destroying three police cars and damaging businesses, Ferguson police said. Some protesters reportedly chanted, "We're ready for what? We're ready for war."

That same month, an officer in Birmingham, Alabama, was beaten unconscious with his own gun by a suspect in a car stop. There was gloating on social media. "Pistol whipped his ass to sleep," read one Twitter post. The officer later said that he had refrained from using force to defend himself for fear of a media backlash.

Officers are being challenged in their most basic efforts to render aid. A New York cop in the Bronx tells me that he was trying to extricate a woman pinned under an overturned car in July 2015 when a bystander stuck his cell-phone camera into the officer's face, trying to bait him into an argument. "You can't tell me what to do," the bystander replied when asked to move to the sidewalk, the cop reports. "A few years ago, I would have taken police action," he says. "Now I know it won't end well for me or the police department."

Supervisors may roll up to an incident where trash and other projectiles are being thrown at officers and tell the cops to get into their cars and leave. "What does that do to the general public?" wonders a New York detective. "Every time we pass up on an arrest because we don't want a situation to blow up, we've made the next cop's job all the harder."

Jim McDonnell, head of the Los Angeles County Sheriff's Department, the nation's largest, tells me that the current anti-cop animus puts the nation in a place where it hasn't been since the 1960s. "The last ten years have witnessed dramatic decreases in crime," Sheriff McDonnell says. "Now, in a short period of time, we are seeing those gains undone."

Even the assassination of police officers doesn't appear to cool the antipolice rhetoric. The day after a Houston police deputy, Darren Goforth, was murdered while filling his gas tank in August 2015, Black Lives Matter protesters—as an online video chillingly attests—marched in St. Paul, chanting: "Pigs in a blanket, fry 'em like bacon."

An organizer with the Organization for Black Struggle in St. Louis refused to apologize for the tenor of the movement, while denying that it condoned violence. "Until the police aren't the dangerous force that black people fear, the rhetoric won't change," she told the *New York Times*, after Houston sheriff Ron Hickman, in the wake of Deputy Goforth's murder, pleaded for antipolice protesters to temper their language. A Texas state senator, Garnet Coleman, assailed Sheriff Hickman for showing "a lack of understanding of what is occurring in this country when it comes to the singling out of African-Americans."

The irony is that the historic reduction of crime in the United States since the 1990s was predicated on police singling out African-Americans *for their protection*. Using victims' crime reports, cops focused on violent hot spots; since black Americans are disproportionately the victims of crime, just as blacks are disproportionately its perpetrators, effective policing was heaviest in minority neighborhoods. The cops were there because they do believe that black lives matter.

In the recent eruption of violent crime, the overwhelming majority of victims have been black. The *Baltimore Sun* reported that July 2015 was the bloodiest month in the city since 1972, with 45 people killed in 30 days. All but two were black.

Police officials have told me that they long to hear America's leaders change the tone of the national conversation before respect for the rule of law itself deteriorates even further, and more innocent people suffer as a consequence. So far, they're still waiting.

12

The Ferguson Effect Is Real

One prominent public official raised a firestorm by sounding a contrarian theme on the topic of policing and crime while racially charged anti-cop sentiment ran high. The FBI director, James Comey, was speaking at the University of Chicago Law School in October 2015 when he observed that violent crime was rising in many cities across the country. The likely reason, he said, was a drop in proactive policing. The strident reaction to his comments, not least from the White House, demonstrated how ideological the subject had become.

But Comey was merely confirming the obvious. The Major Cities Chiefs Association (as mentioned above) had recently met in an emergency session to discuss the homicide surge. The blog FiveThirtyEight looked at homicide data from most of the nation's 60 largest cities up through September 2015 and found a 16 percent increase over the same period in 2014. Comey's statement that "most of America's 50 largest cities have seen an increase in homicides and shootings this year, and many of them have seen a huge increase" was therefore hardly news.

It should also not be news that officers have been backing off of discretionary policing. The available data show a decline in police activity. In New York City, summonses for low-level, quality-of-life offenses like public urination and drinking—a prime gauge of proactive enforcement—were down 26 percent in the first half of 2015; arrests in every crime category were down 15 percent as of the end of October 2015. In Los Angeles, arrests were down 10 percent through the same period. Baltimore arrests dropped a third through November 2015; misdemeanor drug arrests were down nearly two-thirds.

Mayors have noticed the results. "We have allowed our police department to get fetal," said Mayor Rahm Emanuel of Chicago in October 2015 during an emergency crime meeting of police chiefs and mayors in Washington, D.C.

Yet Comey's comments, amply backed up by evidence, landed him in hot water. Most remarkably, President Barack Obama had the temerity to accuse him of shoddy, biased analysis. "We do have to stick with the facts," Obama told the International Association of Chiefs of Police in Chicago in late October, in a thinly veiled rebuke to Comey. "What we can't do is cherry-pick data or use anecdotal evidence to drive policy or to feed political agendas." The idea that Obama knows more about crime patterns and policing than the FBI director is ludicrous; the one with a "political agenda" is Obama, who has spent the last two years disseminating the dangerous lie that the criminal-justice system is racially biased.

In November 2015, the acting chief of the Drug Enforcement Administration, Chuck Rosenberg, seconded Comey's observations about the decline in proactive policing. Officers were feeling "trepidation" about ending up on the evening news even if they "do everything right," Rosenberg told reporters. The White House dressing-down was immediate. Rosenberg had spoken "without any evidence," press secretary Josh Earnest retorted.

Other longtime critics of the police have been just as dismissive of the Ferguson effect. These critics simultaneously deny that there is a crime increase, that officers are reluctant to engage, and that such reluctance (if it existed) could have anything to do with the allegedly nonexistent crime increase. The skeptics' hostility to acknowledging the decrease in proactive policing seems puzzling at first blush. After all, they have spent the last year charging that pedestrian stops and quality-of-life enforcement oppress minority communities. The police have gotten the message and are doing much less of both. You would think that this would be a welcome development to the anti-cop Left. Instead, its members vehemently deny that officers are backing off. Why? Because the resulting crime increase shows that policing does, in fact, lower crime.

To be sure, crime has not risen yet to the levels of the early 1990s, as Obama and other critics of the police point out. That is hardly a refutation of the Ferguson effect, however. Crime dropped 50 percent nationally over the last two decades, and it would be highly unusual to give back all that gain in just one year. But a 16 percent homicide increase in at least 60 major cities is startling enough. If present trends continue, we will soon be back to the pervasive urban violence that FBI director Comey described so eloquently in his remarks at Chicago Law School.

13

Black and Unarmed: Behind the Numbers

Since the Michael Brown incident, the *Washington Post* has been gathering data on fatal police shootings of civilians. The paper has spun the numbers as support for the thesis that the police are gunning down unarmed blacks out of implicit bias. In fact, the *Post*'s findings confirm that the Black Lives Matter movement is a fraud.

The *Post* began its database to correct acknowledged deficiencies in existing federal tallies of police shootings. It searched news sites and other information sources for reports of officer-involved homicides. The results: for 2015, the *Post* documented 991 victims of fatal police shootings, about twice the number historically recorded by federal agencies. Whites were 50 percent of those victims, and blacks were 26 percent.

That percentage of black victims is not helpful in proving that policing is racist. Though blacks are 13 percent of the nation's population (and whites, 62 percent), blacks' violent crime rates would predict that at least a quarter of the victims of police killings would be black. Police shootings will be correlated with the prevalence of armed suspects, violent crime, and suspect resistance in a population and area. Blacks were charged with 62 percent of all robberies, 57 percent of all murders, and 45 percent of all assaults in the 75 largest U.S. counties in 2009, while constituting roughly 15 percent of the population in those counties. From 2005 to 2014, 40 percent of cop-killers were black. Given the racially lopsided nature of gun violence, a 26 percent rate of black victimization by the police is not evidence of bias.

Moreover, the vast majority of the 258 black victims of police shootings in 2015 were armed, as were white and Hispanic victims. And 258 is a small fraction of the nearly 6,000 annual black victims of black-committed homicide. Indeed, the percentage of black homicide deaths that result from police killings is far less than the percentage of white and Hispanic homicide deaths that result from police killings: 4 percent of black homicide victims are killed by the police, compared with 12 percent of white and Hispanic homicide victims. A "Lives Matter" antipolice movement, if there is to be one, would more appropriately be labeled "White and Hispanic Lives Matter."

The black percentage of policing victims was greater, however, in the *Post*'s "unarmed" victims category, and that is where the *Post* put its emphasis. In August 2015, the *Post* ran a piece titled "Black and Unarmed: A year after Michael Brown's fatal shooting, unarmed black men are seven times more likely than whites to die by police gunfire." The piece noted, with a hint of regret, that the 24 unarmed black men killed by the police so far that year constituted a "surprisingly small fraction" of the 585 victims of police shootings to date. Furthermore, most of those 585 victims were white or Hispanic (and, again, most were armed). But there *was* a useful ratio for the Black Lives Matter movement: black men accounted for 40 percent of the 60 "unarmed" deaths to date, which helped explain, the *Post* said, "why outrage continues to simmer a year after Ferguson."

By year's end, there were 36 unarmed black men (and two unarmed black women) and 31 unarmed white men (and one unarmed white woman) among the total 991 victims. The rate at which unarmed black men were more likely than unarmed white men to die by police gunfire had dropped to six to one, but the *Post* did not mention that change, and commentators have continued to quote the seven-to-one ratio. The *Post* again highlighted the fact that 40 percent of the unarmed men shot to death by the police were black, which it juxtaposed to the fact that "black men make up only 6 percent of the U.S. population." (A more appropriate benchmark for black men's 40 percent share of unarmed male victims would be black men's roughly 13 percent share of the male U.S. population.)

It is worth looking at the specific cases included in the *Post*'s "unarmed victim" classification in some detail, since that category is the most politically explosive. The "unarmed" label may be literally accurate, but it frequently fails to convey the charged situation facing the officer who used deadly force. In a number of cases, if the victim ended up being unarmed, it was certainly not for lack of trying. At least five black victims had reportedly tried to grab the officer's gun, or had been beating the cop with his own equipment. Some were shot from an accidental discharge triggered by their own assault on the officer. And two individuals included in the *Post*'s "unarmed black victims" category were struck by stray bullets aimed at someone else in justified cop shootings. If the victims were not the intended targets, then racism could have played no role in their deaths.

In one of those unintended cases, an undercover cop from the New York Police Department was conducting a gun sting in Mount Vernon, just north of New York City. One of the gun traffickers jumped into the cop's car, stuck a pistol to his head, grabbed $2,400 and fled. The officer gave chase and opened fire after the thief again pointed his gun at him. Two of the officer's bullets accidentally hit a 61-year-old bystander, killing him. That older man happened to be black, but his race had nothing to do with his tragic death. In the other collateral damage case, officers in Virginia Beach, Virginia, approached a car parked at a convenience store with a homicide suspect in the passenger seat. The suspect opened fire, sending a bullet through an officer's shirt. The cops returned fire, killing their assailant as well as a woman in the driver's seat. If you're chauffeuring someone with a predilection for shooting cops, you have assumed the risk of getting caught in the crossfire. But that female driver also entered the *Post*'s database without qualification as an "unarmed black victim" of police force.

Unfortunately, innocent blacks like the elderly Mount Vernon man probably do face a higher chance of getting shot by stray police fire than innocent whites, but that is because violent crime in their neighborhoods is so much higher. For example, the per capita shooting rate in Brownsville, Brooklyn, is 81 times higher than in Bay Ridge, Brooklyn, a few miles away. This exponentially higher rate of gun violence means that the police will be much more intensively deployed in Brownsville, trying to protect innocent residents and gangbangers alike from shootings. If the police are forced to open fire, in rare instances a police bullet will go astray and hit a bystander. That is tragic, but that innocent's chance of getting shot by the police is dwarfed by his chance of getting shot by criminals.

Other unarmed black victims in the *Post*'s database were so fiercely resisting arrest that the officers involved could reasonably have viewed them as posing a grave danger. In October 2015, a San Diego officer was called to a Holiday Inn in nearby Point Loma, California, after hotel employees ejected a man causing a disturbance in the lobby. The officer approached a male who was casing cars in the hotel's parking lot. The suspect jumped the officer and both fell to the ground. The officer tried to Tase the man, hitting himself as well. The suspect repeatedly tried to wrench the officer's gun from its holster, according to news reports, and continued assaulting the officer after both had stood up. Fearing for his life, the officer shot the man.

Someone who tries taking an officer's gun must be presumed to have the intention to use it. In 2015, three officers were killed by their own gun, which the suspect had wrestled from them. Those three cases represent 7 percent of all felonious firearms killings of police officers in 2015. (The ratio has been similar in past years.) Someone who is fighting for a service weapon represents a lethal danger. Race has nothing to do with it.

In August 2015, an officer from Prince George's County, Maryland, pursued a man who had fled from a car crash. The man tried to grab the officer's gun, and it discharged. The suspect continued to fight with the officer until he was Tased by a second officer and tackled by a third. The shot that was discharged during the struggle ultimately proved fatal to the suspect.

A sheriff's deputy in Strong, Arkansas, responded to a pharmacy burglary alarm early on a January morning. The burglar inside fought with the deputy for control of the deputy's gun and it discharged. The suspect fled the store but was caught outside, at which point the deputy noticed the suspect's gun injury and called an ambulance.

A critic of the police may reject the officers' accounts of deaths at their hands, invoking the videos that discredited police narratives in the shootings of Walter Scott in North Charleston, South Carolina, in April 2015, and of Laquan McDonald in Chicago in October 2014. In the case of Walter Scott, ballistics and autopsy evidence would eventually have undermined Officer Michael Slager's exculpatory story, even without the cell-phone video. But skepticism toward police narratives has now become routine. Equal skepticism is warranted, however, toward witness accounts of allegedly unjustified officer shootings, as demonstrated by the bystander hoax that Michael Brown was gunned down in cold blood by Officer Darren Wilson. Whether one trusts officer accounts more than bystander accounts or vice versa will depend on one's prior assumptions about the police and the community, unless and until there is a critical mass of such conflicting narratives resolved in one direction or the other.

In several cases in the *Post*'s "unarmed black man" category, the suspect had gained control of other pieces of an officer's equipment and was putting it to potentially lethal use. In New York City, a robbery suspect apprehended in a narrow stairwell beat two detectives' faces bloody with a police radio. In Memphis, Tennessee, a 19-year-old wanted on two out-of-state warrants, including a sex offense in Iowa, kicked open a car door during a car stop, grabbed the officer's handcuffs, and hit him in the face with them.

In other instances in the *Post*'s "unarmed black man" category, the suspect's physical resistance was so violent that it could reasonably have put the officer in fear for his life. A trespasser at a motel in Barstow, California, brought a sheriff's deputy to the ground and beat him in the face so viciously that he broke numerous bones and caused other injuries. The suspect refused repeated orders to desist and move away. An officer in such a situation can't know whether he will lose consciousness under the blows to his head; if he does, he is at even greater risk that his gun will be used against him.

An officer in Orlando, Florida, was called about a fight in an apartment complex. The suspect fought so violently with the responding officer that the officer's equipment—including his used Taser, baton, gun magazine, and wristwatch—was torn off and strewn about the scene. In Dearborn, Michigan, a probation violator escaped from officers after committing a theft; later in the day, an officer approached him and he again took off running. A fight ensued, leaving the officer with his gun belt loosened, his equipment from the belt on the ground, and his uniform ripped. The officer was covered with mud and sustained minor injuries. In Miami, a man crashed a taxicab in the early morning hours and took off running onto a highway. During the resulting fight, the driver bit the officer's finger so hard that he nearly severed it; surgery was required to reattach it to the left hand.

Whether these shootings were justified depends on many factors, including the officer's stature in comparison with his assailant's, the officer's degree of exhaustion, whether the officer is on the ground where he is susceptible to being kicked in the head, and what the alternatives are. The *Post* typically omits relevant details about the suspect's violent resistance from its anodyne descriptions of the incidents. The beating in Barstow that broke the officer's bones is described only as a "physical attack" with no mention of the injuries to the officer. In Orlando, the suspect "struggled," but the reader does not learn that the officer's equipment was ripped off him. In Miami, the suspect "bit the officer who approached him"; that this bite nearly severed the officer's finger is left unsaid. The prolonged combat in the New York City stairwell that even the *New York Times* described as "brutal," and that left one detective bleeding from the head and the other bruised and cut in the face, is described merely as the suspect "grab[bing] an officer's radio and striking a detective on the head." Only by digging into the press coverage that is linked on the *Post* database's site can one discover the relevant facts about the altercations.

One can debate the tactics used and the exact moment when an officer would have been justified in opening fire, but these cases are more complicated than a simple "unarmed" classification would lead a reader to believe. A violent fight against an officer is far more fraught than one between two unarmed civilians, due to the officer's gun. "A firearm is involved in every confrontation with a police officer—the one on his hip—and it belongs to the first person who gets it," says Sam Faulkner, a use-of-force trainer who has taught police officers on behalf of the Ohio attorney general.

There are other incongruities in the *Post*'s classification of "black unarmed" victims. A 22-year-old shot at a hotel in Lake Tahoe, California, during a domestic violence call has blond hair, white skin, and freckles in his mug shot. Perhaps he was an albino, but no one seeing him would think he was black. The *Post* includes Victor Emanuel Larosa and Miguel Espinal, among other Hispanic-named victims, in the "unarmed black" category.

The *Post*'s cases do not support the idea that the police have a more demanding standard for using lethal force when confronting unarmed white suspects. According to the press accounts, only one unarmed white victim attempted to grab the officer's gun. In Tuscaloosa, Alabama, a 50-year-old white suspect in a domestic assault call ran at the officer with a spoon; he was Tased and then shot. A 28-year-old driver in Des Moines, Iowa, led police on a chase, then got out of his car and walked quickly toward the officer, and was shot. In Akron, Ohio, a 21-year-old suspect in a grocery store robbery who had escaped on a bike did not remove his hand from his waistband when ordered to do so. Had any of these victims been black, they would have stood a good chance of becoming household names; instead, they are unknown.

Further analysis of the *Post*'s data reveals that police officers are at greater risk from blacks than unarmed blacks are from police officers. Even if we accept the *Post*'s typology of "unarmed" victims at face value, the per capita rate of officers being feloniously killed is 45 times higher than the rate at which unarmed black males are killed by cops. And an officer's chance of getting killed by a *black* assailant is 18.5 times higher than the chance of an unarmed black getting killed by a cop.[‡]

While the nation was focused on the non-epidemic of racist killings by police throughout 2015, the routine drive-by shootings in urban areas were taking their usual toll, often on children, to little national notice. In Cleveland, three children ages five and younger were killed in September. Five children were shot in Cleveland over the Fourth of July weekend. A seven-year-old boy was killed in Chicago that same weekend by a bullet intended for his father. In November, a nine-year-old in Chicago was lured into an alley and killed by his father's gang enemies; the alleged murderer was reportedly avenging the killing of his own 13-year-old brother in October. The father of the murdered nine-year-old refused to cooperate with the police in identifying his son's killers. In August, a nine-year-old girl was doing her homework on her mother's bed in Ferguson

---

‡ The 36 unarmed black male victims of police shootings in 2015 measured against the total black male population (nearly 19 million in mid-2014, per the Census Bureau) amounts to a per capita rate of 0.0000018 unarmed fatalities by police. In comparison, 52 law enforcement officers were feloniously killed while engaged in such duties as traffic stops and warrant service in 2015, according to the National Law Enforcement Officers Memorial Fund. The FBI counted close to 628,000 full-time law enforcement officers in 2014. Assuming that the number of officers did not markedly increase in 2015, the per capita rate of officers being feloniously killed is 0.000081. The Memorial Fund does not have data on the race of cop-killers in 2015, but applying the historical percentages would yield 21 cops killed by blacks in 2015. An officer's chance of getting killed by a black assailant is 0.000033.

when gunfire ripped through her house and killed her. In Cincinnati in July, a four-year-old girl was shot in the head and a six-year-old girl was left paralyzed and partially blind from two separate drive-by shootings. A six-year-old boy was killed in a drive-by shooting on West Florissant Avenue in March in St. Louis. Ten children under the age of 10 were killed in Baltimore in 2015; 12 victims were between the ages of 10 and 17. This is just a partial list of child victims. While the world knows who the thug Michael Brown is, few people outside these children's immediate communities know their names.

The movement launched in Brown's name is a dangerous distraction from the most serious use-of-force problem facing black communities: criminal violence. As long as crime rates in those communities remain so high, officers will be disproportionately engaged there, with all the attendant risks of such deployment. By all means, we must try to eliminate any unjustified use of force by the police. If de-escalation training can safely reduce the application of force in policing, it should be widely implemented. But the biggest takeaway from the *Washington Post*'s database is the salience of suspect resistance in officer use of force, a finding consistent with Justice Department research. A serious "black lives matter" initiative would educate the public about the need to obey police commands. Instead, the incessant refrain that cops are racist could well increase the likelihood that black suspects will violently resist arrest—sometimes at the cost of their lives.

PART TWO

Handcuffing the Cops

The highly publicized antipolice movement that swelled after the shooting death of Michael Brown has made officers around the country more reluctant to engage proactively. But long before August 2014, a campaign against proactive policing was quietly proceeding in the courts and in the U.S. Department of Justice, rooted in the premise that such practices are a violation of civil rights. It is this campaign that poses the greatest threat to the vigilant style of policing that brought great improvements in public safety to New York and other American cities.

A 1994 law gives the Justice Department the authority to seek control of police agencies that have engaged in a "pattern or practice" of constitutional violations. On that basis, the federal government asserted oversight of the Los Angeles Police Department in 2000, aiming to ferret out racial bias. Such a monitoring regime diverts police resources to compliance requirements and away from fighting crime. The Obama administration took this model and ran with it, opening an unprecedented 23 investigations of police departments since 2009. In February 2016, the administration sued Ferguson for balking at the consent decree it sought to foist on the city; in March, the city caved in and agreed to be federally monitored.

In New York, a cluster of civil rights groups began seeking to control the police department through judicial power in 2008. The main target of the activists' ire was the policing tactic commonly known as "stop-and-frisk," which is better described as "stop, question, and frisk." The Supreme Court had authorized the tactic in *Terry* v. *Ohio* (1968), which held that a cop may briefly detain an individual for questioning if the cop has a reasonable suspicion that he is engaged in criminal activity; if the suspect appears to be armed, the officer may pat him down for weapons. These proactive stops contributed significantly to New York City's record-breaking crime drop by interrupting crimes in progress and deterring gangbangers from carrying guns.

The activist attorneys charged that the NYPD's stop, question, and frisk practice was racially biased. The majority of stop subjects in New York City were minorities—a function of the fact that the vast majority of crime takes place in minority communities. Opponents of "stop-and-frisk" maintained that police activity should essentially match population distributions, rather than crime. Whites are a third of New York City's population, for example, so a comparable portion of police stops should have white subjects, even though whites commit almost none of the city's street violence.

In August 2013, a U.S. district court judge, Shira Scheindlin, agreed with the argument for racial proportionality and declared the NYPD a constitutional renegade. That case, *Floyd* v. *New York*, was just one of three involving stop, question, and frisk that were in Scheindlin's courtroom in 2013; the judge had already decided for the plaintiffs in *Ligon* v. *New York*, a more narrowly focused suit, in January. A few months after her decision in *Floyd*, the Second Circuit Court of Appeals removed Scheindlin from the *Floyd* litigation on the ground that she had violated the appearance of judicial impartiality by soliciting *Floyd*'s filing. Nevertheless, New York's mayor Bill de Blasio and police commissioner William Bratton accepted Scheindlin's ruling and the federal oversight that resulted from it. By 2015 (as previously noted), stops were down 95 percent from their 2011 high, and cops were reporting that guns were rampant on the streets. Murders and shootings surged until Bratton saturated shooting hot spots with officers.

Activists in New York and elsewhere are now campaigning against Broken Windows policing, with the claim that it, too, discriminates against minorities. The fact that black and Hispanic communities generate the bulk of public-order complaints is again ignored. Black Lives Matter protesters nationally have taken up the crusade against pedestrian stops and Broken Windows policing. The agitation against these practices exacerbates the Ferguson de-policing effect.

14

Targeting the Police

A deputy attorney general in the Clinton administration, in 2000, slapped the Los Angeles Police Department with federal oversight based on the 1994 law designed to curb a "pattern or practice" of constitutional violations. The Justice Department's attorneys never uncovered any systemic constitutional abuses in the LAPD, as required by that law, despite having commandeered hundreds of thousands of documents (and having lost ten boxes of sensitive records). Nevertheless, for the next 12 years, the LAPD would operate under a draconian federal consent decree governing nearly every aspect of its operations, at a cost of over $100 million in contracting fees and in manpower diverted to mindless paper-pushing.

The deputy attorney general who forced federal control on the LAPD in 2000 was none other than Eric Holder, who would later preside over a Justice Department determined to make the Los Angeles consent decree the model for future oversight of police departments. In June 2010, the assistant attorney general for civil rights, Thomas Perez, told a conference of police chiefs that the Justice Department would be pursuing "pattern or practice" takeovers of police departments much more aggressively than the Bush administration, eschewing negotiation in favor of hardball tactics seeking immediate federal control. Perez hired nine additional attorneys to beef up his division's search for alleged police agency racism and to sue agencies that don't capitulate to federal demands.

To see what this would mean for the nation's police, one need look no further than the Los Angeles Police Department's travails with the Justice Department.

The LAPD consent decree was a power grab from day one. The first thing that DOJ demanded as part of its new authority over the LAPD was the collection of racial information on every stop that the L.A. officers make—even though the corruption scandal that provided the pretext for the consent decree had nothing to do with race or alleged "racial profiling."

The 180-clause decree mired the LAPD's operations in red tape, apparently on the theory that if cops are left to actually fight crime, rather than writing and reviewing reports, they will run amok violating people's rights. Today, an L.A. officer can hardly nod at a civilian without filling out numerous forms documenting his salutation for later review. If he returns fire at a gangbanger, his use of force will be more intensely investigated for wrongdoing than the criminal shooting that provoked the officer's defensive reaction in the first place.

The LAPD spent approximately $40 million trying to comply with the decree in its first year and close to $50 million annually for several years thereafter. It pulled 350 officers off the street to meet the decree's mountainous paperwork requirements. Nevertheless, it struggled to meet the fanatical standards for compliance imposed by the federal monitor overseeing the decree, who demanded that virtually 100 percent of the arbitrary deadlines for filing reports be met on time, regardless of whether the supervisors who missed their deadline by a few days were otherwise occupied with a triple homicide investigation. In 2006, the federal court to which the monitor reported deemed the department out of compliance with the decree and extended its term. In 2009, the court ended federal control on many of the decree's provisions, yet continued federal oversight on issues relating to "biased policing," among other matters, until January 2011. Facing the potential final expiration of the consent decree, the Justice Department made its most preposterous charge against the LAPD yet, in a desperate last-minute bid to retain its power over the force.

According to DOJ's civil rights division, the LAPD was not investigating racial profiling complaints with sufficient intensity. The department seemed to tolerate a "culture that is inimical to race-neutral policing," said the federal attorneys. These accusations were nothing short of delusional. The LAPD is arguably the most professional, community-oriented police agency in the country, having been led for most of the last decade by modern policing's premier innovator, William Bratton. Moreover, it investigates every racial profiling allegation with an obsessive thoroughness that stands in stark contrast to the frivolity of most profiling accusations. No matter how patently fabricated, every racial profiling complaint receives days of painstaking investigation up through multiple chains of command. A complainant can outright admit making up the profiling charge in retaliation for being arrested, and the LAPD's special profiling investigation body, the Constitutional Policing Unit (CPU), will continue diligently poring over his complaint as if it had been made in good faith. After the department logs a whopping average of 100 hours on each complaint, devoting more resources to these knee-jerk accusations than to any other kind of alleged officer misbehavior, the LAPD's civilian inspector general will audit the department's work with a two-part, 60-question matrix, subjecting claims made by arresting officers to a reflexive skepticism unmoored from reality. The goal of this byzantine process? To find any possible way not to dismiss complaints as unsubstantiated.

Here is a typical profiling allegation and its disposition: A driver who had been cited for tinted windows denied in his racial profiling complaint that his windows were tinted and claimed that he was stopped only because he was black. He said that he was detained for an excessive 45 minutes. The arresting officers estimated that the stop lasted 15 minutes; electronic records revealed that it lasted a reasonable 18 minutes. Department personnel interviewed the complainant twice; the arresting officers were closely interrogated; and the CPU canvassed local businesses around the stop for video of the interaction. The CPU then made an appointment to photograph the driver's car to confirm that his windows were not tinted; the driver failed to appear at the appointment and later called the LAPD to say that he wanted no further contact from the department on his profiling complaint.

Leaving aside the devastating hole that the complainant blew in his own credibility by withholding his car, the complaint was logically problematic to begin with. If the driver's windows were tinted, the cops could not have seen his race, especially since the stop occurred at midnight. Indeed, the complainant himself reported that he had to keep his window rolled down during the stop so that the officer could see into the vehicle. But if the windows were not tinted, it strains credulity that an officer would cite a driver for a violation that could be so easily disproved simply by presenting the car.

Nevertheless, the LAPD's inspector general, Nicole Bershon, after reviewing the voluminous case history, concluded that the accused officer should not be cleared of the profiling charge and that the department should reopen the investigation—though there was nothing more to investigate. Because the car's windows had not been inspected, she said, the officer's claim that he could not see the driver's race before stopping him could not be adjudicated. Bershon, however, rehabilitated the driver's credibility on a wholly speculative theory: because the sergeant who logged the profiling charge asked the driver in passing if he was making the complaint to avoid paying the tinting fine, the complainant lost confidence in the process, Bershon hypothesizes, and as a result went AWOL with his car. Of course, the complainant had already shown enough confidence in the process to sit for two interviews. It was only when it came time to present his car that his painful disillusionment, in Bershon's imaginary scenario, manifested itself.

Predictably, Bershon criticized the intake sergeant for questioning the complainant's motives, however flippantly. In an ideal world, to be sure, no police officer would ever express the slightest personal opinion in his interactions with civilians. But a station house is not an ideal world; it is peopled with human beings whose daily exposure to the full, sorry range of human behavior breeds in them a certain degree of cynicism. Regrettably, that cynicism occasionally breaks through the surface. The notion of cutting officers any slack for such failings—which, in light of their public service, are relatively minor—is, of course, out of the question.

It is this insanely credulous and costly process for investigating racial profiling complaints that the Obama Justice Department claimed to find insufficiently rigorous, in a disturbing harbinger for other police departments. The most damning flaw of the LAPD's elaborate anti-profiling apparatus, from DOJ's perspective, was that it corroborated almost none of the already-minuscule number of racial profiling complaints that the department receives each year. (In 2009, the department received 219 racial profiling complaints out of nearly 200,000 arrests and more than 580,000 citations.) To the Washington attorneys, the paucity of confirmed complaints proved that the investigative process was inadequate, if not in bad faith, since it was a given to the Justice Department staff that the LAPD, like every other police department, routinely violates people's rights. The possibility that the vast majority of Los Angeles officers operate within the law was simply not credible to the DOJ.

Such a preordained conclusion is not surprising, since the career attorneys who investigate police departments for constitutional violations are possibly the most left-wing members of the standing federal bureaucracy. They know, without any felt need for prolonged exposure to police work, that contemporary policing is shot through with bias. During the Bush administration, political appointees to the civil rights division reined in the staff's eagerness to investigate police departments for racial profiling, since the profiling studies routinely served up by the ACLU and other activist organizations were based on laughably bogus methodology. After those appointees left the Justice Department, however, the staff attorneys in the policing section were back in control. And the assistant attorney general for civil rights, after declaring that civil rights advocacy groups would once again function as the "eyes and ears" of the department, publicly embraced the advocates' specious methodology for measuring biased law-enforcement actions.

Civil rights activists invariably use population data as the benchmark for police activity—measuring the rate of police stops for various racial groups, say, against the proportion of those groups in the local population. If the stop rate for a particular group is higher than its population ratio, the activists charge bias. Such a population benchmark could only be remotely appropriate, however, if racial crime rates were equal. They are not. In Los Angeles, for example, blacks commit 42 percent of all robberies and 34 percent of all felonies, though they are 10 percent of the city's population. Whites commit 5 percent of all robberies and 13 percent of all felonies, though they are 29.4 percent of the city's population. Such crime disparities—which are repeated in every big city—mean that the police cannot focus their resources where crime victims most need them without disproportionate enforcement activity in minority neighborhoods, but it is crime, not race, that determines such police deployment.

In September 2010, Thomas Perez, the assistant attorney general for civil rights, announced a litigation campaign against school districts for so-called disciplinary profiling—disciplining black students at a higher rate than white students. He used student population ratios as the benchmark for appropriate rates of student discipline. "The numbers tell the story," he said. "While blacks make up 17 percent of the student population, they are 37 percent of the students penalized by out-of-school suspensions and 43 percent of the students expelled."

Actually, those numbers don't tell the story. The real story behind black student discipline rates is higher levels of violence and misbehavior in school, a reality that Perez ignored completely. DOJ's future assessment of police stops and other enforcement actions will likewise inevitably ignore higher rates of black crime.

DOJ's assertion that the culture of the LAPD is "inimical to race-neutral policing" exploits this same blindness to the facts of crime. The Justice Department seized on a single exchange between two cops who were caught on tape discussing a profiling complaint brought against a fellow officer. One says: "So what?" The other responds that he "couldn't do [his] job without racially profiling." To the feds, this exchange can have only one meaning: these and other cops are randomly hauling over blacks and Hispanics to harass them. But if the officers were involved in gang enforcement, as almost any officer patrolling in the city's southern and eastern sections will likely at some point be, attention to a suspect's race and ethnicity is unavoidable, since L.A.'s gangs are obsessively self-defined by skin color. Until Los Angeles gangs give up their fealty to racial identity, they can expect police officers trying to protect the public from their lethal activities to take their race and ethnicity into account in identifying them.

• • •

The greatest beneficiary of the campaign against police departments will be the police monitoring business. Police monitors, paid for by the locality but reporting to a federal court, range from attorneys to former police officials; they are ostensibly jointly selected by the locality and the Justice Department, but repeat business depends on not antagonizing their DOJ backers. The industry has already perfected such fee-generating practices as billing eight hours to summarize a one-hour meeting. Detroit's federal monitor collected $120,000 to $193,000 a month for her services, for a cool $13 million, which the city has tried to recover after discovering that she consorted with the mayor during her tenure as monitor. The New Jersey State Police spent $36 million to build the racial profiling monitoring system demanded by the Clinton Justice Department and $70 million running it. Oakland's federal monitor pulled in nearly $2 million for two years overseeing the financially strapped department, which now allocates 18 officers for internal affairs investigations but only 11 for homicides. Oakland's monitor had previously worked for DOJ's pattern-or-practice section and was rehired there, where she can be expected to impose similar staffing priorities on other departments. With the revival of the L.A. model of indefinitely renewable, rigidly prescriptive consent decrees, the monitoring business can expect to clean up even further.

There are police departments that could benefit from expert advice by actual police professionals on such issues as use of force, but these are unlikely to draw the attention of the Justice Department. Five-man departments in rural areas where the police chief is the mayor's brother-in-law may well have developed questionable habits, such as walloping suspects who talk back to their arresting officers. Perez said that he wanted to pursue "high-impact" cases, however—meaning big-city departments with a national media presence, even if those departments are already permeated by layers of internal and external safeguards against abuse. Justice Department attorneys homed in on the New York Police Department after convening a closed-door session with the city's anti-cop activists to discuss the multicultural NYPD's alleged failings toward immigrant populations. In 2012, as we have seen, the DOJ imposed a sweeping consent decree on the New Orleans Police Department after investigating charges of civil rights violations.

If the Justice Department were serious about police reform, it would publish its standards for opening a pattern-or-practice investigation so that police agencies could take preventive action on their own. It has never done so, however, because it has no standards for opening an investigation; the initial recommendation to do so is based on the whims of the staffers, such as: "I feel like going to Seattle, and my Google sweep picked up a few articles on the police there," or "My buddy at the NAACP Legal Defense and Educational Fund called me and asked us to open up an investigation in Des Moines." Once the federal attorneys show up in town, for what can be a multiyear fishing expedition through thousands of documents, they rarely disclose to the police department what exactly they are looking for. Meanwhile, the local press engages in a frenzy of speculation about which racist practices the feds are investigating and pressures the department to cave in to federal control.

While DOJ pursues the phantom of widespread police racism, the real abuse in minority communities gets no attention from the civil rights division. In Los Angeles on Halloween 2010, five-year-old Aaron Shannon, Jr. was showing off his Spiderman costume in his family's South Central backyard when he was fatally shot by two young thugs from the Kitchen Crips gang. Aaron was randomly selected in retaliation for an earlier gang shooting; his family had no known gang ties. DOJ's pattern-or-practice attorneys had nothing to say about such grotesque violence even as they were rebuking the LAPD for its alleged inadequacies investigating profiling complaints. And if the LAPD had stopped known gang members around the Shannon home after the Halloween homicide in order to seek intelligence about the shooting, every stop that the officers made would have been tallied against the department in DOJ's racial profiling calculus, simply because the Kitchen Crips and their rivals are black.

Though reform police chiefs like William Bratton and the NYPD's Ray Kelly brought crime down to near-record lows by 2014, violence has continued to afflict minority communities at astronomically higher levels than white communities. The public discourse around policing has focused exclusively on alleged police racism to the neglect of a far more serious and pervasive problem: black crime. If a fraction of the public attention that has been devoted to flushing out supposed police bias had been devoted to stigmatizing criminals and revalorizing the two-parent family, the association between black communities and heavy police presence might have been broken. Instead, the Obama Justice Department has retreated further from honesty.

15

Courts v. Cops

In 2013, a federal judge contemplated three lawsuits asserting that the New York City Police Department's practice of stopping, questioning, and sometimes frisking suspects was unconstitutional and racist. U.S. District Judge Shira Scheindlin issued the first of her rulings in that trilogy of suits on January 8, holding that the NYPD routinely made illegal trespass stops in the Bronx. The ruling was a bad enough blow for the NYPD in its own right, but even more disturbing as an augury of things to come. The decision made it clear that Scheindlin would rule against the city in every stop-and-frisk case before her, jeopardizing the police department's ability to fight crime.

Ligon v. *New York* challenged a decades-long program that authorizes New York police officers to patrol private buildings for trespassers and other lawbreakers. The Trespass Affidavit Program (TAP) tries to give low-income tenants in high-crime areas the same protection against intruders that wealthy residents of doorman-guarded buildings enjoy. According to the New York Civil Liberties Union (NYCLU), however, police officers routinely abuse their power under TAP by stopping and arresting minority residents and their guests on suspicion of trespass without any legal justification.

The NYCLU didn't come close to proving its case. But the litigation's most disturbing failure was its blindness to the realities of inner-city crime.

• • •

Debbie McBride has nothing but contempt for the litigation over the Trespass Affidavit Program. McBride is a street-hardened building superintendent in the heart of the South Bronx zone targeted by the NYCLU. When asked about TAP, also known as the Clean Halls program, she doesn't mince words. "I love it!" she roars. "I'm serious, I *love* it. Me being a woman, I feel safe. I can get up at 4 AM and start working."

McBride represents a type that seemingly lies outside the conceptual universe of the advocates and their enablers in elite law firms and the media: the black inner-city crusader for bourgeois order. In 1999, McBride moved from Brooklyn to her present residence in the Mount Hope section of the Bronx. Her own intersections with street life had left her a three-time victim of rape and blind in one eye from assault—a boyfriend had struck her for refusing to try heroin—but she still wasn't prepared for the South Bronx. "I had had none of this before," she says. "It was like *New Jack City*. People were selling crack openly in the lobby." She asked fellow tenants how long the lobby's drug trade had been going on. Thirty years, they answered. McBride, "desperate" about her building's lawlessness (as she puts it), started attending community meetings at the NYPD's 44th Precinct and secretly partnering with a local cop to get rid of the drug dealers. "I used to give him the nod," she recalls. The officer made so many arrests in her building that he won a promotion to detective.

In 2004, a new owner took over McBride's building and offered her the superintendent's job. "I don't know nothing about plumbing," she warned him, but his instinct for character proved flawless. Today, she roams her building's immaculate halls, searching for stray cigarette butts, with a bouquet of black trash bags tied to her belt. Her biggest concern, however, is not trash but trespassers, since many indoor crimes are committed by nonresidents. Accordingly, McBride has an inviolate rule: no one loiters inside or outside her building, not even tenants. "We're not playing here," she says. "People try to get in, saying: 'I'm looking for so-and-so.' But I throw everyone out, because I'm not going back" to the way things were.

The Trespass Affidavit Program, which the new owner immediately signed up for, buttresses McBride's determination to keep the building safe. "I'm so happy that the cops are here," she says. The feeling is apparently mutual. "The cops love me because I'm the bitch super. 'We love coming into your building,' they say, 'because there's none of the piss and stuff that goes on in other buildings.'" In the summer of 2013, TAP officers helped restore order to the tiny inner courtyard of McBride's building. Teenagers had been jumping over the back gate to have sex on the asphalt, the cleanest spot on the block. "It was crazy," she tells me. "Do you know how many people I called the cops on?" The trespassers didn't go quietly. "'We hate you, you fucking bitch,' they'd say. 'Tell that to your mama,' I said, 'but get out of my backyard.'"

To get the sharpest sense of what trespass means in high-crime neighborhoods, one must talk to the elderly. Mrs. Sweeper, a petite woman with hoop earrings and close-cropped hair, is a tenant of McBride's building. She has been confined to a wheelchair since losing a foot to cancer, but her greatest impediment to mobility comes from fear: she dreads strangers lingering in and around her building. "As soon as [people] see that there's no po-lice around, they ask you to let them into the lobby or to hold the door for them," she observes from her airy, light-filled apartment, decorated with a Prayer for Obama on the wall and a Ringling Brothers toy elephant in the credenza. "'I'm waiting on someone,' they say." And then, if the trespassers gain access, all hell breaks loose: "You can smell their stuff in the hallway; they're cussing and urinating. Then *I* don't want to come in because I'm scared. I'm scared just to stick my key in the door."

The solution to such threatening disorder, in Mrs. Sweeper's view, is the police: "As long as you see the po-lice, everything's A-OK. The building is safe; you can come down and get your mail and talk to decent people." TAP officers climb the stairwells and check the roof and elevators in Mrs. Sweeper's building two or three times a week, but she wants to see them much more frequently. Several summers ago, the 44th Precinct erected a watchtower on the block to deter the gunfire that broke out after dark. "It was the peacefulest summer ever," she recalls. "I could sit outside at night. I wish we'd get our po-lice back. Puh-leez, Jesus, send them back!"

By 2013, crime in the 44th Precinct had dropped 73 percent since 1993, when the NYPD began intensely analyzing crime data through the management process known as CompStat and asking its officers to intervene when they noticed suspicious behavior. But McBride and other area watchdogs know that the sky-high violence levels of the early and mid-1990s could return at any moment. These sentinels of civilization fight a daily battle against lawlessness, scouring the horizon for any signs that disorder is on the rise.

An example of what they guard against is evident a few blocks from McBride's building. A low-riding sedan, blaring hip-hop, is parked next to the Jaylin Barber Shop and a graffiti-splattered bodega; across the street on Morris Avenue is Taft High School, infamous for its violence and its truant students. Seven young males are sitting in and standing around the car, several of them talking on cell phones. A beer bottle flies out of the car's open door and rattles down the sidewalk.

A goateed, barrel-chested man in an orange bomber jacket steps forward to speak for the group. "The Clean Halls program? I'm familiar with it," he says. Why is that? "Because I'm a product of my own environment," he says with Officer Krupke-esque bathos. "I'm victimized every day"—by the police, presumably. Asked what he's doing hanging out on the street, he responds coyly: "That's a little overboard; that's personal." He does volunteer this: "I run the streets. I'm out here every day, morning to night. I'm a businessman." In fact, less than an hour before and a block away, this businessman had greeted me with his best customer-service demeanor: "Howya doin'?"—the usual opening line of the street drug peddler. He seems not to recall that earlier encounter.

Trade must be slow, because Bob, as he mockingly says I should call him, keeps insisting that I put a few twenties in his outstretched palm for a "good story" about the police. "If I put six holes in someone's head, I'm the bad guy. But the cops beat the shit out of my cousin here and they sittin' there eating they fucking lobster every day. They cowards." Bob then announces, out of the blue: "You're here for Kieron; he's getting paid." Kieron Johnson is one of the nine named plaintiffs in *Ligon* v. *New York*, and he lives on the street where Bob propositioned me to buy drugs. In another of that day's coincidences, I had by chance run into Johnson leaving his building just before my encounter with Bob. If Johnson *were* getting paid for his involvement in the suit, the attorneys would be violating the law. The Bronx Defenders, the nonprofit group that recruited Johnson for *Ligon* and that is litigating the suit alongside the NYCLU, denies the charge.

Bob's interest in *Ligon* goes beyond acquaintance with its participants; his business will be affected by its outcome. If the NYPD loses much of its stop, question, and frisk power, life will get a lot easier for the Bobs of the world. Police officers are familiar with their methods: loitering in front of residential buildings, repeated entering and exiting to retrieve stashed merchandise and to close deals out of public sight. Cops also know that people hanging out on the street in crime hot spots, especially at night, are often up to no good. It is precisely to deter such behavior that officers stop and question people, including for trespass.

The advocacy community sees only racism in the fact that the bulk of trespass and other stops happen in minority neighborhoods. But that racism charge ignores the statistical truth that crime, too, is disproportionately concentrated in those neighborhoods, leading to requests from residents like Mrs. Sweeper for protection. Dismissing the idea that the cops are racist, Debbie McBride points to her 20-year-old nephew Richie, who has lived with her for four years since leaving foster care in Brooklyn. Richie comes home from his computer-design classes at Hostos Community College four nights a week, but he's never been stopped by the police. Nor did they ever stop him when he was living in East Flatbush, Brooklyn. "They don't bother him because he's going to school, he's not hanging out," McBride says. On the other hand, "you have six youths on the corner with their pants hanging off their butts, drinking, they're not even from the block." Why are they stopped? "I'm going to keep it real with you: it's the look, it's the jiggaboo. They look and act thuggish. And many of them have warrants."

Many people besides McBride understand what the police are doing, though they rarely show up in the *New York Times*. Victor, a 21-year-old resident of McBride's building, has been stopped a couple of times. "I guess they doing they jobs," he acknowledges. "That's why it's safer: they doing they jobs." Mrs. Sweeper's adult son Michael has been patted down once or twice, but like Victor, he doesn't get worked up about it. "The police are pretty respectful," he says.

• • •

The fierce desire of so many inner-city residents for safe neighborhoods was absent from the plaintiffs' case in *Ligon* v. *New York*. Instead, the plaintiffs' attorneys—who included members of the white-shoe law firm Shearman & Sterling—presented a monochromatic picture of an out-of-control, poorly managed police department irrationally harassing innocent pedestrians. It's worth examining the procedural maneuver by which *Ligon* ended up in trial at all, since it illustrates how the political, legal, and media components of the campaign against the NYPD reinforce one another.

In 2012, agitation against the NYPD's stop-and-frisk policies was picking up steam. A coalition of politicians and left-wing advocacy groups, including the lawyers in the three stop-and-frisk suits, announced an initiative to tie down the police with new bureaucracy and rules on stops. The city council held hearings on the proposed new legislation and on the NYPD's stop practices. The candidates for the 2013 mayoral election competed to see who could denounce police racism the most demagogically. And the *New York Times* went into ecstatic overdrive, pumping out editorials, columns, and news articles accusing the NYPD of routinely abusing blacks and Hispanics.

But throughout this fervor, the three lawsuits remained out of the public eye, plodding through the usual pretrial process of behind-the-scenes motions and depositions. The first and most sweeping of the suits, *Floyd* v. *New York*, which challenged all stop, question, and frisks in the city, wasn't even scheduled for trial yet, though it had been filed in 2008. The next two cases—*Davis* v. *New York*, filed in 2010, challenging trespass stops and arrests in and around public housing, and *Ligon*, filed in March 2012, challenging trespass stops and arrests in and around private buildings—would arrive in court later still. What was needed to bolster the anti-stop cause was an actual trial, which would produce a parade of mediagenic witnesses claiming that the police had illegally harassed them.

So the *Ligon* attorneys made a clever move: they petitioned for a preliminary injunction, even though the case had originally been filed, like the previous two cases, as a regular class-action lawsuit. A party seeking a preliminary injunction argues that he's suffering such ongoing and irreparable harm that a judge needs to hear a truncated version of his case immediately, to enjoin the defendant from further harming him before the regular trial gets under way. The NYCLU never explained why the harm suffered by the *Ligon* plaintiffs was any more irreparable and urgent than that suffered by the *Floyd* and *Davis* plaintiffs, who had been waiting for years for a court hearing. The gambit paid off, however, catapulting *Ligon* into the courtroom ahead of the earlier two cases.

Judge Scheindlin's justification for allowing the preliminary-injunction motion to proceed spoke volumes about her interest in the interlocking trio of cases. Scheindlin had recently granted class certification in *Floyd*, meaning that the attorneys could purport to represent (potentially) hundreds of thousands of plaintiffs, without having to prove their individual cases, and could seek more sweeping judicial oversight of the department. The city had rightly appealed that class-certification order. Now Scheindlin used the city's appeal to hold it hostage. Yes, she acknowledged, preparing for the preliminary-injunction hearing in *Ligon* would be "costly and time-consuming" for the city. But the trial in *Floyd*, she pointed out, "may be indefinitely postponed as a result of the City's decision to appeal this Court's class certification order." If the city didn't like having to prepare for a preliminary-injunction hearing in *Ligon*, she said, it could either agree to an injunction in *Ligon* immediately, without a hearing, or else drop its appeal of the *Floyd* class certification and "permit a trial without delay" in *Floyd*.

If a federal judge hadn't delivered the ultimatum, it would be tempting to call it blackmail. Most tellingly, each of the two unacceptable options that Scheindlin gave the city for avoiding a preliminary-injunction trial would guarantee major press attention to the stop, question, and frisk issue. (Scheindlin, by the way, had encouraged the filing of *Floyd* in the first place as a continuation of an earlier stop-and-frisk lawsuit that she had also presided over, even assuring the attorneys in that earlier suit that she would take jurisdiction over the follow-up case.)

Carving a preliminary-injunction action out of the original *Ligon* complaint provided the NYCLU with an additional advantage besides jumping the queue into the courtroom. The original complaint had challenged trespass stops and arrests both inside and outside Trespass Affidavit Program buildings throughout the city. But the preliminary-injunction motion challenged only trespass stops *outside* TAP buildings, and only in the Bronx. This narrower focus meant that the NYCLU could dismiss the citywide training that the NYPD was conducting on how to do stops properly. That training, according to the motion, was insufficiently targeted at the supposedly unique problem of outdoor trespass stops in the Bronx—even though the legal standard for making a stop is the same in all contexts.

To its credit, the city didn't buckle under Scheindlin's demand that it drop its appeal of the *Floyd* class certification. Instead, it opted to fight the preliminary-injunction version of *Ligon* at trial. The resulting two weeks of hearings in autumn 2012 showed in microcosm just how weak the advocates' case against the NYPD was.

• • •

A central claim in the anti-stop-and-frisk crusade is that NYPD officers regularly accost countless squeaky-clean New Yorkers without cause. It should be easy, then, to assemble an army of Eagle Scout–like victims of police aggression. But four of the nine named plaintiffs in *Ligon* had criminal histories, not even counting their juvenile records; the plaintiffs' nonparty witnesses had similarly troubled stories. Plaintiff "W. B." had already been arrested ten times, despite being only 17, and placed by a court in a juvenile detention home. In December 2015, "W. B." was federally indicted for stomping a 16-year-old gang rival to death in April 2012, six months before the *Ligon* trial began. No wonder the *Ligon* attorneys did not put him on the stand.

The Ledan family was typical of the *Ligon* plaintiffs and witnesses. Forty-one-year-old Letitia Ledan, a named plaintiff who lived in the crime-plagued River Park Towers, had been arrested about 15 times. In the early 1990s, she pleaded guilty to the attempted sale of crack; in the late 1990s, she was convicted of narcotics possession. In 2000, she pleaded guilty to loitering for purposes of prostitution and to using an alias in connection with that arrest. In the early 2000s, she pleaded guilty to the criminal possession of a weapon. In December 2003, she pleaded guilty to the possession of burglary tools. In 2007, she was convicted of aiding in the commission of a felony. Her sometime husband, Antoine Ledan, a nonparty witness, had racked up between ten and 20 criminal convictions over the last 15 years. Antoine was supposed to testify about an incident in which police stopped him and Letitia at River Park Towers, but the NYCLU never called him, claiming without explanation that he was "unavailable." Letitia's brother—36-year-old Roshea Johnson, another plaintiff in the case—had been arrested 21 times. He served six months in prison in the early 1990s for robbery; in the mid-1990s, he was convicted of assault, robbery, and using an illegal alias and served about five years in prison. In July 2003, he was convicted of evading the cigarette tax; in 2011, of cocaine possession; and in 2012, of menacing.

The city had argued that the plaintiffs' criminal backgrounds were relevant to assessing their credibility, since it gave them a motive to defame the police. But Scheindlin, construing precedent with excruciating narrowness, allowed virtually none of the plaintiffs' criminal histories into the record, even though the federal rules of procedure provide for liberal admission of evidence when a judge, not a jury, is hearing a case.

Another commonplace in New York's advocacy community holds that the NYPD's stop-and-frisk policies are inflicting widespread emotional devastation. The head of the Children's Aid Society, for instance, claimed at an event in October 2012 (in which I participated) that stops were producing posttraumatic stress disorder among young minority males. Such trauma, one might think, would be burned in the victims' memories. But the plaintiffs had only the vaguest recollection of when nine of the 11 stops alleged in *Ligon* had occurred—often stating nothing more specific than a year—or of the number and gender of the officers who had stopped them. Whatever details the plaintiffs did provide often changed wildly from one recounting to the next.

That vagueness made it difficult for the NYPD to defend itself by locating the officers who had conducted nine of the alleged stops. (The remaining two stops had resulted in arrests and were therefore easier to corroborate.) The department tried valiantly to find the officers, though. One of the many revelations to emerge from the *Ligon* trial is that the NYPD has an entire office devoted to defending the department against federal civil rights class-action lawsuits. The Special Litigation Support Unit, which reports to the Deputy Commissioner of Legal Affairs, is staffed by detectives whose only job is to respond to the information requests of attorneys prosecuting civil rights cases against the police department—requests that can require obtaining, analyzing, and delivering millions of documents.

The unit's supervisor, Sergeant Robert Musick, testified on the stand about his staff's enormous effort to find information corroborating the stops that would lead to the officers. Initially, there were 45 of these alleged stops; the attorneys whittled them down to 11 only *after* the police department had spent weeks trying to document the other 34. The department's high-powered Office of Management Analysis and Planning, responsible for sophisticated crime analysis, pitched in to help, though it certainly had more important things to do.

One reason that it was so hard to find evidence of the alleged stops was an earlier, successful NYCLU crusade to require the police department to expunge suspects' names from its electronic stop database if their stops didn't lead to arrests. The resulting 2010 data-purging law left the Special Litigation Support Unit with two ways to find the stops alleged in *Ligon*: it could search the electronic database for every possible variant of the stop addresses given by the plaintiffs; or it could manually search months' worth of the forms that officers fill out by hand after stops (called UF-250s), which do contain the suspects' names. The unit also scoured precinct roll-call rosters for any semblance of the officers vaguely described by the plaintiffs.

Despite the unit's Herculean efforts, it found zero documentation of the nine stops that hadn't resulted in arrests. The NYCLU would explain this lacuna by claiming that the officers involved in the undocumented stops negligently failed to fill out UF-250s. But in other anti-NYPD contexts, the NYCLU regularly argues that department productivity quotas are driving officers to make illegal stops, just so that they can fill out UF-250s and hit their targets. Those two propositions are in tension, to say the least.

There are two other possible explanations for the absence of documentation of the *Ligon* stops: the stops never occurred; or they never rose to the level of intrusiveness that requires an officer to complete a UF-250. And if a stop isn't sufficiently coercive to require a UF-250, it also can't provide the basis for a constitutional challenge. Scheindlin, however, simply asserted in her ruling that the department had not tried hard enough to locate the officers involved.

In the two instances in which the city was able to identify the officers, their testimony undercut the plaintiffs' story. Abdullah Turner, an unemployed, 25-year-old high school dropout, claimed to have been stopped for trespass while merely standing outside a residential building in the Bronx. He and his friend Anginette Trinidad had taken a detour there on their way to a party, he claimed, so that Trinidad could drop off a sweater that she'd borrowed from a friend. Because that friend "didn't like new faces," in Trinidad's words, Turner waited outside. As Turner was talking on his cell phone, an officer allegedly snatched it out of his hand and demanded identification. Soon, Trinidad exited the building. Asked by the officers if she was carrying anything unlawful, she admitted to a bag of marijuana and an illegal gravity knife. The officers arrested her for drug and weapons possession and charged Turner with trespassing, even though, by his account, he had never been inside the building.

According to the officers' testimony, however, they had observed Turner inside the lobby for two or three minutes, pacing back and forth and constantly peering up the stairs. One of the officers had made drug and trespass arrests at the building before; its block was well known in the precinct for gun and drug crimes. When Turner exited the building, the officers approached and asked him if he lived there or knew anyone there. Turner allegedly answered that he had come with his friend, who was upstairs buying marijuana. The officers' initial observations of Turner could easily justify stopping him to ask about his presence in the building; a possible nonresident pacing the unsecured lobby of a drug-infested building is precisely the kind of visitor who would disturb a Mrs. Sweeper and whom officers should look out for.

The nine undocumented stops were no more helpful to the plaintiffs' case. Take Kieron Johnson's alleged encounter with the cops. The 21-year-old unemployed high school dropout claimed that sometime in 2010, he was waiting for his friend Jovan Jefferson, another *Ligon* plaintiff, outside Jefferson's building (which is across from his own) in the middle of the day in order to play basketball. Two officers jumped out of a police car, asked if Johnson had been inside the building, demanded identification, rifled through his wallet, and patted him down. But as Johnson himself admitted, the officers who stopped him were truancy officers, and they asked him why he wasn't in school. Not only is that a legitimate question for truancy officers to ask a teenager standing on a residential street in the middle of a school day; it also means that the stop didn't concern trespass and thus didn't belong in the lawsuit at all.

Because of that stop and others like it, Johnson testified, he has "barely gone outside" for three years. It was therefore a remarkable coincidence that in my one unannounced visit to Johnson's building in November, this hermit, a slender young man with a slight beard, should have been on his way out of the lobby. Johnson's account to me of his encounters with the law was even more jumbled than those that he'd given in the course of the lawsuit. He mentioned previously undisclosed arrests and court appearances and claimed that the police had beaten up his friend Jefferson during one of the stops, something that Jefferson himself had never alleged.

If Johnson is correct at least about how often police officers make trespass and other stops on Selwyn Avenue, where he and Jefferson live, it's easy to see why they do. Bob's drug solicitations a few paces down from Johnson's building is just the start of the reasons. Minutes before Johnson entered his lobby, a wizened elderly man and a 34-year-old female resident had reported to me that trespassing teens regularly invade the building to smoke marijuana, despite the landlord's efforts to kick them out—precisely one of the signs of disorder that so frighten Mrs. Sweeper. As for Jefferson's building across the street, there are "more crackheads there," Johnson said, speculating that perhaps the police who stopped him had thought that he was a dealer. Jefferson himself, who was convicted of trespass in 2009 and had been arrested seven times since 2007, was given a judicial reprieve from a marijuana sales conviction in April 2012.

•   •   •

Judge Scheindlin credited all of the plaintiffs' testimony, despite its vagueness and occasional inconsistency, and rejected all of the officers' rebutting testimony. But even if those 11 alleged trespass stops occurred exactly as the plaintiffs claimed, they still represent only a tiny percentage of the several hundred thousand stops conducted in the Bronx over six years, hardly amounting to the kind of systemic police abuse that would require judicial intervention. That's where Columbia law professor Jeffrey Fagan came in. Fagan is the advocates' stop-and-frisk expert of choice; he has provided the statistical ammunition in several stop suits against the NYPD. His specialty is analyzing UF-250 forms en masse, seeking to show that cops are engaged in illegal, racially biased stops, though his methodology for reaching that conclusion is in constant flux. In *Ligon*, for which he was paid $375 an hour, he looked at the UF-250s for 1,663 trespass stops outside TAP buildings in the Bronx in 2011 and concluded that nearly 63 percent of them were illegal.

As an initial matter, it's absurd to determine the constitutionality of a stop according to the way that an officer filled out a UF-250. Even if busy officers in high-crime precincts completed the form as thoroughly as possible, its abbreviated categories would often fail to capture the specificity of the officers' observations that justified the stop.

But sometimes even the UF-250 is precise enough to show how little Fagan understands the world of Debbie McBride and Mrs. Sweeper. Fagan deemed unconstitutional a trespass stop whose suspect had been observed "pulling door open forcibly with no key," as the police officer wrote in the UF-250. Before another supposedly unconstitutional stop, the officer had seen the suspect "trying to enter one building when unab[le]." According to Fagan, the officers' suspicion in both cases that the individual might have been trespassing wasn't "reasonable"—the constitutional standard for making a stop. Time for a thought experiment: the doorman of a building where a Shearman & Sterling partner lives sees someone apparently trying to force his way into the lawyer's home and does nothing about it. How long does the doorman keep his job? Answer: not long, even though the lawyer's neighborhood is undoubtedly a lot safer than the South Bronx. Yet according to the Shearman & Sterling team on *Ligon*, a police officer—an officer trying to provide inner-city residents with some fraction of the security that the liberal elite take for granted—could have no reasonable basis for suspecting that someone trying to force his way into a residential building in a high-crime area is committing trespass.

In several dozen of the stops that Fagan deemed illegal, the officer knew that a particular building had experienced a string of indoor robberies and saw the suspect making "furtive movements" (in the language of the UF-250) outside that building. Fagan and the plaintiffs argued that such circumstances would provide "reasonable suspicion" only for a *robbery* stop, not for a trespass stop. But so many indoor robberies are committed by trespassers that it makes perfect sense to suspect trespass in a robbery-plagued building. Fagan's crabbed view of officer discretion would shut down crime prevention entirely.

Scheindlin accepted Fagan's conclusions that police in the Bronx routinely make illegal trespass stops outside TAP buildings. But to issue a preliminary injunction against the department, she also had to find that the NYPD was "deliberately indifferent" to such abuse.

It was here that the *Ligon* trial entered its most surreal phase. Commanders from the highest level of the NYPD were treated on the stand like dolts or recalcitrant children if they failed to recall one document that the NYCLU had plucked out of the thousands that flood through the department each year—even though their responsibilities in one day exceed anything that an NYCLU attorney shoulders in 12 months.

Delegation is a concept with which the NYCLU and Judge Scheindlin seemed unfamiliar. Deputy Chief Brian McCarthy is the executive officer of the NYPD's Patrol Services Bureau, tasked with overseeing 25,000 patrol officers in eight borough commands. Scheindlin could barely contain her incredulity when the mild-mannered McCarthy, answering a question that has zero relevance to his job, said that he wasn't sure what year a particular section of the massive *Field Training Guide* for rookie officers had first appeared. "You don't know?" she asked, her voice dripping with condescension. "How long has it been around, decades? How long have you been in your position?" At another point, Christopher Dunn, the NYCLU's lead attorney, asked McCarthy if he personally reviewed UF-250 forms. Very rarely, McCarthy answered. It's ludicrous, of course, to suggest that a deputy chief ought to scrutinize the hundreds of thousands of UF-250s written every year. Dunn nevertheless persisted: "Do you recall a single instance where you reviewed a stop that you knew was TAP-related?" When McCarthy explained that top brass reviewed selected arrests during weekly CompStat meetings and would therefore necessarily discuss TAP arrests if they came up, Dunn struggled to contain his impatience. "Let me go back," he said slowly, enunciating each syllable so as to be sure of being understood by this cretin. "You mentioned yesterday that every arrest was brought to the precinct for desk officer review. . . ."

As aggressive as they were, the NYCLU's efforts to expose an NYPD oblivious to its constitutional obligations backfired—or so most disinterested observers would have concluded. Witness after witness attested to the department's self-scrutiny. Long before the NYCLU filed *Ligon*, the NYPD had sharply increased its training and oversight related to stop, question, and frisks in general and to trespass stops in particular. The department's self-analysis and accountability put the NYCLU in the position of trying to outpace what the NYPD was already doing. Hence the activists' strategy of carving out a speciously narrow category of stops in its preliminary-injunction motion. Have NYPD brass ordered platoon commanders to critique stops at TAP buildings? Yes, but that's not good enough, the NYCLU retorts; what are they doing to ensure that *trespass* stops *outside* TAP buildings in the *Bronx* are under review? Have patrol supervisors been commanded, when possible, to drive to TAP buildings after arrests there to make sure that the arrests were done properly? Yes, but big deal, sniffs the NYCLU; we see nothing in that order about *outdoor trespass stops* in the *Bronx*! This strange one-upmanship doesn't just ignore the logical truth that the general contains the particular. It's also deeply solipsistic, as it's based on the delusion that the NYPD's policies should mirror the activists' categories, which sprouted from legal strategy, rather than policing expertise.

Nowhere were the NYCLU's solipsism and ambition more evident than in its proposed remedies, a grab bag of new procedures that would remake the department's chain of command. The NYCLU preposterously demanded, for example, that an official in the chief of patrol's office be designated to review every UF-250 for a trespass stop outside a Bronx TAP building and then report on his findings. Whom would he report to? Why, to the NYCLU, of course, which would also receive copies of every UF-250 under review. Who better to understand trends in crime and strategic response?

But the NYCLU hadn't justified this demand for special treatment for a particular kind of stop. It never demonstrated that trespass stops were so different from stops in general, or that *outdoor* trespass stops were so different from trespass stops in general, or that the *Bronx* had a unique problem with outdoor trespass stops. It was simply throwing out improvised protocols and hoping that some would stick. Dunn made another of these demands in his closing arguments to the court, suggesting that Scheindlin require police supervisors in the Bronx to meet face-to-face with every officer who makes a trespass stop outside a TAP building to discuss that stop. (Currently, supervisors are supposed to review the

UF-250s but don't need to speak with the officers.) This arbitrary accretion of red tape was too much even for Scheindlin, who asked Dunn: "If every stop requires an interview with a supervisor, how is any policing going to get done in this town? You're doubling the time on every stop." Hilariously, Dunn responded with saccharine concern: "We're particularly sensitive to the demands on the NYPD's time." Two weeks later, when the NYCLU filed its final proposals with the court, the demand for face-to-face meetings had disappeared.

It hardly mattered. Scheindlin agreed with the NYCLU that the NYPD had been "deliberately indifferent" to the law and proposed a slightly modified set of additional training and supervision protocols. She stayed their effect, however, until *Floyd* reached its own remedies phase. Most strikingly, she invited plaintiffs' counsel from all three suits to collaborate on new citywide stop, question, and frisk rules. This proposal was a remarkably frank admission, despite Scheindlin's protestations to the contrary, of how she thought the remaining cases would come out.

• • •

After the *Ligon* ruling in January 2013, the NYCLU's executive director, Donna Lieberman, exulted that the case represented "a major step toward dismantling the NYPD's stop-and-frisk regime." Sadly, she was right. Scheindlin went on to declare the department's entire stop, question, and frisk practice unconstitutional in her *Floyd* ruling that summer. Even if future mayoral administrations are supportive of proactive policing, they will have to contend with the judicial restraints on the police department that Mayor Bill de Blasio happily accepted when he entered office in 2014.

This outcome threatens New York City's unmatched public-safety triumph. No other police department in the country came close to achieving what the NYPD had done since the early 1990s: New York's crime drop during that period was twice as deep and lasted twice as long as the national average. By early June 2015, however, murders were up 20 percent and shootings up 9 percent in the city. Gun crime had risen for two years in a row, the first two-year consecutive increase in nearly two decades. Mayor de Blasio and Commissioner Bratton were noticeably panicking;

New Yorkers should not worry about the surge in violence, they said, because its victims were predominantly gangbangers.

Bratton unleashed all the manpower available to him. He jumpstarted by a month a summer program of high-visibility policing that flooded shooting zones with cops. These additional resources were expected to discourage criminals by their mere presence on the street, rather than by making pedestrian stops. Given the manpower uniquely available to the NYPD, it worked. The shooting surge flattened out, and by the end of 2015, murders were up by "only" 6 percent. Bratton and de Blasio declared victory.

Critics of stop, question, and frisk have seized on 2015's final crime tally as evidence that pedestrian stops are unnecessary. But if Bratton had not had the officers with which to saturate emerging violence zones—and the overtime funding to pay for them—the crime trajectory of the first half of 2015 would have continued throughout the year. With another 1,000 cops slated to enter the force by 2016, Bratton may be able to keep a lid on crime by using command presence even more intensively, though that remains to be seen.

The lesson from the stop, question, and frisk lawsuit trilogy and its aftermath is that policing matters—whether it's proactive intervention into suspicious activity, or merely projecting law and order with a conspicuous presence. For now, Debbie McBride has a message for the local teens who try to intimidate cops: "People complain: 'Why are the cops here?' To protect you; they come here to protect you." That's something the NYCLU needs to hear, too.

16

The Great Stop-and-Frisk Fraud

Seven months after U.S. District Judge Shira Scheindlin ruled against the New York Police Department in *Ligon* v. *New York*, she announced her decision on the most sweeping of the three lawsuits challenging the department's practice of stopping, questioning, and sometimes frisking suspicious individuals. The plaintiffs in *Floyd* v. *New York* charged that this practice was driven by race, not crime. Scheindlin issued her ruling for the plaintiffs on August 12, 2013. In reaching her decision, she relied heavily on the arcane statistical models of Professor Jeffrey Fagan, as she did in *Ligon*. Let us take a careful look at Fagan's role in the trial, the actual numbers behind his scholarship, and the methods he used to reach his conclusions—which might be characterized as a tutorial on lying with statistics.

Scheindlin could not have reached her verdict based on the case's 12 individual complainants alone. Even if she had concluded that the named plaintiffs were all stopped because of their race—a finding that would have required ignoring the considerable evidence supporting their stops—that judgment would still have left her far from the requisite inference that their police encounters were emblematic of the 4.4 million stops that the NYPD had conducted since 2004.

That's where Fagan came in, again. He was tasked with showing en masse that those 4.4 million stops were made not because the officers suspected that the individuals stopped were engaged in criminal activity but because most of those individuals were black or Hispanic. The models he constructed to prove such bias were an apt symbol of the lawsuit itself: wholly detached from the realities of crime and policing in New York.

• • •

The Center for Constitutional Rights and the elite law firm of Covington & Burling, the attorneys in *Floyd*, faced an inconvenient truth: the stop rate for blacks was actually lower than their violent crime rate would predict. Blacks, who constitute 23 percent of the city's population, commit two-thirds of all violent crimes and three-quarters of all shootings, according to victims and witnesses, but they were only 53 percent of all stop subjects in 2011. Whites, who constitute 34 percent of the city's population, made up 9 percent of all stops in 2011, though they commit only 5 percent of all violent crimes and less than 2 percent of all shootings.

Fagan, however, needed to show that race, not crime, predicts police activity. Given the facts arrayed against such a proposition, it was no surprise that for days, Scheindlin's courtroom was filled with debates over "exponentiated coefficients," "P values," "Z scores," "zero-inflated models" and "Vuong tests," as Fagan tried to explain and defend his computer formulas. The judge candidly admitted to being lost at times, as would be anyone who was not steeped in advanced statistics.

But you don't have to have a Ph.D. in econometrics to spot the flaws in Fagan's techniques. For starters, he fed into his statistical black box all the 4.4 million stops from the last eight years, even though his own extremely superficial analysis of the forms that officers fill out after a stop had concluded that nearly nine-tenths of those stops appeared to be lawful, and only 6 percent clearly unlawful. Those lawful stops should have been excluded from his regression analysis, since they cannot form the basis for concluding that the officers making the stop substituted race for reasonable suspicion.

The errors in Fagan's models got worse from there. He refused to consider the race of New York's criminal suspects in evaluating whether the police were making stops based on skin color rather than behavior. Such information, however, is an essential component of any racial profiling analysis. Males are 91 percent of all stop subjects, but no one accuses the police of sex discrimination because it is acceptable to acknowledge that males commit the lion's share of crime.

Fagan justified his refusal to take criminal suspect data into account on the ground that the data are incomplete, but the race of suspects is known for 98 percent of the city's shootings, 98 percent of drug crimes, and 85 percent of all violent crimes—precisely the offenses that overwhelmingly drive the NYPD's deployment decisions. Only in property crimes is the race of a majority of suspects unknown, but there is no reason to think that the racial makeup of unknown property offenders differs from the makeup of known property offenders.

Fagan's treatment of the relationship between crime and police response was even further from reality. His model used crime data from the previous calendar month to predict stops in the current month: if a stop was made on May 31, for example, he assumed that crime data for April should explain it. Such a huge time lag ignores the essence of the NYPD's data-driven policing revolution, in which the most up-to-the-minute crime information determines tactics. Officers on one tour will be working off information gathered on the previous tour, not just off crime data from six weeks ago. A gang shooting will immediately trigger a local influx of officers, who will make an elevated number of stops to try to apprehend the shooter and avert a retaliatory shooting. In Fagan's model, however, if there were no shootings in the previous month, the spike in stops from this month's shooting will appear unmotivated by crime and thus likely to be a function of race.

Fagan made no distinction between domestic and gang homicides, even though the former, unlike the latter, have no impact on street patrols. (The vast majority of homicides committed by whites are domestic-violence cases. Domestic violence, by definition, does not trigger street stops, but the absence of such post-domestic-homicide stops will improperly show up as pro-white police bias in Fagan's model.) His model did not properly represent Commissioner Ray Kelly's biggest policing innovation: so-called Impact Zones, where a high concentration of rookie officers walked the beat in the city's most dangerous neighborhoods and made stops if they witnessed suspicious behavior. Impact Zones were located virtually exclusively in minority neighborhoods; the higher number of officers available to observe criminal activity would result in more stops. Fagan's model, however, saw only the stops without accounting for the strategy behind them.

With these and other important details of the NYPD's operations stripped away, resulting in a set of mathematical equations that are blind to the ways that gang culture influences communities and law enforcement, Fagan's "negative binomial regression analysis" purported to show that the number of stops in a neighborhood is a function of the race of the residents, not of local crime conditions. No wonder that when he finally estimated the exact number of stops that would result from an increase in an area's black population, he reached a result wildly out of sync with the real world. His model predicted that a census tract with an 85 percent or higher black population would experience 120 stops a month; the actual average in such tracts is 19 stops. The plaintiffs offered no examples of tracts with 120 stops.

• • •

The handpicked named plaintiffs in *Floyd* made no more compelling a case for declaring the NYPD a constitutional reprobate than did Fagan's regression models (which the city's attorneys and expert witnesses ably discredited). David Floyd, the lead plaintiff, was presumably the clearest victim of race-based oppression that the attorneys could find. He was stopped in February 2008 outside his home in the South Bronx. (Floyd is an activist with the Black Panther–inspired Copwatch, as well as a member of a black nationalist group that pledged solidarity with the late Venezuelan "revolutionary leader" Hugo Chávez. Floyd and the Center for Constitutional Rights had already sued the police on a civil rights claim when the organization named him lead plaintiff in its class-action litigation.)

Three NYPD officers observed Floyd and another man jostling the door of a basement apartment, unsuccessfully trying a series of keys on a large key chain; one of the men kept looking over his shoulder at the street. (As it turned out, Floyd's downstairs neighbor had locked himself out of his apartment, and Floyd had picked up the landlady's keys to help him get back in.) According to Floyd's lawyers, the officers could have had no reason other than racism to approach and ask the two men what they were doing—despite actions that looked consistent with a home invasion, in an area that had recently seen a pattern of burglary. If this was an unconstitutional stop, the department might as well give up trying to prevent crime and let the community fend for itself.

Another named plaintiff, Nicholas Peart, a 24-year-old "facilitator" for a Harlem youth program, was added to the *Floyd* suit late in the game, following the Center for Constitutional Rights' otherwise unsuccessful effort in 2012 to bulk up its case. According to an op-ed that Peart wrote for the *New York Times* after he joined the litigation, he was stopped on the night of his 18th birthday while sitting on a bench at Broadway and 96th Street in Manhattan with two friends. Squad cars pulled up, and an officer yelled, "Get on the ground!" Peart then found himself on the ground, he wrote, with a gun pointed at him. The officer removed Peart's wallet from his pocket to check his ID; sarcastically said "Happy birth-day" after noticing his birth date; and then left after briefly questioning Peart's companions.

What Peart didn't mention in his op-ed was that the officer had just received a radio call reporting that three men with a gun in the immedi-ate vicinity had been overheard planning a robbery and that one of the suspects was described as wearing a tank top and blue shorts. Peart was in a tank top and blue shorts. The officer had even replayed the radio call to Peart and his friends to explain his actions. Moreover, the officer had unholstered his gun only after the group repeatedly disobeyed his com-mand to get on the ground.

Plaintiffs' counsel apparently believed that if someone matches the description of a gun suspect, officers should wait until a victim is actu-ally shot before acting on the call. In deciding for the plaintiffs, Judge Scheindlin essentially supported this view, disregarding the realities of life for law-abiding residents of crime-plagued communities who support proactive policing and were not represented in *Floyd*.

• • •

Ivan De Bord, a youthful apartment superintendent in the South Bronx, is typical of those unrepresented New Yorkers. De Bord was stopped many times when he was a teen. "When you're young, you react a little different, but it's obvious that they always have a reason to stop. I can see that in my work at the building," he says. "They know who's who." Are the cops overaggressive? "Now that I see the area here, I understand why they're aggressive sometimes." De Bord was stunned at the crime and disorder in the Bronx when he moved from Manhattan for his current job: "I was in shock. It's insane; I've never seen anything like it." De Bord's building has been colonized by a group of former tenants who hang out in the lobby "smoking [weed], selling drugs, peeing everywhere, not respecting people, playing dice," he says. "It's very bad. A lot of the tenants are scared; they don't want to live in the building any longer." After Judge Scheindlin ruled against the city in *Ligon* v. *New York* in January 2013, the cops backed off from proactive policing, De Bord reports, but things have been slowly returning to normal. "The police could modify [the stop program] a little bit, but I'm totally with them stopping and searching. It's one of the best things they have."

Dorrien Christiani, a dapper former mail carrier, began attending community council meetings at the 28th Precinct in 2011, worried about drug dealing outside the methadone clinics in his Central Harlem neighborhood. Asked if the cops are overaggressive, he raises his eyebrows over his wire-rimmed glasses. "So I've heard," he responds skeptically. "I feel the NYPD does an excellent job. You have some good cops and some mediocre cops, as in all occupations."

Earl Cleveland, a retired bus driver who lives in the South Bronx, has a simple message for the mayor: "Public safety, I consider that Number One. The city shouldn't take a chance. You cannot turn your back on crime; it's here. You need law enforcement, and they should make stops."

Perhaps younger people have a different perspective? Some do; others don't. Creash, a roly-poly 13-year-old, waits for a bus in East Flatbush, Brooklyn. Over the previous three nights (in March 2013), rioters looted and trashed stores near the bus stop in response to a fatal police shooting of a 16-year-old gang member named Kimani Gray, who had pointed a pistol at the officers; it was recovered at the scene. "I feel safer with the police," Creash says. "There's a whole bunch of gangbangers around my school. That's why the police are over there. When I see an officer, I be like: 'Hey, good job!'" A tall 15-year-old from the Caribbean named Mikey is striding past the 67th Precinct's police station, another target of the Flatbush rioters the night before. "The police leave me alone because I'm a good kid," he says.

The advocates regularly attack the NYPD's enforcement of quality-of-life laws, especially those prohibiting marijuana. And who might be asking for such enforcement? People like Johnny, a young man in the South Bronx who complained to a 41st Precinct community council meeting in March 2013 about a "stench" of marijuana whenever he left his building. At the same meeting, a young woman reported that people were loitering around the back exit of a nightclub in her neighborhood: "They be smokin' weed, playin' music, a lot of stuff happens." The 41st Precinct is 98 percent black and Hispanic. If the police respond to these requests for public order by questioning or arresting the people about whom the community is complaining, they cannot help but generate racial stop data that the Center for Constitutional Rights will use against them.

The time and energy spent on the *Floyd* trial, and on Fagan's abstruse analyses, were a sad diversion from the real problem facing the city's black and Latino residents: the persistence of senseless victimization. During closing arguments on May 20, 2013, no one referred to the fatal shooting just two days earlier of a 14-year-old girl returning from a friend's birthday party in Queens. A gunman had sprayed a bus with bullets, one of which entered the girl's right temple. Judge Scheindlin did her best to keep such incidents far from the courtroom, but they occasionally seeped in when officers described the mob violence or the reports of a gunman at large that had preceded a stop.

The NYPD's response to the bus murder in South Jamaica, Queens, would generate more stop data that could be used against the department in another racial profiling lawsuit, but it was precisely such high-intensity policing that brought the city's murder rate down nearly 80 percent over a period of twenty years. The vast majority of lives saved thanks to that falling homicide rate were black and Hispanic.

The ruling against the NYPD in *Floyd* perpetuated the misconception that the police disproportionately patrol some neighborhoods out of bias. But those are precisely the neighborhoods where peppering a city bus with bullets is not as extraordinary an incident as it ought to be. They are also the places that were most affected by the spike in violence that followed the court rulings against "stop and frisk." Until society is willing to address the family breakdown that generates such violence, it will continue to fall to the police to provide social control where fathers no longer do so.

PART THREE

The Truth About Crime

As a budding sociologist, Alice Goffman spent six years living in a black inner-city neighborhood in Philadelphia during the 2000s—an experience chronicled in her acclaimed book *On the Run: Fugitive Life in an American City*. Her portrait of young crack dealers being "persecuted" by the cops and the courts was intended as an indictment of a racist criminal-justice system. What Goffman actually exposed, however, was a community torn apart by family breakdown and criminality. When the police retreat from such neighborhoods or decline to enforce the law, the result is not less crime but more. (Since *On the Run* appeared in 2014, Goffman has been credibly accused of fabricating some of her damning anecdotes about the police.)

A straight line can be drawn between family breakdown and youth violence. In Chicago's poor black neighborhoods, criminal activity among the young has reached epidemic proportions. It's a problem that no one, including the Chicago Police Department, seems able to solve. About 80 percent of black children in Chicago are born to single mothers. They grow up in a world where marriage is virtually unheard of and where no one expects a man to stick around and help raise a child. This section examines the criminogenic environments that define many of America's dysfunctional inner cities.

17

Chicago's Real Crime Story

Barack Obama has exploited his youthful stint as a Chicago community organizer at every stage of his political career. As someone who had worked for grassroots "change," he said, he was a different kind of politician, one who could translate people's hopes into reality. The media lapped up this conceit, presenting Obama's organizing experience as a meaningful qualification for the Oval Office.

In September 2009, a cell-phone video of Chicago students beating a fellow teen to death coursed over the airwaves and across the Internet. None of the news outlets that had admiringly reported on Obama's community-organizing efforts mentioned that the beating involved students from the very South Side neighborhoods where the president had once worked. Obama's connection to the area was suddenly lost in the mists of time.

Yet a critical blindness links Obama's activities on the South Side during the 1980s and the murder of Derrion Albert in 2009. Throughout his four years working for "change" in Chicago's Roseland and Altgeld Gardens neighborhoods, Obama ignored the primary cause of their escalating dysfunction: the disappearance of the black two-parent family. Obama wasn't the only activist to turn away from the problem of absent fathers, of course; decades of failed social policy, both before and after his time in Chicago, were just as blind. And that myopia continues today, guaranteeing that the response to Chicago's current youth violence will prove as useless as Obama's activities were a generation ago.

• • •

One year out of college, Barack Obama took a job as a community organizer, hoping for an authentic black experience that would link him to the bygone era of civil rights protest. Few people know what a community organizer is—Obama didn't when he decided to become one—yet the term seduces the liberal intelligentsia with its aura of class struggle and agitation against an unjust establishment. Saul Alinsky, the self-described radical who pioneered the idea in Chicago's slaughterhouse district during the Great Depression, defined community organizing as creating "mass organizations to seize power and give it to the people." Alinsky viewed poverty as a political condition: it stemmed from a lack of power, which society's "haves" withhold from the "have-nots." A community organizer would open the eyes of the disenfranchised to their aggrieved status, teaching them to demand redress from the illegitimate "power structure."

Alinskyite empowerment suffered its worst scandal in 1960s Chicago. The architects of the federal War on Poverty created a taxpayer-funded version of a community-organizing entity, the so-called Community Action Agency, whose function was to agitate against big-city mayors for more welfare benefits and services for blacks. Washington poverty warriors, eager to demonstrate their radical bona fides, funneled hundreds of thousands of dollars into Chicago's most notorious gangs, who were supposed to run job-training and tutoring programs under the auspices of a signature Alinskyite agency, the Woodlawn Organization. Instead, the gangbangers maintained their criminal ways—raping and murdering while on the government payroll, and embezzling federal funds to boot.

The disaster failed to dim the romance of community organizing. But by the time Obama arrived in Chicago in 1984, an Alinskyite diagnosis of South Side poverty was doubly irrelevant. Blacks had more political power in Chicago than ever before, yet that power had no impact on the tidal wave of dysfunction that was sweeping through the largest black community in the United States. Chicago had just elected Harold Washington, the city's first black mayor; the heads of Chicago's school system and public housing were black, as were most of their employees; black power broker Emil Jones, Jr. represented the South Side in the Illinois State Senate; Jesse Jackson would launch his 1984 presidential campaign from Chicago. The notion that blacks were disenfranchised struck even some of Obama's potential organizees as ludicrous. "Why we need to be protesting and carrying on at our own people?" a prominent South Side minister asked Obama soon after he arrived in Chicago. "Anybody sitting around this table got a direct line to City Hall."

Pace Alinsky, such political clout could not stop black Chicago's social breakdown. Crime was exploding. Gangs ran the housing projects— their reign of thuggery aided by ACLU lawsuits, which had stripped the housing authority of its right to screen tenants. But the violence spread beyond the projects. In 1984, Obama's first year in Chicago, gang members gunned down a teenage basketball star, Benjy Wilson.

The citywide outcry that followed was heartfelt but beside the point. None of the prominent voices calling for an end to youth violence—from Mayor Washington to Jesse Jackson to school administrators—noted that all of Wilson's killers came from fatherless families (or that he had fathered an illegitimate child himself). Nor did the would-be reformers mention the all-important fact that a staggering 75 percent of Chicago's black children were being born out of wedlock. The sky-high illegitimacy rate meant that black boys were growing up in a world in which it was normal to impregnate a girl and then take off. When a boy is raised without any social expectation that he will support his children and marry his children's mother, he fails to learn the most fundamental lesson of personal responsibility. The high black crime rate was one result of a culture that fails to civilize men through marriage.

Obama offers fleeting glimpses of Chicago's social breakdown in his autobiography, *Dreams from My Father*, but it's as if he didn't really see what he recorded. An Alinskyite group from the suburbs, the Calumet Community Religious Conference, had assigned him to the Roseland community on the far South Side, in the misguided hope of strong-arming industrial jobs back to the area. Roseland's bungalows and two-story homes recalled an era of stable, two-parent families that had long since passed. Obama vividly describes children who "swaggered down the streets—loud congregations of teenage boys, teenage girls feeding potato chips to crying toddlers, the discarded wrappers tumbling down the block." He observes two young boys casually firing a handgun at a third. He notes that the elementary school in the Altgeld Gardens housing project had a center for the teen mothers of its students, who had themselves been raised by teen mothers.

Most tellingly, Obama's narrative is almost devoid of men. With the exception of the local ministers and the occasional semi-crazed black nationalist, Obama inhabits a female world. His organizing targets are almost all single mothers. He never wonders where and who the fathers of their children are. When Obama sees a group of boys vandalizing a building, he asks rhetorically: "Who will take care of them: the alderman, the social workers? The gangs?" The most appropriate candidate—"their fathers"—never occurs to him.

Surrounded with daily evidence of Roseland's real problem, Obama was nevertheless at a loss for a cause to embrace. Alinskyism, after all, presupposes that the problems afflicting a poor community come from the outside. Obama had come to arouse Roseland's residents to take on the power structure, not to persuade them to act more responsibly. So it was with great relief that he noticed that the Mayor's Office of Employment and Training (MET), which offered job training, lacked a branch in Roseland: "'This is it,' I said. . . . 'We just found ourselves an issue.'" So much for the fiction that the community organizer merely channels the preexisting will of the "community."

Obama easily procured a local MET office. It had as much effect on the mounting disorder of the far South Side as his better-known accomplishment: getting the Chicago Housing Authority to test the Altgeld Gardens project for asbestos. In an area that buses wouldn't serve at night because of fears that drivers would get robbed or hit by bricks, perhaps asbestos removal should have been a lower priority, compared with ending the anarchy choking off civilized life. In fact, "there is zero legacy from when Obama was here," says Phillip Jackson, director of the Black Star Project, a community group dedicated to eliminating the academic-achievement gap. Jackson, like other local leaders, is reluctant to criticize Obama, however. "I won't minimize what Obama was doing then," he says.

In 1987, during Obama's third year in Chicago, 57 children were killed in the city, reports Alex Kotlowitz in his book on Chicago's deadly housing projects, *There Are No Children Here*. In 1988, Obama left Chicago, after four years spent helping "people in Altgeld . . . reclaim a power they had had all along," as the future president put it in *Dreams from My Father*. And the carnage continued.

• • •

Two particularly savage youth murders in 1994 drew the usual feckless hand-wringing. An 11-year-old Black Disciples member from Roseland, Robert "Yummy" Sandifer (so called for his sweet tooth, the only thing childlike about him), had unintentionally killed a girl while shooting at (and paralyzing) a rival gang member. Sandifer's fellow Black Disciples then executed him to prevent him from implicating them in the killing. A month later, after five-year-old Eric Morse refused to steal candy for an 11-year-old and a ten-year-old, the two dropped him from a 14th-story window in a housing complex, killing him. Eric's eight-year-old brother had grabbed him in an effort to keep him from falling, but lost his hold when one of the boys bit him on the arm. None of the perpetrators or victims in either case came from two-parent families.

A year after these widely publicized killings, and on the eve of Obama's first political campaign, the aspiring state senator gave an interview to the *Chicago Reader* that epitomized the uselessness of Alinskyism in addressing black urban pathology—and that inaugurated the trope of community organizer as visionary politician. Obama has attacked the Christian Right and the Republican Congress for "hijack[ing] the higher moral ground with this language of family values and moral responsibility." Yeah, sure, family values are fine, he says, but what about "collective action . . . collective institutions and organizations"? Let's take "these same values that are encouraged within our families," he urges, "and apply them to a larger society."

Even if this jump from "family values" to "collective action" were a promising strategy, Obama overlooks a crucial fact: there are almost no traditional families in inner-city neighborhoods. Fathers aren't "encouraging" values "within our families"; fathers are nowhere in sight. Moving to "collective action" is futile without a core of personal responsibility on which to build. Nevertheless, Obama leapfrogs over concrete individual failure to alleged collective failure: "Right now we have a society that talks about the irresponsibility of teens getting pregnant," he told the *Reader*, "not the irresponsibility of a society that fails to educate them to aspire for more."

The same rhetorical leapfrogging has governed the response by the Obama administration and the Chicago political establishment to the city's current teen violence. Compared with the 1990s, that violence was way down when Obama took office—114 children under 17 were killed both in 1993 and in 1994, while 50 were in 2008. But the proportion of gang-related murders has gone up since the late 1980s and 1990s, when the Chicago police, working with federal law enforcement, locked up the leaders of Chicago's most notorious gangs. Those strong leaders, it turns out, exercised some restraint on their members in order to protect drug profits. "Back then, you knew what the killings were about," says Charles Winston, a former heroin dealer who made $50,000 a day in the early 1990s in the infamous Robert Taylor Homes. "Now, it's just sporadic incidents of violence." The Black Star Project's Phillip Jackson compares the anarchy in Chicago's gang territories to Somalia: "There are many factions," he says, all fighting one another in unstable, shifting configurations.

In the early 2000s, the number of assaults reported in and around schools increased significantly, according to Wesley Skogan, a political scientist at Northwestern University. School dismissal time in Chicago triggers a massive mobilization of security forces across the South and West sides, to try to keep students from shooting one another or being shot by older gang members. Police officers in bulletproof vests ring the most violence-prone schools, and the Chicago Transit Authority rejiggers its bus schedules to try to make sure that students don't have to walk even half a block before boarding a bus.

Each street in a neighborhood possesses a mystical significance to its juvenile residents. What defines their identities isn't family, or academic accomplishments or interests, but ruthless fealty to small, otherwise indistinguishable pieces of territory. Roseland's 123rd Street is the 12-Treys' turf, 119th Street belongs to the 11-9s, and 111th Street is in an area of Roseland called "the Ville." Gang members from the Ville aren't supposed to cross 119th Street; doing so will provoke a potentially lethal challenge. School-reform initiatives may have contributed to increasing tensions on the streets by shutting down failing schools and sending students into enemy territory; the demolition of Chicago's high-rise housing projects in the 2000s likewise disrupted existing gang groupings.

• • •

In September 2009, that now-notorious cell-phone video gave the world a glimpse of Barack Obama's former turf. Teenagers—some in an informal school uniform of khaki pants and polo shirts, others bare-chested—swarm across a desolate thoroughfare in Roseland; others congregate in the middle of it, indifferent to the SUVs that try to inch by, horns blaring. Against a background din of constant yelling, some boys lunge at one another and throw punches, while a few, in leisurely fashion, select victims to clobber on the torso and head with thick, eight-foot-long railroad ties. Derrion Albert is standing passively in the middle of a knot on the sidewalk when one boy whacks him on the head with a railroad tie and another punches him in the face. Albert falls to the ground uncon-scious, then comes to and tries to get up. A boy walking by gives him a desultory kick. Five more cluster around him as he lies curled up on the sidewalk; one hits him again with a railroad tie, and another stomps him on the head. Finally, workers from a nearby youth community center drag Albert inside. Throughout the video, a male companion of the videogra-pher reacts with nervously admiring "damns."

In the Alinskyite worldview, the school system was to blame, not the students who committed the violence. Several years before, Altgeld Gardens' high school, Carver High, had been converted to a charter military academy. Students who didn't want to attend were sent to Fenger High School in the Ville, several miles away. Students from Altgeld Gardens and from the Ville fought each other with knives and razors inside Fenger High and out, their territorial animosity intensified by minute class distinctions. Ville children whose mothers use federal Section 8 housing vouchers to rent homes look down upon housing-project residents like those from the Gardens. The morning of the Albert killing, someone fired a gun outside Fenger. During the school day, students sent one another text messages saying that something was likely to "jump" after school. When students from the Gardens, instead of immediately boarding a bus home, walked down 111th Street—the heart of Ville territory—the fighting started. Derrion Albert had a loose affiliation with Ville students; the students who killed him were from the Gardens.

South Side aldermen and the usual race claque accused the school bureaucracy of insensitivity and worse in expecting Altgeld Gardens and Ville children to coexist without violence. In a pathetic echo of 1950s civil rights protests, Jesse Jackson, cameras in tow, rode a school bus with Altgeld Gardens students from their homes to Fenger High, demanding that Carver be converted back to a neighborhood school. No one pointed out that the threat from which Jackson the Civil Rights Avenger was protecting black students came from other black students, not from hate-filled white politicians. Obama's former organizing group, the Developing Communities Project, led noisy parent protests, demanding that Carver accept all comers from Altgeld Gardens and reduce its military component to a quarter of the school. James Meeks, a race-baiting South Side pastor and an Illinois state senator, staged his own well-photographed bus tour, taking suburban officials through Roseland and past Fenger to demonstrate the "adversity" that Fenger students faced compared with suburban kids—though the greatest adversity comes from the violence that students inflict on each other.

Other protests sent an even more muddled message. After a day when a dozen fights in Fenger High School provoked a security clampdown and five arrests, a group of parents and students staged a two-day boycott of classes, complaining of excessive discipline and harsh treatment from the guards. "They put us on lockdown for two hours because of a little fight," senior DeShunna Williams told the *Chicago Sun-Times*. "It was just an ordinary fight." Schools can restore safety only by strict discipline and zero tolerance for violence, however. If parents and students protest whenever such discipline is enforced, they undercut their own call for greater safety.

Mayor Richard Daley initially rejected the protesters' demands. "The day when the city of Chicago decides to divide schools by gang territory, that's a day when we have given up the city," he said. But the Chicago Public Schools soon promulgated a policy letting Fenger students transfer out of the school. Few parents took advantage of the option for their children, despite the weeks of agitation for it. Meanwhile, the school system allocated millions of additional dollars to protect Fenger students from one another. Ten extra school buses now escort the 350 Altgeld teens to and from Fenger every day, and school administrators pressed the Chicago Transit Authority to add more public bus routes around Fenger so that students wouldn't have to wait on the sidewalk for more than a few minutes.

Who wins the award for the most Alinskyite evasion of personal and parental responsibility after Derrion Albert's death? Perhaps not the local protesters but the federal officials dispatched to Chicago for damage control. The videotaped murder, seen around the world, couldn't have come at a worse time for the Obama administration—just over a week before the Olympic Committee was to decide on Chicago's bid to host the 2016 games. On October 1, 2009, the day before Obama was to make his last-minute pitch to the Olympic Committee in Copenhagen, the White House announced that Attorney General Eric Holder and Secretary of Education Arne Duncan would fly to Chicago to deliver a federal response to youth violence. The next day, Chicago lost its bid in the first round of votes, but Holder and Duncan continued to Chicago the following week.

Their message picked up exactly where Obama's 1995 *Chicago Reader* interview left off. "I came here at the direction of the president, not to place blame on anyone, but to join with Chicago, with communities across America in taking responsibility for this death and the deaths of so many other young people over the years," announced Duncan. Of course, the government has been "taking responsibility" for children for several decades now, at a cost of billions of dollars, without noticeable effect on inner-city dysfunction. The feds have funded countless programs in child and youth development, in antiviolence training, in poverty reduction. If "collective action," as Obama put it in 1995, could compensate for the absence of fathers, the black violence problem would have ended years ago.

Holder's remarks were just as irrelevant (though, to his credit, he did pledge $500,000 for beefed-up school security). "We have to ask hard questions, and we have to be prepared to face tough truths," he said, and then proceeded to ignore the hard questions and duck the tough truths. "Youth violence is not a Chicago problem, any more than it is a black problem, a white problem, or a Hispanic problem," he claimed. "It is something that affects communities big and small, and people of all races and all colors. It is an American problem." Tough-truth quotient: maybe 20 percent. No, youth violence isn't just a Chicago problem. Urban school districts across the country flood school areas with police officers at dismissal time. But youth violence is definitely correlated with race. Though rates of youth killings and shootings vary—Chicago children under the age of 17 are killed at four times the rate of New York children, for example—youth violence is disproportionately a "black problem" and, to a lesser extent, a Hispanic one. According to James Alan Fox and Marc Swatt of Northeastern University, the national rate of homicide commission for black males between the ages of 14 and 17 is ten times higher than that of "whites," into which category the federal government puts the vast majority of Hispanics. Black juveniles accounted for 78 percent of all juvenile arrests between 2003 and 2008 in Chicago; Hispanics were 18 percent, and whites, 3.5 percent of those arrests. Recognizing that tough truth is the only hope for coming up with a way to change it.

In Chicago, blacks, at least 35 percent of the population, commit 76 percent of all homicides; whites, about 28 percent of the population, commit 4 percent; and Hispanics, 30 percent of the population, commit 19 percent. The most significant difference between these demographic groups is family structure. In Cook County—which includes both Chicago and some of its suburbs and probably therefore contains a higher proportion of middle-class black families than the city proper—79 percent of all black children were born out of wedlock in 2003, compared with 15 percent of white children. Until that gap closes, the crime gap won't close, either.

•   •   •

Official Chicago's answer to youth violence has also opted for collective, rather than paternal, responsibility. As the Chicago school superintendent at the time of Derrion Albert's murder, Ron Huberman developed a whopping $60 million, two-year plan to combat youth violence. The wonky Huberman, who had created highly regarded information-retrieval and accountability systems for the police department and the city's emergency response center in previous city jobs, turned his passion for data analysis to Chicago's violent kids. Using a profile of past shooting victims that included such factors as school truancy rates and disciplinary records, he identified several hundred teens as having a greater than 20 percent chance of getting shot over the next two years. The goal was to provide them with wraparound social services. (The profile of victim and perpetrator was indistinguishable, but targeting potential victims, rather than perpetrators, for such benefits as government-subsidized jobs was politically savvy.) The program would assign the 300 or so potential victims their own "advocates" to intercede on their behalf with government agencies and provide them with case management and counseling.

In some cities, it's a police officer who visits a violence-prone teenager to warn him about staying out of trouble. Chicago sends a social worker. The Chicago Police Department has kept a low profile during the public debate over teen shootings, ceding primary accountability for the problem to the school system. This hierarchy of response may reflect Chicago's less assertive police culture compared with, say, New York's. "We'd marvel at how the NYPD was getting mayoral support" during Mayor Rudolph Giuliani's tenure, said a former Chicago deputy superintendent. "Mayor Daley is not a cop supporter; it's no secret that he rules the police department with an iron fist." The South Side's black ministers also act as a check on more proactive policing. There have been few calls in Chicago for a more aggressive stop-and-frisk policy to get illegal guns off the street, and the police department hasn't pushed to implement one.

Now, perhaps if Huberman's proposed youth "advocates" provided their charges with opportunities to learn self-discipline and perseverance, fired their imaginations with manly virtues, and spoke to them about honesty, courtesy, and right and wrong—if they functioned, in other words, like Scoutmasters—they might make some progress in reversing the South Side's social breakdown. But the outfit that Huberman picked to provide "advocacy" to the teens at a reported cost of $5 million a year, the Youth Advocates Program (YAP), couldn't have been more mired in the resolutely nonjudgmental ethic of contemporary social work. "Some modalities used in this endeavor," explained YAP, "include: assess the youth and his/her family to develop an Individualized Service Plan (ISP) to address the individual needs of each youth." The organization's CEO, Jeff Fleischer, tried further to clarify the advocates' function: "If a family needs a new refrigerator or a father needs car insurance, it's the advocate's job to take care of it," he told the *Chicago Tribune*. The reference to a "father" is presumably Fleischer's little joke, since almost none of the Chicago victims-in-waiting will have their fathers at home. It's not a lack of material goods that ails Chicago's gun-toting kids, however, or their mothers' lack of time to procure those goods. Providing their families with a government-funded gofer to carry out basic adult tasks like getting car insurance will not compensate for a lifetime of paternal absence.

YAP represents the final stage of Alinskyism: its co-optation by the government-funded social-services industry.

Obama came to Roseland and Altgeld Gardens with the fanciful intention of organizing the "community" to demand benefits from a hostile power structure. But here's that same power structure not just encouraging demands from below but providing the community with its own government-funded advocates to "broker and advocate for each youth and family," as YAP puts it, thus ensuring constant pressure to increase government services.

Huberman's plan for ending youth violence included other counselors and social workers who would go to work in the most dangerous public high schools. He also wanted to create a "culture of calm" in the schools by retraining security guards and by de-emphasizing suspension and expulsion in favor of "peer mediation." Nothing new there: in 1998, Chicago schools announced plans to train students to be peer mediators and to engage in conflict resolution. In fact, everything in Huberman's plan had already been tried, to no apparent effect. You'd think that someone would ask: What's lacking in these neighborhoods that we didn't notice before? The correct answer would be: family structure.

• • •

Needless to say, everyone involved in the beating death of Derrion Albert came from a fatherless home. Defendant Eugene Riley hit Albert with a railroad tie as he lay unconscious on the ground in his final moments. According to 18-year-old Riley's 35-year-old mother, Sherry Smith, "his father was not ready to be a strong black role model in his son's life." Nor was the different father of Riley's younger brother, Vashion Bullock, ready to be involved in his son's life. A bare-chested Bullock shows up in the video wielding a railroad tie in the middle of the street. As for Albert himself, his father "saw him the day he was born, and the next time when he was in a casket," reports Bob Jackson, the worldly director of Roseland Ceasefire, an antiviolence project.

The absence of a traditional two-parent family leaves children uncertain about the scope of their blood ties. One teen who attends the Roseland Safety Net Works' after-school program thinks that she has more than ten siblings by five different fathers, but since her mother lives in North Carolina, it's hard to pin down the exact number. Eight of the ten boys enrolled in Kids Off the Block, another after-school program, don't know their fathers. "The other two boys, if the father came around, they'd probably kill him," says Diane Latiker, who runs the program. If children do report a remote acquaintance with their father, they don't seem to know what he does for a living.

Though teen births have dropped among blacks since the 1990s, unwed pregnancy is still a pervasive reality in Chicago's inner-city high schools. "Last year at Fenger, it was all you heard about—pregnancies or abortions," reports the youth president at Roseland Safety Net Works. In autumn 2009, one in seven girls at Chicago's Paul Robeson High School was either expecting or had already given birth to a child. It's not hard to predict where Chicago's future killers will come from.

A 15-year-old resident of Altgeld Gardens, for example, was sitting at home with her three-month-old boy during the week of Veterans Day this year, having been suspended for fighting. You'd never know it from her baby-doll voice, but this ninth-grade mother runs with a clique of girls at Fenger High "who have no problem taking you out," says Bob Jackson. She lives with her 34-year-old mother, two brothers, and a sister; she sometimes sees her father when he's in town but doesn't know if he has a job. Her son's father, still playing with toys, isn't providing support. She was on her way to pick up free food from the federal WIC program when I spoke with her.

The next stage in black family disintegration may be on the horizon. According to several Chicago observers, black mothers are starting to disappear, too. "Children are bouncing around," says a police officer in Altgeld Gardens. "The mother says: 'I'm done. You go stay with your father.' The ladies are selling drugs with their new boyfriend, and the kids are left on their own." Derrion Albert's mother lived four hours away; he was moving among different extended family members in Chicago. Even if a mother is still in the home, she may be incapable of providing any emotional or moral support to her children. "Kids will tell you: 'I'm sleeping on the floor, there's nothing in the fridge, my mother doesn't care about me going to school,'" says Rogers Jones, the courtly founder of Roseland Safety Net Works. "Kids are traumatized before they even get to school." Some mothers are indifferent when the physical and emotional abuses that they suffered as children recur with their own children. "We've had mothers say: 'I was raped as a child, so it's no big deal if my daughter is raped,'" reports Jackson.

The official silence about illegitimacy and its relation to youth violence remains as carefully preserved in today's Chicago as it was during Obama's organizing time there. A fleeting reference to "parental" responsibility for children is allowed, before the speaker quickly moves on to society's more important role. But anything more specific about fathers is taboo. "I have not been in too many churches lately that say: 'Mom, you need to find yourself a husband, this is not the norm,'" observes Jackson—an understandable if lamentable lacuna, he adds, since single heads of households constitute the vast majority of the congregation. Press coverage of teen shootings may mention a participant's mother, but the shooter and victim may as well be the product of a virgin birth, for all the media's curiosity about where their fathers are. I asked John Paul Jones of Obama's old Alinskyite outfit, the Developing Communities Project, if anyone ever tries to track down the father of a teen accused of a shooting. The question threw him. "Does anyone ever ask: 'Where are the fathers?'" he paraphrased me. A brief silence. "That's a good point."

Some members of Chicago's Left will argue against holding fathers or mothers responsible for their children. "To blame it on the family is totally unfair," says Gwen Rice, a board member of the Developing Communities Project. "I'm tired of blaming the parents. The services for the poor are paltry; it boggles the mind. Historically, you can't expect a parent who can't get a job to do something that someone with resources can do. These problems have histories; there are policies that have mitigated against black progress. What needs to happen is a change in corporate greed and insensitivity." Rice corrects my use of the term "illegitimacy": "There are no illegitimate births," she says.

One activist, however, makes ending illegitimacy an explicit part of his work. "I tell people: 'Unless you get married, you will perish,'" says Phillip Jackson, the Black Star Project's director. An intense, wiry man who looks like a cross between Gandhi and Spike Lee, Jackson organizes events to make fathers visible and valued again, like "Take Your Child to School Day." Yet Jackson is not immune from the Alinskyite tic of looking to government for solutions to problems of personal responsibility (nor does he avoid launching groundless charges of racism). He gathered a crate of petitions to President Obama regarding Chicago's youth violence, some of whose signers are as young as four. "President Obama, please send help for the sake of these young people in Chicago," reads the petition. Asked what he wanted Obama to do, Jackson's answers ranged from a trickle-up stimulus plan to jobs to leadership.

Jobs, whether government-created or not, aren't likely to make much difference in the culture of illegitimacy. As journalist Nicholas Lemann observed over two decades ago in *The Atlantic Monthly*, the black illegitimacy rate has only a weak correlation to employment: "High illegitimacy has always been much more closely identified with blacks than with all poor people or all unemployed people." An Alinskyite approach to the related problems of illegitimacy and crime is only a distraction. Seeking redress and salvation from the "power structure" just puts off the essential work of culture change.

Barack Obama started that work in a startling Father's Day speech in Chicago while running for president in 2008. "If we are honest with ourselves," he said, "we'll admit that . . . too many fathers [are] missing from too many lives and too many homes. They have abandoned their responsibilities, acting like boys instead of men. . . . We know the statistics—that children who grow up without a father are five times more likely to live in poverty and commit crime; nine times more likely to drop out of school and 20 times more likely to end up in prison."

But after implicitly drawing the connection between family breakdown and youth violence—"How many times in the last year has this city lost a child at the hands of another child?"—Obama reverted to Alinskyite bromides about school spending, preschool programs, visiting nurses, global warming, sexism, racial division, and income inequality. And he has continued to swerve from the hard truth of black family breakdown ever since his 2008 speech. The best thing that the president could do for Chicago's embattled children would be to confront head-on the disappearance of their fathers and the consequence in lost lives.

18

Running with the Predators

As the videotaped murder of a teenager in Chicago brought new attention to the scourge of urban violence, a young sociologist was contemplating her experience in a rough urban neighborhood and setting about to explain the disorder. Alice Goffman, daughter of the influential sociologist Erving Goffman, lived in the inner city of Philadelphia from 2002 to 2008, integrating herself into the lives of a group of young crack dealers. Her resulting book, *On the Run*, was published in 2014, and a film or TV adaptation may be on the way. Goffman presents a detailed and startling ethnography of a world usually kept far from public awareness and discourse. But her book is an equally startling—if unintentional—portrait of the liberal elite mind-set. She draws a devastating picture of cultural breakdown within the black underclass, but she is incapable of acknowledging the truth in front of her eyes. Instead, she deems her subjects the helpless pawns of a criminal-justice system run amok.

At the center of *On the Run* are three half-brothers and their slightly older friend Mike, all of whom live in a five-block area of Philadelphia that Goffman names Sixth Street. Sixth Street, we are told, isn't viewed as a particularly high-crime area, which can only leave the reader wondering what an actual high-crime area would look like. In her six years living there, Goffman attended nine funerals of her young associates, and she mentions several others, including one for "three kids" paid for by local drug dealers eager to cement their support in the community.

Goffman contends that it is the legal system itself that is creating crime and dysfunction in poor black communities. Young men get saddled with a host of allegedly petty warrants for having missed court dates, violated their parole and probation conditions, and ducked the administrative fees levied on their criminal cases. Fearful of being rounded up under these allegedly senseless procedural warrants, they adopt a lifestyle of subterfuge and evasion, constantly in flight from an increasingly efficient and technology-enhanced police force. "Once a man fears that he will be taken by the police, it is precisely a stable and public daily routine of work and family life . . . that allows the police to locate him," Goffman writes. "A man in legal jeopardy finds that his efforts to stay out of prison are aligned not with upstanding, respectable action but with being a shady and distrustful character."

Goffman's own material demolishes this thesis. *On the Run* documents a world of law-of-the-jungle mores, riven with violence and betrayal. Far from being the hapless victims of random "legal entanglements"—Goffman's euphemism for the foreseeable consequences of lawless behavior—her subjects create their own predicaments through deliberate involvement in crime.

• • •

In 2002, when Goffman began her acquaintance with Sixth Street, the half-brothers Chuck, Reggie, and Tim were 18, 15, and nine, respectively. All had different fathers by the same crack-addict mother, Miss Linda. Their Section 8 subsidized house reeked of vomit, alcohol, and urine; roaches and ants crawled over the inhabitants as well as the furniture; cat feces covered a kitchen corner. Chuck's and Reggie's arrest records had begun in their early teens; Tim would graduate from middle school to the juvenile courts when he turned 12. Fatherlessness is a virtually universal condition among the young men in Goffman's tale, but gradations exist within it. Chuck's father came around during his early years, which helps explain, says Chuck, "why [Chuck] knew right from wrong and his young brothers did not"—a poignant acknowledgment of the role of fathers in raising sons, even if its premise (that Chuck knows right from wrong) is dubious.

On Sixth Street, drug dealing is tantamount to a bourgeois occupation. Chuck complains that his middle brother, Reggie, lacks the patience for "making slow money selling drugs hand to hand." Instead, Reggie favors armed robberies, to the admiration of his mother, Miss Linda. "He fearless," she says. "A stone-cold gangster." It would be a mistake, however, to think of drug dealing as a peaceful activity. Early on, a disgruntled supplier firebombs Chuck's car. Chuck responds by shooting at the supplier's home. In 2007, at the end of Goffman's chronicle, Chuck is fatally shot in the head while standing outside a Chinese restaurant, one of three shootings that night in Philadelphia. The killer, Goffman writes, was "trying to make it at the bottom rung of a shrinking drug trade."

Accompanying this drug-related violence is a more random violence that springs from dog-eat-dog exploitation and lack of impulse control. In an earlier incident, Goffman's fourth main character, Mike, another crack dealer, is walking home one night with a large wad of cash from a dice game. An armed robber accosts him—presumably tipped off to Mike's stash by the other players. Mike tries to pull his own gun but gets shot in the hip first. Several days later, Mike sees the gunman in a Buick and opens fire. Two days after that, Mike and his attacker drive past each other, guns blazing. Mike's car takes seven bullets, and he starts wearing a bulletproof vest. During another dice game, a young thug from Sixth Street named Tino puts a gun to a fellow player's head and demands his money. His target, Jay Jay, refuses, so Tino, who is high on PCP, kills him. Jay Jay's fellow crew members take to driving up and down Sixth Street firing at residents. Chuck gets shot in the neck—not fatally this time—and his friend Steve is hit in the thigh.

Ned, 43, supports himself in part by stealing credit cards and intercepting checks in the mail. When he and his girlfriend Jean, a crack addict, need money for property taxes, they lure a cousin of Reggie's (Miss Linda's second son) to their house with the promise of gossip about a former girlfriend. Waiting there is a man in a hoodie, who robs the cousin at gunpoint. The unintended punch line of the story: Ned and Jean also get income from working as foster parents, a fact that does not apparently give Goffman pause but that speaks volumes, sadly, about the quality of parenting in the area.

Theft is constant among Sixth Street residents. Mike invited a man he met in prison to play video games at his mother's house. The guest steals the stereo, DVD player, and two TVs. Anthony, another Sixth Street resident, was thrown out by his mother for stealing from her purse.

He was turned in to the police by neighbors on a warrant, after stealing their shoes. When he stayed at Miss Linda's, he grumbled that he couldn't save money because she would steal from him while he slept. Mike gives Anthony crack to sell, but he could not shoot his fellow dealers when they stole from him, since his usual whereabouts at night were widely known, making him an easy target. As a result, he was not a very effective drug dealer.

The mishaps of the characters in Goffman's narrative often resemble farce. Reggie, on the run for a drug crime, takes refuge in his mother's house. Miss Linda instructs him to leave before midnight, but he falls asleep. When a SWAT team arrives, Miss Linda persuades them not to go upstairs, and Reggie jumps out the bedroom window and flees into the alley, like Cherubino leaping from the Countess's window in *The Marriage of Figaro*.

Mike gives himself a birthday party, and the guests start stealing liquor bottles. He sets up sentry on the windowsill, gun in his lap, threatening to pistol-whip the next guy who takes a bottle. But he, too, falls asleep, and a guest lifts a wad of cash from his pocket.

After the police find Reggie cowering in a shed one day, he is sent to the county jail. He wallows in self-pity because his Sixth Street male friends are not visiting him or putting money into his commissary account. "Niggas ain't riding right! Niggas ain't got no respect," he complains to Goffman. "When I come home, man, I'm not fucking with none of these niggas. Where the fuck they at? They think it's going to be all love when I come home, like, what's up, Reggie, welcome back and shit . . . but fuck those niggas, man, they ain't riding for me. I got no rap for them when I touch."

The residents' chaotic sex lives generate further farcical situations— if one can overlook for a moment the consequences for their children. Virtually every male has a baby mom and a simultaneous collection of girlfriends; the females have children and their own series of boyfriends. After a prison term, Mike is sentenced to a halfway house in North Philly. He starts sleeping with a caseworker there named Tamara. Mike violates curfew and winds up back in prison. He tries to ensure that Tamara's visits are on different days from those of Marie, the baby mom of his two children. One day, however, Tamara shows up unexpectedly, "ostensibly,"

Goffman qualifies, to visit her inmate brother. Tamara sees Marie and Mike sitting across from each other and says hello. Marie sizes up the situation and announces loudly: "I ain't drive five fucking hours for this shit." Mike tries to quiet Marie down—like Don Giovanni trying to hush up Donna Elvira—but she retorts: "You fucked her, didn't you." Tamara announces loudly to her brother that she really likes Mike and hopes that he is not still messing with his baby mom, while Marie conspicuously plays with Mike's hair. Mike starts talking loudly to cover up Tamara's monologue to her brother while looking desperately at Goffman to rescue him. Marie stands up and leans in for a kiss, which Mike, cornered, supplies. Tamara ends up in tears.

But the sexual complications usually take on a more depressing aspect. At the hospital where Chuck has died after his head wound, his "on-again-off-again girlfriend," Tanesha, shows up, but everyone wonders "where the hell Chuck's baby-mom Brianna was." Miss Linda asks Goffman to give the Pampers money, which the author had promised her, to Tanesha, who is looking after Chuck's two daughters until Brianna can be located. This is not an arrangement likely to end well.

False incriminations are pervasive. When Mike was 24 and his children were three and six, he started dating a woman from North Philly named Michelle. He had high hopes for her, he tells Goffman, since, as a Puerto Rican, she should be more loyal than the "black chicks" who "love the cops" and turn in their boyfriends. Moreover, Michelle's father and brothers sold drugs, so she was well accustomed to criminal proceedings. Michelle said that she loved Mike more than any man she had ever met, including her three-year-old's father, then serving a ten-year federal prison sentence for an undisclosed crime. But Mike misses a court appointment, and a warrant issues for his arrest. The police find drugs and a gun in his apartment, which he tries to pin on Michelle and her father. The police show Michelle Mike's statement against her, as well as his texts and phone calls to Marie that indicate that he is still involved sexually with his baby mom. Indignant, Michelle tells the police everything she knows about his drug dealing. Mike writes her from jail: "Don't come up here, don't write, don't send no more money [this last mandate entailing heroic self-sacrifice, no doubt]. . . . You thought I wasn't going to find out that you a rat? . . . Fuck it. I never gave a fuck about you anyway. You was just some pussy to me and your pussy not even that good!"

But Mike is the victim of double-crossing as well. He acts as godfather to a young, hoodie-wearing tough named Ronny, a close competitor to Miss Linda's son Reggie for the status of Sixth Street's most loathsome figure. Ronny started carrying a gun at 13 and shot himself in the leg while boarding a bus at 15. He periodically gets kicked out of school for such offenses as hitting his teacher and trying to steal his principal's car. He brags to Goffman that he has slept with women older than she. (Goffman was then 21.) Most of his days are spent running from truant officers and serving suspensions. One night, when Ronny is 16, he and some Sixth Street associates try to break into a motorcycle store on the outskirts of Philadelphia to steal motorbikes. They fail to get into the store and, when their Pontiac doesn't start, are unable to make their getaway. Ronny calls Goffman and Mike at 2 AM to pick him up. (Mike is, at that point, living in Goffman's apartment, along with Chuck.) The silent alarm in the motorcycle dealership has already alerted the police. They arrest Ronny and Mike, and in the station house Ronny falsely incriminates Mike as the mastermind behind the break-in. The police let Ronny go and charge Mike with attempted breaking and entering. Mike spreads the word that Ronny is a snitch. Eager to redeem his reputation, Ronny burgles a house in Southwest Philly with Mike's gun and pays Mike's bail with the proceeds from the stolen TV, stereo, and jewelry.

This lawlessness cascades into the legal economy as well. Health-care workers steal antibiotics and medical supplies from their employers to provide to their fugitive friends who are fearful of being apprehended at a hospital. Regina Austin, a law professor at the University of Pennsylvania, has approvingly referred to such "pilfering employees [who] spread their contraband around the neighborhood" as occupying the "good middle ground between straightness and more extreme forms of law-breaking."

• • •

Goffman looks at this unending stream of lawless behavior and sees only the helpless pawns of a mindlessly draconian criminal-justice system: "Since the 1980s, the War on Crime and War on Drugs have taken millions of Black young men out of school, work, and family life, sent them to jails and prisons, and returned them to society with felony convictions." Actually, it is these men's own consistently bad decisions that remove them from lawful society. "Felony convictions" do not simply fall from the sky; they result from the serious criminal activity—and persistence at criminal activity, at that—required to induce a district attorney actually to seek a felony charge and possibly a trial. If any of Goffman's subjects made a disciplined effort at "school, work, and family life," she forgot to include that detail.

Revealingly, Goffman explains how she arrived at her incongruous interpretation of Sixth Street's malaise. As a graduate student at Princeton, she had been casting about for a theme for her still-growing ethnographic material. Princeton was a "hotbed" of mass-incarceration theory, she says, which holds that American prison practices have "cease[d] to be the incarceration of individual offenders and [have become] the systematic imprisonment of whole groups," in the words of sociologist David Garland. Eureka! Under the tutelage of Bruce Western and other criminal-justice critics (and with obvious influence from the writings of the French historian Michel Foucault), Goffman comes to see that her "project could be framed as an on-the-ground look at mass incarceration and its accompanying systems of policing and surveillance. I was documenting the massive expansion of criminal-justice intervention into the lives of poor Black families in the United States."

Yet Goffman's material refuses to conform to this template. To her credit, she devotes a chapter to "clean people"—individuals who have no dealings with the criminal-justice system. A group of young men on Sixth Street try to steer as clear as possible from the "dirty people." They remain at home at night, playing video games together. They drink beer, rather than smoke marijuana, because there are drug tests at their jobs, which include security guard, maintenance man, and convenience-store clerk. If they lose their jobs, they don't start dealing drugs; they rely on friends and family until they find another position. When they break traffic laws, they pay off their fines and recover their driving licenses before they start driving again. Their unassuming rejection of criminality comes as an enormous relief after the ugly behavior of Goffman's closest associates. Their respect for the law should be celebrated and studied, as Robert Woodson has long advocated.

Remarkably, however, Goffman tries to shoehorn even these law-abiding individuals into her mass-incarceration framework, resulting in the most incoherent passage in the book: "In a community where only a few young men end up in prison, we might speak of bad apples or of people who have fallen through the cracks," she writes. "Given the unprecedented levels of policing and imprisonment in poor Black communities today, these individual explanations make less sense. We begin to see a more deliberate social policy at work. In that context simply bearing witness to the people who are avoiding the authorities and the penal system seems worth a few pages. The people featured here are all, in a variety of ways, leading clean lives in a dirty world. In so doing, they demonstrate that the criminal-justice system has not entirely taken over poor and segregated Black neighborhoods like Sixth Street, only parts of them."

It would be more accurate to say that the clean people demonstrate that lawless behavior and moral breakdown have "not entirely taken over poor and segregated Black neighborhoods like Sixth Street." The fact that the criminal-justice system distinguishes people who break the law from those who do not shows precisely that "individual explanations" for who gets incarcerated are accurate, not mystifying. The clean people do not run from the police because they are not wanted by the police. Even more absurd is Goffman's ascription of a "deliberate social policy" of oppression to the prosecution of crime. If such a policy existed, there would be no reason to make exceptions for anyone.

Goffman's thesis that the supervision of offenders creates more crime also lacks support in her reportage. She claims that the enforcement of warrants for missed court dates, probation violations, and unpaid court fees drives the Sixth Street drug dealers and thieves underground, preventing them from joining the "clean" world. But she never reveals why her subjects miss their court dates. Do those court obligations inflexibly interfere with job schedules in the legal economy? She would have said so. Instead, these drifting drug dealers most likely simply lack the organization and will to make their court appointments. Goffman herself notes that many a Sixth Street resident who blamed his joblessness on his fugitive status made no effort to find work when he had no outstanding warrants. As for testing dirty for drugs in violation of parole or probation conditions, no one forces a parolee to take drugs. Goffman gives us no reason to think that these thugs would behave better with less supervision; nor does she suggest what a court's response should be when they go AWOL.

Goffman's most persuasive critique of the justice system is that court fees are imposed on defendants who lack the means to pay them, resulting in a vicious cycle of judgments for nonpayment and further warrant enforcement and incarceration. (The Justice Department report on the Ferguson Police Department lodged this complaint as well, as noted in Chapter 4, and it is a growing focus of academic attention.) Here too, though, Goffman shows no instance of someone making a good-faith effort to pay his fees. While her young men are not prosperous, she mentions Mike's sizable collection of worldly possessions, which include cars, motorbikes, sneakers, speakers, jewelry, and CDs. Some men may indeed lack the resources to pay their court fines, in which case the system is self-defeating; but it is also quite possible that they choose to spend their money on other things, such as drugs and sneakers.

On the Run unwittingly demonstrates why police presence is heavy in black inner-city neighborhoods. Goffman mentions just one fatal police shooting: Anthony had shot at undercover officers in an alley, thinking that they were gang rivals; they returned fire and killed him. Otherwise, her young black men overwhelmingly die at one another's hands, such as a friend of Chuck's, shot while exiting Goffman's car outside a bar. The clean people of Sixth Street do not complain about the police; indeed, Miss Linda's father, a retired postal clerk, regularly calls the cops on his grandsons and welcomes the heavy police activity in the neighborhood. Even the Sixth Street criminals try to get themselves arrested when the local gang violence becomes too hot, since prisons and jails are the only place they feel safe.

Goffman claims to have witnessed officers beating up suspects 14 times in 18 months of daily observation and asserts that the Philadelphia Police Department has an official, if sub rosa, policy of pummeling suspects who so much as put a finger on an officer. She also claims, without a source, that the cops routinely steal cash during drug raids. Such brutality and corruption, if true, must be punished and eradicated.‡ But such police misconduct, if it exists—as it did in North Charleston, South Carolina, where Walter Scott was shot to death in wholly unjustified circumstances—does not mean that lawful police activity is any less needed in neighborhoods still plagued by violence and other forms of disorder. Philadelphia's high crime rate has been a perennial drag on its economy. Data-driven policing and the incarceration buildup that Goffman and her mentors so decry resulted nationally in the steepest crime drop in modern history (especially in New York), saving countless inner-city lives, both clean and dirty.

At the end of Goffman's book, Reggie and Tim are serving long prison sentences. We have no reason to believe that those punishments were not deserved.

• • •

It is remarkable enough that Goffman, seeing the lawless behavior of Sixth Street's "dirty people," still views them as helpless victims of a racist criminal-justice system. She has clearly been captured by her subjects. After Chuck is killed, she chauffeurs Mike around the neighborhood, Glock in his lap, as he seeks to find and gun down the murderer. She feels "ashamed and sorry" about being white when Miss Linda's extended family complains about there being a white girl in their midst. (Such pervasive antiwhite antagonism is perhaps the best-kept secret about black inner-city culture.) Goffman refuses to give the police information about the crimes she has witnessed.

But it is even more remarkable that so many influential readers have bought Goffman's thesis that law enforcement is the predominant source of trouble in her subjects' lives. Journalist Malcolm Gladwell, lauding the book in *The New Yorker*, draws the conclusion that the criminal-justice system blocks black criminals and their progeny from entering the middle class, unlike its earlier treatment of the Mafia. Harvard's Christopher

---

‡ Goffman's credibility in police matters has been severely undermined, however. Northwestern University law professor Steven Lubet and Yale clinical law professor James Forman tried to confirm many of Goffman's claims about abusive criminal-justice practices with Philadelphia public defenders, prosecutors, and police sources, and they were told that no such practices existed, nor were they even possible.

Jencks, writing in *The New York Review of Books*, rues the "terrible collateral damage inflicted on the young black men of Sixth Street by their interminable struggle with the police"—echoing Goffman's contention that such struggles simply happen, rather than being the result of voluntary behavior. Like Goffman, her well-placed readers focus on the consequences of crime for the criminal and ignore the crime itself.

On the Run could have been a needed corrective to the post-Ferguson conceit of a racist justice apparatus arbitrarily descending on helpless black communities. But it has not been received that way. Instead, the book's reception has demonstrated how unshakably committed liberal elites are to the belief in black victimhood. And that belief, continuously fed to the street by the advocates and the media, means that relations between the police and the community in New York and other American cities will continue to be fraught with tension and danger.

PART FOUR

Incarceration and Its Critics

To listen to the activists, one would think that jails and prisons are filled with pathetic bumblers who just happened to run afoul of the law. Spending time in a jail quickly disabuses a visitor of that fantasy. This section reports from some of the nation's largest penal institutions to reveal a world of incessant aggression and intermittent violence, in which inmates maneuver constantly to subjugate one another and to corrupt their guards. Preventing inmates from assaulting and murdering one another is an enormous management challenge, a task aided in recent years by the information and accountability tools developed during the 1990s policing revolution.

The myths about the criminal-justice system come to a head in the attack on incarceration, an attack that is ultimately driven by race, like virtually every other aspect of the current vendetta against law enforcement. We are living in an age of "mass incarceration," it is said—an irrational, self-defeating condition that sucks up increasingly harmless offenders to feed the prison-industrial complex. In fact, prison remains a lifetime achievement award for persistence in criminal offending. Many criminals are given numerous opportunities for supervision in the community before finally being sent to prison. The prison population, it is said, is the product of a misguided, racist war on drugs. In fact, violent felons and habitual thieves make up the vast majority of prisoners. The overrepresentation of blacks in prison is supposedly due to an ugly strain of racism that infects the entire criminal-justice system, from policing to judging. In fact, the prison population accurately reflects the incidence of crime.

California shows where the nation is headed if the present agitation against incarceration continues. California's powerful prisoner advocacy bar, in conjunction with the federal judiciary, has tied up the state's prisons in costly litigation for decades, with the ultimate goal of massive prisoner releases. The state has been forced to shift large tranches of convicts from prisons to county jails—in turn, forcing jails to release their own inmates back to the streets. A 2014 voter initiative resulted in a further wave of deincarceration, by reclassifying a host of felonies as misdemeanors. Crime is up sharply in California, a product of both the Ferguson effect and the state's deincarceration policies.

If an alternative to prison can be shown to be equally effective in lowering crime, however, it should be implemented. This section concludes by considering the Swift and Certain sentencing movement, the most promising reform idea in corrections. It also proposes universal inmate work to make prison less violent and more conducive to rehabilitation.

19

Is the Criminal-Justice System Racist?

The race industry and its elite enablers take it as self-evident that high black incarceration rates result from discrimination. At a presidential primary debate on Martin Luther King Day 2008, for instance, candidate Barack Obama charged that blacks and whites "are arrested at very different rates, are convicted at very different rates, [and] receive very different sentences . . . for the same crime." Not to be outdone, his opponent Hillary Clinton promptly denounced the "disgrace of a criminal-justice system that incarcerates so many more African-Americans proportionately than whites."

If a listener didn't know anything about crime, such charges of disparate treatment might seem plausible. After all, in 2006, blacks were 37.5 percent of all state and federal prisoners, though they're under 13 percent of the national population. About one in 33 black men was in prison in 2006, compared with one in 205 white men and one in 79 Hispanic men. Eleven percent of all black males between the ages of 20 and 34 are in prison or jail. The dramatic rise in the prison and jail population over the previous three decades—to 2.3 million people at the end of 2007—amplified the racial accusations against the criminal-justice system.

The favorite culprits for high black prison rates include a biased legal system, draconian drug enforcement, and even prison itself. None of these explanations stands up to scrutiny. The black incarceration rate is overwhelmingly a function of black crime. Insisting otherwise can only worsen black alienation and further defer a real solution to the black crime problem.

• • •

In 2005, the black homicide rate was over seven times the rate of whites and Hispanics combined, according to the federal Bureau of Justice Statistics. From 1976 to 2005, blacks committed over 52 percent of all murders in America. In 2006, the black arrest rate for most crimes was two to nearly three times blacks' representation in the population. Blacks constituted 39.3 percent of all violent-crime arrests, including 56.3 percent of all robbery and 34.5 percent of all aggravated-assault arrests, and 29.4 percent of all property-crime arrests. The arrest data in 2013 were virtually the same.

The advocates acknowledge such crime data only indirectly: by charging bias on the part of the system's decision makers. Police, prosecutors, and judges, Obama suggested in the Martin Luther King Day debate, treat blacks differently from whites "for the same crime."

Let's start with the idea that cops over-arrest blacks and ignore white criminals. In fact, the statistics on the race of criminals as reported by crime victims match the arrest data. As long ago as 1978, a study of robbery and aggravated assault in eight cities found parity between the race of assailants in victim reports and in arrests—a finding replicated many times, across a range of crimes. No one has ever come up with a plausible argument as to why crime victims would be biased in their reports.

Moving up the enforcement chain, the campaign against the criminal-justice system next claims that prosecutors overcharge and judges over-sentence blacks. Obama described this alleged post-arrest treatment as "Scooter Libby justice for some and Jena justice for others." Jena, Louisiana, was where a district attorney initially lodged charges of attempted second-degree murder against black students who, in December 2006, slammed a white student's head against a concrete beam, knocking him unconscious, and then stomped and kicked him in the head while he was down. As Charlotte Allen chronicled in *The Weekly Standard*, a local civil rights activist crafted a narrative linking the attack to an unrelated incident months earlier, in which three white students hung two nooses from a schoolyard tree—a display that may or may not have been intended as a racial provocation. This entrepreneur then embellished the tale with other alleged instances of redneck racism—above all, the initial attempted-murder charges. An enthusiastic national press responded to the bait exactly as intended, transforming the "Jena Six" into victims rather than perpetrators. In the seven months of ensuing headlines and protests, Jena became a symbol of systemic racial unfairness in America's court system. If blacks were disproportionately in prison, the refrain went, it was because they faced biased prosecutors—like the one in Jena—as well as biased juries and judges.

Backing up this bias claim has been the holy grail of criminology for decades—and the prize remains as elusive as ever. In 1997, criminologists Robert Sampson and Janet Lauritsen reviewed the massive literature on charging and sentencing. They concluded that "large racial differences in criminal offending," not racism, explained why more blacks were in prison proportionately than whites and for longer terms. A 1987 analysis of Georgia felony convictions, for example, found that blacks frequently received disproportionately lenient punishment. A 1990 study of 11,000 California cases found that slight racial disparities in sentence length resulted from blacks' prior records and other legally relevant variables. A 1994 Justice Department survey of felony cases from the country's 75 largest urban areas (as mentioned in Chapter 8) discovered that blacks actually had a lower chance of prosecution following a felony than whites did and that they were less likely to be found guilty at trial. Following conviction, blacks were more likely to receive prison sentences, however—an outcome that reflected the gravity of their offenses as well as their criminal records.

The media's favorite criminologist, Alfred Blumstein, found in 1993 that blacks were significantly underrepresented in prison for homicide compared with their presence in the arrest data.

This consensus hasn't made the slightest dent in the ongoing search for systemic racism. An entire industry in the law schools now dedicates itself to flushing out prosecutorial and judicial bias, using ever more complicated statistical artillery. The net result? A few new studies show tiny, unexplained racial disparities in sentencing, while other analyses continue to find none. Any differences that do show up are trivially small compared with the exponentially greater rates of criminal offending among blacks. No criminologist would claim, moreover, to have controlled for every legal factor that affects criminal-justice outcomes, says Patrick Langan, former senior statistician for the Bureau of Justice Statistics. Prosecutors and judges observe the heinousness of a defendant's conduct, for example, but a number-crunching researcher has no easy way to discover and quantify that variable.

Some criminologists replace statistics with High Theory in their search for racism. The criminal-justice system does treat individual suspects and criminals equally, they concede. But the problem is how society *defines* crime and criminals. Crime is a social construction designed to marginalize minorities, these theorists argue. A liberal use of scare quotes is virtually mandatory in such discussions, to signal one's distance from primitive notions like "law-abiding" and "dangerous." Arguably, vice crimes are partly definitional (though even there, the law-enforcement system focuses on them to the extent that they harm communities). But the social constructivists are talking about *all* crime, and it's hard to see how one could "socially reconstruct" assault or robbery so as to convince victims that they haven't been injured.

●　●　●

Unfair drug policies are an equally popular explanation for black incarceration rates. Legions of pundits, activists, and academics charge that the war on drugs is a war on minorities—a de facto war, at least, or even an intentional one.

Playing a starring role in this narrative are federal crack penalties, the source of the greatest amount of misinformation in the debate on race and incarceration. Crack is a smokable and highly addictive cocaine concentrate, created by cooking powder cocaine until it hardens into pellets called "rocks." Crack produces a faster—and more potent—high than powder cocaine, and it's easier to use, since smoking avoids the unpleasantness of needles and is more efficient than snorting. Under the 1986 federal Anti-Drug Abuse Act, getting caught with five grams of crack carried a mandatory minimum five-year sentence in federal court; to trigger the same five-year minimum, powder-cocaine traffickers would have to get caught with 500 grams. On average, federal crack sentences were three to six times longer than powder sentences for equivalent amounts. (In 2010, Congress upped the crack amount that triggered a five-year sentence to 28 grams.)

The media love to target the federal crack penalties because crack defendants are likely to be black. In 2006, 81 percent of federal crack defendants were black, while only 27 percent of federal powder-cocaine defendants were. Since federal crack rules are more severe than those for powder, and crack offenders are disproportionately black, those rules must explain why so many blacks are in prison, the conventional wisdom holds.

But consider the actual number of crack sellers sentenced in federal court each year. In 2006, for example, 5,619 crack sellers were tried federally, 4,495 of them black. It's going to take a lot more than 5,000 or so crack defendants a year to account for the 562,000 black prisoners in state and federal facilities at the end of 2006—or the 858,000 black prisoners in custody overall, if one includes the population of county and city jails. From 1996 to 2000, the federal courts sentenced more powder traffickers (23,743) than crack traffickers (23,121). Crack/powder disparities at the state level cannot explain black incarceration rates, since only 13 states distinguish between crack and powder sentences, and they employ much smaller sentence differentials than the federal courts.

The press almost never mentions the federal methamphetamine-trafficking penalties, which were identical to those for crack—five grams of meth netted you a mandatory minimum five-year sentence—and which now, after the sentencing revisions in 2010, are much more severe. In 2006, the 5,391 sentenced federal meth defendants (nearly as many as the crack defendants) were 54 percent white, 39 percent Hispanic, and 2 percent black. But no one calls the federal meth laws anti-Hispanic or antiwhite.

Nevertheless, the federal crack penalties dominate discussions on race and incarceration because they seem to provide a concrete example of egregious racial disparity. This leads to a commonplace syllogism: crack penalties have a disparate impact on blacks; disparate impact is racist; therefore, crack penalties are racist. This syllogism became particularly prominent after the U.S. Sentencing Commission's 2007 decision to lighten federal crack penalties retroactively in the name of racial equity.[‡]

The press covered this development voraciously, serving up a massive dose of crack revisionism aimed at proving the racist origins of the

‡ In 2014, the commission retroactively reduced federal trafficking sentences for all drugs by an average of two years; releases under the retroactive change began in November 2015.

war on crack. Crack was never a big deal, the revisionist story line goes. But when Boston Celtics draft pick Len Bias died of a crack overdose in 1986, the media went into overdrive covering the crack phenomenon. "Images—or perhaps anecdotes—about the evils of crack, and the street crime it was presumed to stoke," circulated, as the *New York Times* archly put it in a December 2007 article. There ensued a "moral panic" (criminologist Michael Tonry's term) over an imaginary threat from a powerless minority group. Whites feared that addicted blacks would invade their neighborhoods. Sensational stories about "crack babies" surfaced. All this hysteria—according to the revisionist narrative—resulted in the unnecessary federal crack penalties.

Since the 1980s, the story continues, pharmacological experts have determined that powder and crack show "more similarities than differences," in the *Times'* words, and that crack is no more damaging to fetuses than alcohol. The belief that crack was an inner-city scourge was thus a racist illusion, and the sentencing structure built to quell it a racist assault. Or, as U.S. District Judge Clyde Cahill put it, in what one hopes is not a representative sample of the federal judicial temperament: "Legislators' unconscious racial aversion towards blacks, sparked by unsubstantiated reports of the effects of crack, reactionary media prodding, and an agitated constituency, motivated the legislators . . . to produce a dual system of punishment."

Leave aside the irony of the press's now declaring smugly that the press exaggerated the ravages of crack. (The same *New York Times* that now sneers at "images—or perhaps anecdotes—about the evils of crack" ran searing photos of crack addicts in 1993, one of them featuring a woman kneeling before a crack dealer, unzipping his fly, a baby clinging to her back; such degraded prostitutes, known as "strawberries," were everyday casualties of the epidemic.) The biggest problem with the revisionist narrative is its unreality. The assertion that concern about crack resulted from "unconscious racial aversion towards blacks" ignores a key fact: black leaders were the first to sound the alarm about the drug, as Professor Randall Kennedy of Harvard Law School documents in *Race, Crime, and the Law*. Congressman Charles Rangel, representing Harlem, initiated the federal response to the epidemic and warned the House of Representatives in March 1986 that crack had made cocaine "frightening[ly]" accessible to youth. A few months later, Congressman Major Owens of Brooklyn explicitly rejected what is now received wisdom about media hype. "None of the press accounts really have exaggerated what is actually going on," Owens said; the crack epidemic was "as bad as any articles have stated." Congressman Alton Waldon, from Queens, then called on his colleagues to act: "For those of us who are black this self-inflicted pain is the worst oppression we have known since slavery. . . . Let us . . . pledge to crack down on crack." The bill that eventually passed, containing the crack/powder distinction, won majority support among black congressmen, none of whom, as Kennedy points out, objected to it as racist.

These politicians were reacting to a devastating outbreak of inner-city violence and addiction unleashed by the new form of cocaine. Because crack came in small, easily digestible amounts, it democratized what had been a rarefied drug, making an intense high available to people with very little money. The crack market differed radically from the discreet phone transactions and private deliveries that characterized powder-cocaine distribution: volatile young dealers sold crack on street corners, using guns to establish their turf. Crack, homicides, and assaults went hand in hand; certain areas of New York became "like a war zone," said Robert Stutman, a retired special agent from the Drug Enforcement Administration, on PBS's *Frontline* in 2000. The large national spike in violence in the mid-1980s was largely due to the crack trade, and its victims were overwhelmingly black inner-city residents.

Though the elites are furiously rewriting crack history, many people who lived through it are not. In April 2007, Los Angeles prosecutor Robert Grace won the conviction of a crack dealer who had raped and strangled to death ten "strawberries" between 1987 and 1998. The "crack epidemic was one of the worst things that happened to the black and brown community," Grace asserts. Matthew Kennedy managed an infamous public-housing project in Watts during the crack epidemic. "Some of us remember how bad it was," he says. When children avoid school for fear of getting shot by drug gangs, "you've just lost that generation." Lawrence Tolliver has witnessed his share of shootings outside his South Central barbershop. "Sometimes it was so bad you had to scout the horizon like a gazelle at a watering hole in Africa," he recalls.

It takes shameless sleight of hand to turn an effort to protect blacks into a conspiracy against them. If Congress had ignored black legislators' calls to increase cocaine-trafficking penalties, the outcry among the groups now crying racism would have been deafening. Yes, a legislative bidding war drove federal crack penalties ultimately to an arbitrary and excessive point; the reduction of those penalties is appropriate. But what led to the crack-sentencing scheme wasn't racism; it was legal logic. Prosecutors rely on heavy statutory penalties to induce defendants to spill the beans on their criminal colleagues. "An amazing public spirit is engendered when you tell someone he is facing 150 years to life but has the possibility of getting out after eight if he tells you who committed a string of homicides," says Walter Arsenault, who headed the Manhattan district attorney's homicide-investigation unit in the 1980s and 1990s.

Race activists endlessly promote the claim that the draconian federal crack laws are sweeping up mere sad sacks with a little extra crack to spare. But anyone who fits that description is exempt from the federal sentencing scheme. Traffickers with only a modest criminal history who didn't injure others or have a gun when arrested can escape the mandatory federal sentences if they don't lie to the government about their offense (and there is no requirement to rat out others). In 2006, only 15.4 percent of crack-cocaine defendants qualified for this safety-valve provision, compared with 48.4 percent of powder-cocaine offenders; in 2000, even fewer crack defendants qualified—12.6 percent. Crack sellers seldom merit the escape clause because their criminal histories tend to be much more serious than those of powder sellers and because they're more likely to have or use weapons. The legislative distinction between crack and powder sellers, it turns out, had a firm grounding.

Equally misleading is the criticism that few crack "kingpins" can be found in federal prison. This is actually not surprising given that "kingpins" in the traditional sense—heads of major drug-importing rings—don't exist in the crack world. Crack is not imported but is cooked up locally. Its supply and distribution scheme is more horizontal than vertical, unlike that of powder cocaine and heroin. Federal crack enforcement wasn't about stopping the flow of illegal drugs into the country; it was about stopping urban violence. And that violence was coming from street dealers.

Critics follow up their charges about crack with several empirical claims about drugs and imprisonment. None is true. The first is that drug enforcement has been the most important cause of the rising incarceration rate since the 1980s. Yet even during the most rapid period of prison population growth—from 1980 to 1990—36 percent of the growth in state prisons (where 88 percent of the nation's prisoners are housed) came from violent crimes, compared with 33 percent from drug crimes. Since then, drug offenders have played an even smaller role in state prison expansion. Violent offenders accounted for 53 percent of the census increase from 1990 to 2000, and all of the increase from 1999 to 2004.

Next, critics blame drug enforcement for rising racial disparities in prison. Again, the facts say otherwise. In 2006, blacks were 37.5 percent of the 1,274,600 state prisoners. If you remove drug prisoners from that population, the percentage of black prisoners drops to 37 percent—half a percentage point, hardly a significant difference. (No criminologist, to the best of my knowledge, has ever performed this exercise.)

The rise of drug cases in the criminal-justice system has been dramatic, it's important to acknowledge. In 1979, drug offenders were 6.4 percent of the state prison population; in 2004, they were 20 percent. Even so, violent and property offenders continue to dominate the ranks: in 2004, 52 percent of state prisoners were serving time for violence and 21 percent for property crimes, for a combined total over three and a half times that of state drug offenders. In federal prisons, drug offenders went from 25 percent of all federal inmates in 1980 to 47.6 percent of all federal inmates in 2006. Drug-war opponents focus almost exclusively on federal rather than state prisons because the proportion of drug offenders is highest there. But the federal system held just 12.3 percent of the nation's prisoners in 2006.

• • •

So much for the claim that blacks are disproportionately imprisoned because of the war on drugs. An even more audacious argument is that incarceration itself causes crime in black neighborhoods, and therefore constitutes an unjust and disproportionate burden on them because blacks have the highest prison rate. This idea has gained wide currency in the academic world and in anti-incarceration think tanks. Professor

Jeffrey Fagan of Columbia Law School (whom we met as in "expert witness" in earlier chapters) offered a representative version of the theory in a 2003 law review article coauthored with two public-health researchers. Sending black males to prison "weakens the general social control of children and especially adolescents," Fagan writes. Incarceration increases the number of single-parent households. With adult males missing from their neighborhoods, boys will be more likely to get involved in crime, since they lack proper supervision. The net result: "Incarceration begets more incarceration [in] a vicious cycle."

A few questions present themselves. How many convicts were living in a stable relationship with the mother (or one of the mothers) of their children before being sent upstate? (Forget even asking about their marriage rate.) What kind of positive guidance for young people comes from men who are committing enough crimes to end up in prison, rather than on probation (an exceedingly high threshold)? Further, if Fagan is right that keeping criminals out of prison and on the streets preserves a community's social capital, inner cities should have thrived during the 1960s and early 1970s, when prison resources contracted sharply. In fact, New York's poorest neighborhoods—the subject of Fagan's analysis—turned around only in the 1990s, when the prison population reached its zenith.

Fagan, like many other criminologists, conflates the effects of prison and crime. Neighborhoods with high incarceration rates suffer disproportionate burdens, he claims. Firms are reluctant to locate in areas where many ex-convicts live, so there are fewer job opportunities. Police pay closer attention to high-incarceration zones, increasing the chance that any given criminal within them will wind up arrested. Thus, incarceration "provides a steady supply of offenders for more incarceration."

But if business owners think twice about setting up shop in those communities, it's because they fear crime, not a high concentration of ex-convicts. It's unlikely that prospective employers even know the population of ex-cons in a neighborhood; what they *are* aware of is its crime rates. And an employer who hesitates to hire an ex-con is almost certainly reacting to his criminal record even if he has been given community probation instead of prison. Likewise, if the police give extra scrutiny to neighborhoods with many ex-convicts, it's because ex-cons commit a lot of crime. Finally, putting more criminals on probation rather than sending them to prison—as Fagan and others advocate—would only increase law-enforcement surveillance of high-crime neighborhoods.

This popular "social ecological" analysis of incarceration, as Fagan and other criminologists call it, treats prison like an outbreak of infectious disease that takes over certain communities, felling people on a seemingly random basis. "As the risks of going to jail or prison grow over time for persons living in those areas, their prospects for marriage or earning a living and family-sustaining wage diminish as the incarceration rates around them rise," Fagan says. This analysis elides the role of individual will. Fagan and others assume that if one lives in a high-incarceration—that is, high-crime—area, one can do little to avoid prison. But even in the most frayed urban communities, plenty of people choose to avoid "the life." (These are the "clean people" discussed in Chapter 18.) Far from facing diminished marriage prospects, an upstanding, reliable young man in the inner city would be regarded as a valuable catch.

No one doubts that having a criminal record—whether it results in community probation or prison—is a serious handicap. People convicted of crimes compete for jobs at a clear disadvantage with those who have stayed crime-free. But for all the popularity of the view that the system is to blame, it's not hard to find dissenters who believe that individuals are responsible for the decision to break the law. "My position is not hard," says public-housing manager Matthew Kennedy. "You don't have to do that crime." Kennedy supported President Bill Clinton's controversial 1996 "one-strike" rule for public housing, which allowed housing authorities to evict drug dealers and other lawbreaking tenants on their first offense. "I'm trying to protect the good people in my community," Kennedy explains. "A criminal record is preventable. It's all on you." Kennedy has no truck with the argument that it is unfair to send ex-offenders back to prison for violations of their parole conditions, such as staying away from their gang associates and hangouts. "Where do they take responsibility for their own actions?" he wonders. "You've been told, 'Don't come back to this community.' Why would you come back here? You've got to change your ways, change the habits that got you in there in the first place."

Though you'd never know it from reading the academic literature, some people in minority communities even see prison as potentially positive for individuals as well as for communities. "I don't buy the idea that there's no sense to prison," says Clyde Fulford, a 54-year-old lifelong resident of the William Mead Homes, a downtown Los Angeles housing project. Having raised his children to be hardworking, law-abiding citizens, Fulford is a real role model for his neighborhood, not the specious drug-dealing kind posited by the "social ecological" theory of incarceration. "I know a lot of people who went to prison," Fulford says. "A lot changed they life for the better. Prison was they wake-up call." Is prison unavoidable and thus unfair? "They knew they was going to pay. It's up to that person." What if the prisoners hadn't been locked up? "Many would be six feet under."

• • •

Robert Grace, the Los Angeles prosecutor, is acutely aware of the fragility and preciousness of the rule of law. "As a civilized society, we can't allow what's happening in Latin America to take over here," he says. "Venezuela and Mexico are awash in appalling violence because they don't respect the law." Thus, when prominent figures like Barack Obama make sweeping claims about racial unfairness in the criminal-justice system, they play with fire. "For any political candidate to make such claims out of expediency is wrong," Grace says. "If they have statistics that back up the claim, I'd like to see them. But to create phony perceptions of injustice is as wrong as not doing anything about the real thing."

The evidence is clear: black prison rates result from crime, not racism. America's comparatively high rates of incarceration are nothing to celebrate, of course, but the alternative is far worse. The dramatic drop in crime in the 1990s, to which stricter sentencing policies unquestionably contributed, has freed thousands of law-abiding inner-city residents from the bondage of fear. Commerce and street life have revived in those urban neighborhoods where crime has fallen most.

The pressure to divert even more offenders from prison, however, will undoubtedly grow. If a probation system can finally be crafted that provides as much public safety as prison, we should welcome it. But the continuing search for the chimera of criminal-justice bigotry is a useless distraction that diverts energy and attention from the crucial imperative of helping more inner-city boys stay in school—and out of trouble.

20

The Jail Inferno

Jails are the ideal testing ground for romantic myths about incarceration, including the notion that a racist society is locking up large numbers of innocent people who just happened to be in the wrong place and have the wrong skin color. Other myths present a false picture of what happens once a convict is locked up. Michel Foucault asserted in *Discipline and Punish*, academia's most celebrated book on incarceration, that jails and prisons subject inmates to constant, spirit-crushing surveillance. If you were standing in the well of a jail on New York's Rikers Island as profanities rained down on you from the cells above, you would realize the incompleteness of the claim. The truth is that surveillance goes both ways in correctional facilities. Inmates watch their keepers as intensely as they are watched, and usually much more malignly.

As policing has gotten more efficient at nabbing wrongdoers, it has pumped a growing volume of increasingly troubled individuals into the jail system. Governing that population is a management challenge more complex than that faced by any other criminal-justice institution. Yet jails, unlike prisons, remain largely out of sight and out of mind. This public ignorance is unfortunate, because jails have been evolving important principles for controlling criminal behavior of late—ideas that directly contradict the Foucauldian critique.

To understand the difficulties of running a large jail, imagine that your job is personally to shepherd each of the thousands of commuters streaming through New York's massive Penn Station to their trains safely and on time . . . except that the commuters are all criminals who keep changing their travel plans, and their trains, to which they don't want to go, have no fixed timetables. A cross-section of the entire universe of criminal offenders, from the most hardened murderer to the most deranged vagrant, cycles through the nation's 3,365 jails. But the majority of jail inmates show up with no predictable release date, since they have as yet only been charged with a crime and are awaiting a trial that may or may not occur and whose duration is unknown. Even before their trials begin, they may make bail at any moment and be released. Planning for pretrial detainees is therefore no easy task. "The ones who stay less than 36 hours drive you out of your mind," says Michael P. Jacobson, a former corrections commissioner in New York City. "You think: 'Couldn't you have made bail ten hours ago rather than coming into my facility?'" Prisons, by contrast, hold only post-conviction defendants who have been found guilty or pleaded guilty and have been sentenced to a known term of more than a year. (Prisons and jails differ as well in their government overseers: the former are run by states and the federal government, the latter by cities and counties.)

Jail administrators are obligated to get pretrial detainees back and forth to court on time and to keep them safe until their cases are completed. But pretrial detainees are just less than two-thirds of the nation's approximately 780,000 jail inmates. The remainder consists of post-conviction defendants with a sentence of a year or less, who serve their time in jail; post-conviction defendants sentenced to more than a year and awaiting transfer to prison; parolees and probationers who have violated their conditions of release; illegal immigrants detained for U.S. Immigration and Customs Enforcement; and inmates in transit between prisons.

These populations show up at all hours, often with no background information on who they are. Their turnover rate is extremely high: jails process as many admissions and releases in two months as state and federal prisons (which hold about 1.5 million inmates) process in a year. Managing that "churning mass of humanity" is a nightmare, says Jacobson, who now directs the Institute for State and Local Governance at the City University of New York. "So many arrestees lead unbelievably disorganized lives"—but as soon as they enter a jail, the jail becomes responsible for their well-being.

• • •

Two men in street clothes amble down the wide, buffed corridor of the Otis Bantum Correctional Center, one of ten razor-wired fortresses on Rikers Island that together hold nearly 14,000 inmates. They're as odd a couple as any pair of Shakespearean rustics: one short and white, with mismatched eyes that look as though they've been squished by a pickup truck; the other tall and black, with a gap-toothed smile spreading broadly across his craggy face. The very picture of bonhomie and goodwill, the two flag down a passing official to share the happy news: they have just made bail after a day inside and are going home. "Congratulations!" replies Mark Cranston, deputy chief of staff operations. "Now please don't come back to my hotel again."

The chances that they will honor Cranston's cheerful request are slight. At Rikers, 40 percent of all inmates return within a year of release. Such recidivism is typical; all jails have "frequent fliers" who cycle through repeatedly. "I see these guys leave, and they're back in two days," says Gerald, a slender, already-sentenced drug offender in a green uniform who is swabbing the floors of the Otis Bantum intake area. Fifteen men are standing, sitting, or lying down in a holding pen inside the bustling intake office. Plexiglas covers one side of the cell to protect the staff from "splashing" incidents—drinks or bodily fluids thrown at them by cell occupants. One tall detainee in a Yankees jacket is talking on a phone that reaches into the cell, trying to line up bail. As Gerald cleans, he keeps his distance from the new admits. "This place can get you in trouble; there's no need to get involved," he says.

Over the next few days, Rikers officials will try to gather as much information as they can on the men in the pen, seeking to determine how securely to house them and whether they need medical or psychological care. They will analyze their criminal records, intake questionnaires, medical examinations, and current behavior. Such inmate classification is the cutting edge of jail management. Jails are only now starting to recognize the importance of rigorously analyzing information to maintain order, just as policing has in the last decade. Some jails still practice "open bed" classification, housing an inmate wherever there is an empty bed or, at best, separating felony and misdemeanor pretrial detainees.

But careful inmate classification acknowledges that a Mike Tyson in on a drunk-driving charge, say, is likely to be more dangerous than many a felony auto thief—and should be housed accordingly.

At Rikers, new inmates spend up to 72 hours under observation in quasi-quarantine, until the results of their tuberculosis and other medical tests come back. Outside one such quarantine area, a square, windowed dormitory filled with rows of mussed beds, a sentenced inmate working as a suicide-prevention aide roams the hall every ten minutes, checking on new admits suspected of suicidal tendencies. Inside, a pallid transvestite with widely set eyes, several missing teeth, and a curtain of hennaed hair stares intently at a group of visitors. Though he claims that he has just been slapped for not providing a sexual favor to another inmate, the 28-year-old heroin addict otherwise isn't worried about getting attacked. "At Rikers, unlike New Jersey, they cater to you," Della says. "They won't put me in protective custody here"—isolating an inmate for his own safety, that is—"or make me feel like an animal." (Recent studies suggest that rape among inmates is far less prevalent than was previously claimed.)

•   •   •

The spread of quality-of-life policing has brought a more mentally unstable, troubled population into jails—one that mental hospitals would have treated before the deinstitutionalization movement of the 1960s and 1970s shuttered most state mental hospitals. In fact, jails have become society's primary mental institutions, though few have the funding or expertise to carry out that role properly. Mental illness is much more common in jails than in prisons; at Rikers, 28 percent of the inmates require mental health services, a number that rises each year. "People are coming right off the streets with a whole range of street problems," Jacobson reports. "You have to deal with them immediately and figure out: 'Are you a dangerous lunatic, or just tough?'"

Jail administrators worry constantly about inmates' killing themselves—in 2008, Rikers spent $5.3 million in overtime pay for officers to sit watch, 24 hours a day, outside the cells of potential suicides. Mentally ill jail inmates stay longer than other inmates because of pretrial competency hearings and other self-induced complications. One mentally ill Rikers inmate has been incarcerated for five years, during which time he has staged numerous diversionary courtroom dramas to defer his case. Another "has defied all efforts to safely get her to court by injuring herself every time a hearing is approaching," sighs Helena Smith, an assistant deputy warden who oversees a Rikers mental health ward.

The Kent County Correctional Facility—a pair of squat, striped cylinders housing 1,300 inmates in Grand Rapids, Michigan—is a leader in correctional mental health care. Mental clinicians sit in on every intake interview, and they have access to mental health records on every inmate dating back to 2003, an unparalleled degree of medical record-keeping. Every morning, clinicians and corrections supervisors discuss each detainee who has been placed in a suicide cell—a camera-monitored cell lacking a table or any kind of fixture that the inmate could use to hang himself. The discussion sounds as though it is taking place in a hospital, not a jail.

The head clinician brings up a picture of a bedraggled female on a PowerPoint screen. "Miss Wilson is a frequent flier," she begins. "I tried to direct her to the positive aspects of her life; she said she didn't have any." "Does she have a place to go?" asks a supervisor. "She wouldn't engage with me," the clinician answers. A series of men appear on the screen. "Derek wanted someone to talk to; he has a strained relation with his child's mother. I allowed him some time to process those thoughts and feelings. Mr. Taylor continues to be evasive. He smiles and reported that he doesn't want to hurt himself, but if he had to move, he would make no promises for his safety. He says he hears voices, but he doesn't tell me what they say."

The night before, a man just sentenced to life imprisonment for second-degree murder had been moved into a suicide cell under protest. He now lies on Cell 34's green bunk, under a long horizontal slit of a window, tightly wrapped in a blanket like a shroud, his face invisible; a dictionary, slippers, manila envelopes, and rolls of toilet paper litter the floor. In his old cell, a dozen sheets of paper are attached with toothpaste to a wall, each displaying a softly shaded word: Judas, guilt, death, sinner, empty, fear, pain, lust, hope? A blob of green-and-white soap on the wall holds a pencil. This convict has required more than 1,000 staff interventions during his 20-month stay, over ten times the number of incidents that a typical non–mentally ill inmate would generate over a comparable period.

Outside the convict's cell, other mentally ill inmates wander around the cell block's dayroom (the common area where inmates not on lockdown spend their time) following a group-therapy discussion; a few sit at a table with a jigsaw puzzle. John, an elfin Sudanese drunk driver who looks as though he has been dusted in flour, complains in barely comprehensible English about getting bossed around and says that he refuses to take showers. Spencer, a 45-year-old unmarried father in on an assault-and-battery charge that he won't discuss, says with an affectless, unblinking gaze that he has tried to get a job but gets too stressed out to hold it.

A few mentally ill inmates defeat all efforts to get them to take their medication. They cannot be forced to do so without a court order, but they refuse to go to court, thus requiring a judicial order to extract them from their cells. Others hide the pills or spit them out. Once treated and sobered up, some mental-needs inmates become model prisoners, while others remain difficult to control. The question of whether mentally ill inmates are disproportionately violent is a fraught topic. The Wisconsin state auditor reported in March 2009 that mentally ill state prisoners commit nearly 80 percent of assaults on staff, though they are 30 percent of the state prison population. At Rikers, the rate of fights in the mental health observation units is 12 times greater than in the general population.

One day in February, a black-uniformed search team is mustering outside Rikers Island's redbrick Robert M. Devoren Center after an assault by a mentally ill teen. A delusional 17-year-old robbery suspect who fancies himself "King the Punisher" has slashed a fellow adolescent's ear with a razor fashioned from radiator metal. A perennial troublemaker, the assailant has been at Rikers for two years while his trial stretches on. Now the elite search team, drawn from security officers across the island, will scour every crevice of the jail for more weapons, while the victim goes into protective custody. The assailant is at a court hearing as the search team gathers; when he returns, officials will try to bring a new charge of attempted murder against him.

Two of Rikers Island's "punitive segregation" wings—areas where inmates who have broken the rules stay confined up to 23 hours a day in a single cell—are devoted to mentally ill detainees, like King the Punisher. IMPROVE THE MOMENT, exhorts a mural leading into the two wings, located in the George R. Vierno Center, a low tan building with blue corral-type rails on top. The most violent mentally ill offenders, almost all of whom have assaulted staff, are housed in the Mental Health Assessment Unit for Infracted Inmates (MHAUII), a long, double-tiered room of cells with heavy doors. The hatches in the middle of the doors where officers deliver food are bolted like safes because they also serve as complicated mechanisms for handcuffing inmates.

Before a detainee can leave the MHAUII for a visit to a doctor or other appointment, he must be handcuffed and searched for weapons, all while isolated beyond striking range of another human being. He is first cuffed from behind through his food tray while in his cell, and then escorted to a small cage containing a battered gray magnetometer. There he is uncuffed through an opening in the cage and asked to strip and walk through the magnetometer. After dressing again, he is recuffed through the cage. Even these precautions don't always protect officers. A cuffed and scanned inmate on his way to the health clinic has just kicked an officer in the face, cutting him deeply. That inmate will now have leg irons as well as handcuffs when outside his cell.

The violence of MHAUII inmates exceeds the jail's capacity to punish it. No Rikers inmate may spend more than 30 days at a time in punitive segregation, but the most recalcitrant accumulate far more punitive time (known at Rikers as "bing days") than they can pay in a single stretch. The average MHAUII resident owes 303 bing days; one current inmate owes 4,000. When an inmate with a backlog of punitive segregation leaves the island, his debt stays on the books. If he returns, he'll go right back to punitive segregation to start paying down his bing days again.

Even in punitive segregation, mentally ill Rikers inmates continue to receive treatment from a clinical psychologist and a psychiatrist, who try to persuade them to enter behavior-modification therapy. As a reward for good behavior, a group of MHAUII detainees in orange jumpsuits clusters around a TV set in a tall glassed-off room. Outside several cells on the block, single officers sit on stools, each staring at the cell's door. Rikers, unlike Kent County, may not film inmates on suicide watch inside their cells; instead, it must post an officer outside each cell, 24 hours a day. One such detainee, a jailhouse bully awaiting trial on gun, assault, and drug charges, is curled up in a ball under his green mattress, while his monitor sits watching.

. . .

Surveillance of this kind, said Foucault in *Discipline and Punish*, turns inmates into powerless subjects of the "disciplinary" state. Foucault called jails and prisons "Panopticons" after a circular prison model conceived by the eighteenth-century philosopher Jeremy Bentham, allowing guards to observe a large number of inmates from a central position.

But jails and prisons are also reverse Panopticons; to walk around one is to be under constant observation from the inmates. The moment that Deputy Warden Thomas Hall enters another Rikers punitive segregation unit, inmates watching from their cells unleash a torrent of obscenities: "Fucking Hall!" "Call Hall!" While the authorities' surveillance of inmates is often protective—as in the ubiquitous suicide watches—the inmates' surveillance of the authorities can be aimed at corrupting them. Like surveillance, power in jails flows between officers and inmates in multiple directions.

Rikers Island's most dangerous inmate stands watching at his cell door in Twelve Main, a small, square space that contains the island's maximum-security prisoners. Lee Woods, tall and well built, with a broad mouth, has just been sentenced to life in prison for the murder of New York police officer Russel Timoshenko. Woods was driving a stolen SUV with two other thugs on the night of July 9, 2007, when Officers Timoshenko and Herman Yan pulled it over. Gunfire burst from the SUV. Timoshenko died of face and neck wounds five days later, and Yan was seriously injured. Now the former Bloods leader and career criminal stares impassively at some visitors, a white T-shirt tied rakishly around his head, as a corrections officer sits outside his cell.

Woods is in Twelve Main—where the walls are made of reinforced steel so that inmates can't rip out sinks and toilets for weapons—because of the eerie power he exercises over corrections officers. After his arrest for the Timoshenko murder, he arrived at Rikers owing 3,000 bing days, accumulated from 14 assaults on staff, three arson attempts, and several contraband violations during previous stays. In earlier state-prison stints, he had devised homemade razor blades and thrown feces at staff. Yet on his current visit to Rikers, this monster managed to seduce at least six staff members to break the rules on his behalf. Two rookie officers brought him marijuana, tobacco, and alcohol; another two officers supplied him with a cell-phone memory chip and a handcuff key (which was discovered inside his bowels by a magnetometer); a female officer exchanged photos with him during her frequent stops outside his cell (a violation of fraternization rules); and a captain let him make a phone call without supervision. When news of Woods's treatment broke in the summer of 2008, New York police officers were so angry that they allegedly went on a ticket-writing spree against vehicles belonging to the Department of Corrections, a separate entity from the NYPD.

Woods could corrupt his keepers because of the two-way nature of surveillance and power in jail. "You're in a mirror as a corrections officer," says Rikers captain Sean Jones. "The inmates watch you continuously; they can get a heads-up on you before you get one on them. They know when you get a haircut, whether you're wearing your wedding ring any longer. 'Your hair looks great today,' they'll say, or 'I see you took your ring off.'" If a supervisor berates an officer, they will appear to sympathize.

The goal is to gain control of the officer. An inmate's most potent method of corruption is to persuade an officer to break the rules for him. "Inmates know that once they get a corrections officer to do something for them, even if it's just bringing them a cheeseburger from McDonald's, they own the officer," says Frank Straub, the former police commissioner of White Plains, New York. It is illegal to bring an inmate so much as a stick of gum, as corrections officers learn from their first day in the academy. But there will always be a few officers who are turned by a skilled con man. The manipulators test officers quickly—looking for a sign of weakness or perhaps kindness to exploit, or using intimidation to try to bring an officer to heel. "Inmates say it all the time: 'I'll see you when I get out,'" says Jones.

The threat can be realistic because at Rikers, as at other urban jails, inmates and officers often share community ties. The Rikers workforce is predominantly minority; there is a tradition in black families of correctional work, dating from the time when police and fire departments were less friendly to blacks. Given the black incarceration rate, the chance that an officer and an inmate know each other is not negligible. For some officers, familiarity with an inmate or intimacy with the culture of crime raises the risk of malfeasance, and not just because of fear of retribution when the inmate is released. The president of the New York corrections officers' union, Norman Seabrook, addressed the problem of fraternization on the union's website. "Are you just willing to surrender all that you've worked for and all that your family is proud of," he asked, "just because of some individual who lives down the street from you and you want to be a part of some acceptable click [*sic*]?" The 1 percent of officers "who say it's ok to bring in that cell phone or that contraband for an inmate, because they are 'friends'" put the lives of their colleagues at risk, Seabrook warned. "Today it's a cell phone; tomorrow it's a 9 millimeter."

The results of any favoritism, even if it's less shocking than bringing contraband to a cop-killer, are disastrous for a jail. "When a corrections officer builds a relation with an inmate, the system starts to collapse," says Straub, who has studied corruption in New York prisons. "The whole process is undermined."

• • •

Four months after the contraband scandal involving Lee Woods came to light, 18-year-old Christopher Robinson was killed in his Rikers cell by three fellow adolescents, on October 18, 2008. Investigation into the murder revealed a different locus of corruption.

Officers Michael McKie ("Mack") and Khalid Nelson ("Nel"), with help from Officer Denise Albright ("Mama A"), had licensed 12 young thugs ("the Team") to enforce discipline on their cell blocks by means of an extortion racket. New inmates had a choice: they could join "the Program," which meant forking over a percentage of their commissary accounts and telephone privileges to the Team; or they could receive "spankins" (beatings) in their cells. Nelson and McKie taught the Team how to beat the holdouts so as to avoid bruises that supervisors might detect. Team members got to dictate who sat on which chairs in the dayroom, who went to the bathroom and when, and who could go into and out of his cell. Lowly lookouts policed the communal seating areas, "pop-off dummies" delivered the beatings, and the top dogs controlled the housing areas. In exchange for their extortion privileges, Team members were to keep order on the wing.

Throughout the history of corrections, officers seeking to maintain order have tried to exploit the brutal authority that inmates exercise over one another. Mississippi and Louisiana prison officials, among others, issued pistols to selected prisoners to keep other inmates in line in the 1940s and 1950s, writes John DiIulio in *Governing Prisons*, with predictable results. A respected Texas prison commissioner, George Beto, tried to civilize this so-called con-boss system in the 1960s by more carefully choosing the inmates who would perform staff functions, but the same abuses developed, including quasi-official beatings of noncompliant inmates. Other institutions had more informal means of delegation. Captain Randy Demory of the Kent County Correctional Facility (in Michigan) recalls the small South Dakota jail where he once worked: "A guard got a local college football player out of a cell and put him into another cell with instructions to 'settle these boys down.' The football player took care of business and was rewarded with extra food."

McKie and Nelson's "Program" had a particularly dire outcome. Rikers officials had transferred Christopher Robinson into McKie and Nelson's housing unit in an effort to disrupt Robinson's own violent behavior toward fellow inmates in a different cell block. Accustomed to being the top dog himself, he refused to join the Program. Two days later, three inmates known as "Pop Brim," "Ant Luv," and "Fire" beat him to death.

Delegation arrangements like the Program are no longer officially tolerated, yet they keep breaking out. Why? Perhaps because keeping a lid on inmate violence is so difficult. After all, the other benefits to corrections officers from such schemes appear modest. Police corruption usually entails considerable financial gain for the dirty cop; but in jail, there are few deep pockets. At best, McKie and Nelson were freed from the necessity of patrolling the cell block every hour or so. They were undoubtedly lazy (and probably also part of the same criminal culture to which their charges belonged), but what we should learn from the Program scandal is just how great the challenges for corrections officers are. Left to its own devices, inmate society is not carnivalesque spontaneity, as the Foucauldians might have us believe, or grassroots democracy, as proponents of the misguided 1970s and 1980s "prisoner self-governance" movement suggested, but *Lord of the Flies* cruelty in which the strong try to control and exploit the weak.[‡]

The symbols of detainee power would be laughable if the means of attaining them weren't so dangerous. Power-seeking inmates will try to control bathroom use and food consumption. Low-status inmates will wind up excluded from the dayroom. Commissary accounts, with which inmates purchase snacks and personal hygiene items from the jail store, are an obvious target for extortion. And chairs are a particularly useful tool of domination. A detainee sitting on a stack of four chairs is broadcasting: "I'm king." A battle-gray adolescent dayroom at Rikers recently got rid of its freestanding chairs in favor of a green cement picnic table with attached benches. "The inmates were trying to control the seating: stacking chairs and not allowing certain people to sit," says Edmund Duffy, the tall, energetic warden who runs the jail where Christopher Robinson was murdered. Eliminating movable chairs solved another problem as well: they're the first thing grabbed during a fight.

The predatory drive is particularly strong among younger inmates. Not only are young detainees in thrall to their hormones, but only the worst of the worst adolescent criminals go to jail, rather than to the far milder juvenile-justice system. Three-quarters of the adolescent detainees at Rikers are awaiting trial for the top felonies, such as homicides, shootings, and robberies, a far higher percentage than in the detainee population at large.

In such a world, ordinary objects must be viewed as potential weapons—such as a King of Hearts card containing a razor blade made from a battery shell that had just been discovered during one of my trips to Rikers—and attacks can come at any time. Moments before I entered Rikers' Central Punitive Segregation Unit, which houses non–mentally ill infractors, an inmate had thrown an unknown liquid at a guard—it could have been water or urine—angry that he had to wait to use the showers. Red lights flashed throughout the facility, and a team in riot gear trotted by to make sure that the unit stayed calm, as the inmate looked coolly around while being escorted to a medical evaluation.

[‡] In June 2015, New York City agreed to a federal monitor for Rikers as part of a settlement of a lawsuit charging the jail's guards with a "culture of violence," in the words of U.S. Attorney Preet Bharara, against adolescent inmates. The head of the corrections officers' union, Norman Seabrook, criticized the deal for ignoring "inmates who commit crimes while jailed."

Simply directing the movement of bodies in a jail can be a monumental task. Officers work alone or in pairs, vastly outnumbered by the inmates. One evening at the intake area of Rikers' Anna M. Kross Center, a 1960s facility whose anachronistic baby-blue geometric security gates appear to have been inspired by Mondrian, several dozen inmates press their faces against the barriers of six small pens, their features barely visible through the fine blue mesh. A table outside the pens is strewn with the recent admits' sneakers, MP3 players, and jeans. A wiry inmate with dreadlocks in an orange jumpsuit shouts at a visitor, "You have food poisoning, too!" as he is escorted from a pen into the main jail. The detainees are all on different trajectories to and from court, the Bellevue mental hospital, and punitive segregation, and all need to be searched or are waiting to be fed. Getting 20 bodies from court and through the search procedures without a fight requires considerable command presence and finesse, especially if some inmates have previously been separated for security reasons.

Now, imagine that you are a corrections officer in such a situation. Your safety depends on inmates' cooperation. But there's a very fine line between saying, "Hey, guy, work with me here," and letting an inmate call the shots. Time and again, officers have crossed that line, trying to solve the inmate-control problem by ceding authority for order maintenance to the inmates themselves. "It's not easy managing this kind of humanity," says former corrections commissioner Jacobson. "One way to do it is to make deals between yourself and the people."

Observers are divided over how devastating a managerial failure the Robinson case represents. Most acknowledge that in an institution as large as Rikers, some bad things will happen, despite management's best efforts. Bernard Kerik, whose accomplishments as New York corrections and police commissioner in the 1990s have been tarred by a federal conviction for corruption and tax fraud, is the most damning. "If the supervisors were doing their job, there is no way that you could have enforcers," he says. "Where was the captain? If he was making his rounds, inmates should have told him."

Martin Horn, who served as corrections commissioner in the 2000s, disagrees. The corruption scandal that led up to Robinson's murder was essentially undetectable, he argues. The noise of opening and shutting heavy gates to cell blocks means that supervisors can't secretly enter a housing area, and participants had a system of signals to alert one another about approaching visitors. "I have to rely on the integrity of my officers," says Horn. "Without integrity, all the staff in the world won't make a difference." The ethic among inmates and officers against informing further complicates efforts to detect corruption, Horn adds: "There may be no secrets in a jail, but there's also no snitching." A month before Robinson's death, the mother of an inmate on the McKie-Nelson wing told Rikers officials that her son's eye socket had been fractured after he refused to join the Program—but when questioned by authorities, the inmate responded, "I ain't talkin'." Horn doesn't know whether other officers were aware of the ring, though the likelihood that no other adults saw what was happening seems small. In a paramilitary organization, however, bad news does not flow easily up the chain of command; a jail leader constantly needs to figure out ways to extract the facts on the ground, such as showing up at 3 AM to talk to inmates and staff.

Compared with New York police-corruption cases—such as the Dirty 30 in the NYPD's 30th Precinct in the early 1990s, in which more than two dozen officers were stealing drugs and money from West Harlem drug dealers—the McKie-Nelson affair is peanuts and does not discredit Commissioner Horn's achievements overseeing the most complex jail facility in the country.[‡] He drove violence down at Rikers through data-driven managerial accountability; the jail bears no resemblance to the inmate-dominated anarchy of the mid-1990s. In 1995, there were more than 1,000 inmate slashings; in 2008, there were 21, with a total population down by just 2,000 or so. Horn kept the facility clean and orderly through rigorous attention to prisoner classification and Broken Windows–type detail. New York City's jail-homicide rate is a small fraction of Baltimore's, Philadelphia's, Chicago's, or Los Angeles's.

Nevertheless, revelations of officially sanctioned favoritism toward inmates further suggest that top management has lost contact with some operations on the ground. The most damning disclosure concerns the royal treatment that the politically influential Hasidic rabbi Leib Glanz secured for Jewish inmates, benefits that included an elaborate, catered bar mitzvah in a Manhattan jail for the son of an inmate; semiweekly

---

‡ Horn left the commissioner's job in 2009, criticizing cuts in staffing.

feasts for Jewish inmates in the rabbi's office; and inmate use of the rabbi's private phone to call girlfriends and bookies, according to the *New York Post*. When such special treatment is conducted with the approval of jail officials, as Glanz's apparently was, it is even more destructive of correctional fairness than surreptitious favors passed from a guard to an inmate—and when targeted at an already-resented ethnic or religious group, it is the most inflammatory of all.

• • •

However outrageous the Jewish dispensation in the New York City jail system was, the more common problem throughout corrections is inmate misbehavior and secret guard corruption. Such corruption is best prevented by ensuring order through discipline and as much information-gathering on inmates as possible. These principles remain abhorrent to a Foucauldian perspective on corrections, but they're essential to sound management.

Foucault criticized visual surveillance as an oppressive encroachment on inmate autonomy. In fact, visual surveillance has only a limited effect on inmate behavior and leaves officers largely ignorant about what happens on the cell block. The D1A pod in the Kent County Correctional Facility is a semicircle of cells on the second floor of a maroon atrium, holding the jail's most assaultive inmates. It's a pie-slice-shaped version of Bentham's Panopticon: guards stay behind a glass barrier observing the cells in front of them, emerging only for their prescribed tours of the cell block. An occupant of Cell 37 had chiseled out the plate holding his window to the point where he could stick his hand out. Every time he heard the guard entering the cell area, he would replace the plate with a papier-mâché version made out of toilet paper. "The incident resolved for all time the question: 'Do we know what's going on inside the cells?'" observes Captain Demory.

More important than visual surveillance is information-gathering. Just as the NYPD started debriefing every suspect it arrested in the 1990s to collect knowledge about unsolved crimes, progressive corrections officials recognize the need for grassroots information in fighting jail crime. "We teach our officers that the most important thing they can do is to listen to the inmates," says Rikers deputy warden Thomas Hall. "Jot things down: Who's Big Daddy, or Red-O? Feed it up the chain so we can figure out who's running things, who the predators and victims are. When someone gives you information, be receptive; don't shut it off." The Kent County jail reports the information it gathers to the Grand Rapids Police Department; in 2008 there were 70 reports about unsolved crimes, including 23 homicides and six robberies.

The imperative to be open to information from inmates is in tension with officers' instinct to erect a wall between themselves and their charges, a useful check against corruption. Corrections officers develop a strong degree of skepticism toward everything they hear. "If it's not verifiable, you have to take it as not true until you can prove otherwise," says Rikers captain Sean Jones. Indeed, officials can develop a hair-trigger authority reaction to the barrage of claims and requests that they face. As Ernest Lewis, assistant warden of New York's Westchester County jail, walks through a high-security area, a wiry inmate with a history of making trouble shouts through a barred cell: "I'm about to lose my cool. Can I switch to a pen?" In a flash, the previously relaxed warden turns on his command presence: "You better chill out," he warns.

• • •

Despite the complexity of the officer-inmate relationship, an emerging philosophy of correctional design, "direct supervision," seeks to break down the physical and psychological barriers between officers and inmates. In traditional prisons and jails, the corrections officer stays behind a barrier at a workstation, emerging only to make his rounds on a predetermined schedule, while inmates spend their day either in their cells or in a group dayroom. "It's difficult to manage behavior under such conditions," says Demory, "because for 59 minutes of the hour, the inmates control the turf." The traditional design's passive management style is good at containment but not at shaping the culture, he adds. Demory wouldn't let me into the remotely supervised high-security D1A pod because the inmates, beyond the influence of the guards, would likely start exposing themselves and throwing bodily fluids when I entered. "Right now, it's settled down; the officers like it nice and quiet," he explained.

In a direct-supervision facility, by contrast, when inmates congregate out of their cells, the corrections officer is in the same space, either at an accessible workstation or circulating among them, like a community-policing cop walking his beat. The objective is to break down any distinction between the territory of inmates and of officers; the officer is supposed to talk with inmates, set the tone, and intervene immediately in aggression and misbehavior.

The direct-supervision model has had impressive results in managing one of Rikers Island's most difficult populations. A few dormitories of the adolescent jail are devoted to a program in which officers engage constantly with detainees to try to encourage self-control and respect for authority. One day in February 2009, about 50 teenagers enrolled in the Institute for Inner Development sit quietly on immaculately made cots that extend in three rows down a long, shady hall; a fellow inmate is mopping the floor. Francis X, a slender, goateed officer, speaks deliberately and with mellow self-assurance to the group: "I have to say that y'all are quite remarkable. You make me proud. You've only been here for a week or two, but there's already a trust factor here." Officer X invites me to point to a boy at random. I choose a hefty boy with soft features. "Rodriguez, stand up!" X commands. "Why do you want to be here, Rodriguez?" Awkwardly, but still audibly, Rodriguez, in on a drug charge, answers: "To try to learn discipline, to try to change. I came here saggy, I came here with a temper, but if you get jail time, this is the place to be." Another boy is summoned to stand. "Sharif, tell me something about maturity, brother!" Sharif is awaiting sentence on an attempted murder and armed robbery charge. "When I came here, I was running around, but Brother Francis told me what I was doing was wrong and how to humble myself to others. Hopefully, I'll take Brother Francis's teaching when I go upstate. When I come out, I'll be an adult."

In the next wing, a laid-back female officer, Anisah Watkins, leads a rambling discussion with young inmates. A few lay their heads down on their folded arms—the classic ghetto gesture of classroom indifference—while another is lying on his bed. In short order, the discussion tacks from what it means to grow up too fast (it means "you grew up with no father," a boy suggests) to sexual relations between boys and girls ("sometimes the mom had babies just like her teen daughter") to the need to be prompt and organized in life (here the only insights come from the officer). The boys push back against the implacable Watkins, complaining that the regimen in the Institute for Inner Development is too strict.

She calmly reminds them: "That's how it's gonna be down here; it's not going to change."

"We're trying to take the urban street that's inbred in the detainees and file it down, soften it a bit, in order to make them productive members of society," says Officer Alfonzo Miller, a tall, composed man standing in a glass vestibule overlooking another Institute for Inner Development dorm. Still, Rikers officials stress that the main purpose of the Institute is maintaining order, not reducing recidivism when detainees get out. It has accomplished that goal, lowering the fight rate in what was once the jail's most violent area. One boy ejected from Officer X's wing for violence now wants back in. Patrick, a diminutive 17-year-old gun defendant, presses his face against the light-green bars of his cell in the Administrative Segregation Unit and calls Warden Duffy over. As a gesture of courtesy, Duffy opens the food-tray door and starts to bend down toward it (some inmates prefer to speak through the open slot, where there is no screen). Patrick remains standing, however, and asks Duffy in hushed tones if he can get back into the Institute. "I want to get my GED. It's hard to focus here. I need structure," he says. "With a high school diploma, you can get a good job." Duffy says that he doesn't know if there's still room in the program but that he'll look into it.

Direct-supervision theory is evolving further in the direction of community-policing concepts. "Place-based management," for instance, teaches officers to think of themselves as owners of the housing units they supervise. They're accountable for everything that happens on their watch, just as a community-policing officer should feel responsible for what happens on his beat. Too often, says Demory, who trains jail officials in the concept for the National Institute of Corrections, "if a fight breaks out, the officer thinks, 'They're just fools,' rather than, 'I'm the manager. How did that happen?'"

• • •

Very few jails offer rehabilitation-oriented programming for the pretrial population because the length of pretrial detainees' stay is unknown and usually brief. Merely getting them safely to and from their legal appointments on time consumes most jails' attention and budgets. However, the Westchester County jail, a redbrick hilltop facility north of

New York City and surrounded by geese, has launched an antiviolence program for adult pretrial detainees that combines direct supervision with intense group therapy.

The 44 inmates in the Resolve to Stop the Violence Project (RSVP) are all awaiting trial on murder, rape, robbery, and other top felonies or have just been sentenced and await transfer to prison upstate. On Monday mornings, they sit in a large oblong circle in the light-filled atrium of their two-tiered cell block, arms crossed, orange-jumpsuit-clad legs splayed out in front of them, paying close attention to an unusual conversational ritual. Pat, a designated inmate leader, begins: "I heard you say, Fred, that I discounted you. You said you were angry. Can I ask you a clarifying question?" Fred's response is less than clear, but Pat presses on: "Can I propose an agreement that we support each other and let us nurture each other?" Another man chimes in: "Can I validate that I heard you say that you propose an agreement that you support each other?" A third inmate picks up: "I support you validating the agreement that they support each other," and everyone claps.

The men are performing their "one-on-ones," public interactions between two inmates who bring up any tense moments they've recently had with each other, discuss what they learned the previous week about controlling and expressing their emotions, and announce what they intend to learn as the day progresses. The conversational conventions would undoubtedly be familiar to group-therapy habitués; but without such therapy experience, the self-referentiality of the discussion seems like a madly literalistic enactment of social-contract theory.

The participants turn to the future. "Now can I give you some feedback, Greg?" the leader starts. "My kernel of truth is that I'm excited because I'm expecting a visit on Saturday." Greg responds: "Pat, can I give you some feedback? Would you like me to validate it? I heard you say that your kernel of truth is that you are happy because you are expecting a visit; my kernel of truth is that I'm happy, too." Pat replies: "I heard you say that you heard me say that I'm asking for validation; however, you said . . ." Some members of the ring aren't paying rapt attention to this exchange. A facilitator rebukes them: "Is that respectful that you are talking while these brothers speak?" The inattentive detainees soberly apologize.

That men with a criminal inability to control violent impulses can participate in this artificial ritual, known as "conscious languaging," with seeming sincerity says a lot about human malleability. What will remain of these conversational mannerisms when they collide with the code of the streets is unknown. But program director Eddie Concepcion says that the inmates are already bringing their new language to court. "A detainee will say to the judge: 'I hear you say that if I take this plea, I can go home. Can I ask you a clarifying question?' The court personnel are blown away. Usually these guys are cussing out the judge."

RSVP aims to train the inmates to think twice about their reactions before acting on them and to take responsibility for everything that they do. If a participant even hints at blaming drugs, alcohol, or anger for his past violence or a present conflict, program leaders will call him out. "Every day, we remind them that they are violent and are responsible for being violent," Concepcion says. The early data on post-release outcomes of the Westchester RSVP showed the rate of infractions among its members to be a small fraction of those among the inmate population at large. Graduates who have been sent upstate to prison have requested the RSVP manuals so that they can start their own groups there. And the San Francisco prototype of RSVP does boast a significant impact on recidivism: the one-year rearrest rate for violent offenses dropped 82 percent for participants who spent 16 weeks in the program; participants who spent less time in the program had higher rearrest rates.

• • •

The challenges of running jails exceed anything that the academic world—and most of us—can begin to understand. In addition to the huge problems of logistics and safety that jails present on their own, commissioners also face a well-organized inmates' rights lobby that fights commonsense antiviolence measures. Until recently, for example, New York City officials weren't allowed to put pretrial detainees in uniform, which made detecting contraband more difficult. Commissioner Horn struggled to win the right to monitor detainees' phone calls. Adolescents arrive at Rikers with their criminal histories largely concealed from officials to protect their privacy, hindering the determination of their security risk.

But the order that the lobbyists, academic critics, and neo-Foucauld-ians see as oppressive is inmates' only hope for safety and even, perhaps, rehabilitation. The recent insights of urban policing—that order matters, that small violations lead to greater crimes, and that information must be gathered and analyzed—are all equally pertinent to jails, where chaos and corruption always threaten.

21

California's Prison-Litigation Nightmare

Anti-incarceration activists in California won a major victory in 2009 when three federal judges announced that the state must release upward of 46,000 prisoners within two years. The late Supreme Court justice Antonin Scalia dubbed this "perhaps the most radical injunction issued by a court in our nation's history." It was the culmination of two decades of nonstop litigation by prisoner advocates, who argued that the poor health care in California prisons violated the constitutional ban on cruel and unusual punishment.

Since that release order in 2009, California has added well over $1 billion in new prison health-care facilities; correctional experts have declared the state's inmate care among the nation's best; and the prison population has dropped by more inmates than are housed in all but a few states. The state has radically reconfigured its criminal-justice system to comply with the court order—and crime has increased. Yet the judicial triumvirate shows no signs of relinquishing its hold on the prisons, despite repeated requests from Governor Jerry Brown to do so. The dramatic struggle between Brown and the federal judiciary has prefigured the broader deincarceration movement that continues to gain steam nationally.

• • •

California has long been the epicenter of prison litigation. But for cataclysmic force and sheer staying power, nothing beats two massive and inextricably intertwined class-action lawsuits, the first of which began in

1990. The Prison Law Office, California's leading prisoner rights organization, filed a suit arguing that the mental health care provided to the state's mentally ill inmates violated the U.S. Constitution. A second Prison Law Office suit in 2001 extended the argument to the entire prison health-care system. Hundreds of judicial orders have flown forth from these two cases, specifying such management arcana as bed planning. Each order was preceded by a furious exchange of motions between the plaintiffs' attorneys and the state, and was followed by more dueling motions over compliance. Taxpayers pick up both sides' legal bills, which, from 1997 to 2009 alone, excluding payments to experts, cost $38 million.

The federal judge presiding over the mental health–care case, *Coleman* v. *Brown*, installed a special master to oversee mental health treatment. By 2013, the master's fees totaled $48 million. The judge overseeing the general health-care case, *Plata* v. *Brown*, put all prison health care under the control of a federal receiver, with the power to set budgets and make policy. (Though filed long before Brown returned to the governor's office, the cases now bear his name.) The receiver has forbidden the prison system's central management from speaking with prison doctors and medical staff without his permission and outside the presence of his own attorneys—a wildly dysfunctional arrangement. California's per prisoner spending on medical treatment is six times that of Texas, four times that of the federal government in its prisons, and three times that of New York. Health care makes up one-third of California's prison budget.

Notwithstanding undisputed improvements in care, the Prison Law Office expanded its litigation strategy in 2006. Overcrowding, it now argued, was the primary source of the remaining deficiencies in medical treatment. California's prisons had, in fact, been overbooked for years. Starting in the early 1980s, a series of voter initiatives increased sentences for habitual offenders, a reaction to the quadrupling of the murder rate over the previous decade and a half. (That crime increase coincided with an early effort to divert lower-level criminals from state lockup.) Those lengthened sentences nearly doubled the prison census from 1988 to 2006, but the legislature failed to authorize a construction budget to keep up. "I've seen some bizarre overcrowding," an inmate in an Orange County jail recalled. "At one point in Chino, we were given blankets and told to pitch a tent in the rec yard." Gyms and hallways in lockups across the state were converted into dormitories; the staff struggled to keep order.

In 2006, Governor Arnold Schwarzenegger declared that the prisons were in a state of emergency, the prerequisite to transferring inmates out of state. Stress on infrastructure from the 162,000 inmates increased the risk of power outages and sewage spills, the proclamation stated, which, in turn, threatened to spread infectious diseases to the public.

The Prison Law Office leveraged Schwarzenegger's order to seek a mass release of state inmates, as provided for by the federal Prison Litigation Reform Act. That act, passed in 1996, sought to rein in the judicial micromanagement of prisons by requiring, among other measures, that prisoner-release motions be heard by a specially convened three-judge panel composed of the federal judge already overseeing a prison-reform case and two outside jurists. The two additional judges would counterbalance any bias that the presiding judge might bring. The attorneys asked the judges overseeing *Coleman* and *Plata*—respectively, Lawrence Karlton‡ and Thelton Henderson, both senior U.S. district judges—to convene a prisoner-release panel. Both agreed that a panel was needed; each put himself on it. This would be the first three-judge court constituted over the objections of a government defendant since passage of the Prison Litigation Reform Act.

With a majority already constituted by the two judges who deemed the panel necessary and who happened to be among the most activist trial judges on the West Coast, the only question was who would be the third jurist. The nod went to Stephen Reinhardt, a circuit judge, presumably by random assignment. Reinhardt is not just one of the most liberal judges on the West Coast; he is arguably one of the most liberal judges in the country. Given the entire federal judiciary from which to pick, writes University of Michigan law professor Margo Schlanger, "it would have been hard to populate a court more likely to be favorable to the prisoner plaintiffs than the . . . three judge court." (For the record: I had the enormous privilege of clerking for Judge Reinhardt and stand in awe to this day of his supreme intelligence and almost musical ear for language.)

•   •   •

After a one-month trial in which the state and the plaintiffs presented dramatically conflicting testimony about the need for a large-scale

---

‡ Judge Karlton died in July 2015.

prisoner release and its likely effect on public safety, the panel found in August 2009 that prison overcrowding was the "primary cause," in the language of the Prison Litigation Reform Act, of the alleged constitutional violations in health care. The panel ordered the state to reduce the prison population—which, during the trial, stood at 156,000—to 137.5 percent of the system's design capacity within two years, a benchmark that the panel estimated could require releasing up to 46,000 prisoners. (The issue of "design" versus "operational" capacity has bedeviled California throughout the prisoner-release litigation. The state perversely continues to define its own "design capacity" according to the notion that every cell should house only one inmate, even if it was designed for two, and even though the federal government and every other prison system routinely use double celling. In 2010, the system's "design capacity" was for 84,181 inmates; its "operational capacity," based on the intended use of cells, was 149,624 inmates. By the time the panel issued its order, the prison population had fallen to 150,118 inmates—or within spitting distance of operational capacity.)

Jerry Brown, the attorney general at the time, denounced the court ruling: "This order, the latest judicial intrusion by the federal judiciary into California's prison system, is a blunt instrument that does not recognize the imperatives of public safety, nor the challenges of incarcerating criminals, many of whom are deeply disturbed." California appealed to the U.S. Supreme Court. In May 2011, a five-to-four majority, led by Anthony Kennedy, affirmed the panel's population cap in a decision titled *Brown v. Plata*. Justice Kennedy, already on record as a critic of contemporary incarceration policies, found that the health care provided by the state's prisons fell "below the evolving standards of decency that mark the progress of a maturing society" and that only a reduction in the inmate census would cure that constitutional violation. The majority's ruling was the first time that the Supreme Court had ever ordered a prisoner release, and the Court went big.

Justice Scalia's blistering dissent claimed that the panel's "factual" finding that a prisoner release would likely improve public safety, not harm it, was grounded in the judges' policy preferences, rather than in any true findings of fact. Justice Samuel Alito, also dissenting, charged that the panel's decree represented precisely the judicial overreach that the Prison Litigation Reform Act "was enacted to prevent." The judges had a duty to assess the constitutionality of prison health care at the time they issued their release order; instead, they based their remedy on outdated evidence from as long as 14 years ago, including the conditions of a facility that had been replaced. The panel cited mortality figures from 2005, but likely preventable deaths had fallen 83 percent by 2007. From 2001 to 2007, 37 state prison systems had an average mortality rate higher than California's, without calling down the federal judiciary's wrath. In an observation that would only grow more apt over the next two years, Alito noted that the lower court had ignored the extremely high standards for finding an Eighth Amendment violation. The panel had cited, among other pieces of evidence, the lack of "appropriate confidentiality" during medical intake exams. Since when, Alito wondered, does a prison's failure to provide private consultation rooms constitute "cruel and unusual punishment"?

• • •

In a harbinger of battles to come, the now-affirmed three-judge panel rejected the state's initial plan for meeting the 137.5 percent cap as too flexible and required it to start submitting monthly as well as semiannual population-reduction reports. That requirement itself spawned a subgenre of rapid-fire dueling motions, with such titles as "Defendants' Opposition to Plaintiffs' Renewed Motion for an Order Requiring Defendants to Demonstrate How They Will Achieve the Required Population Reduction by June 2013."

Meanwhile, the panel's population-reduction order had triggered profound criminal-policy changes. In May 2011, at the urging of now-governor Brown, the Democrat-controlled California legislature passed what Stanford University law professor Joan Petersilia calls the "biggest penal experiment in modern history." Assembly Bill 109, known as "realignment," would lower the prison count by sentencing certain felony offenders to county jail instead of state prison and by virtually eliminating parole supervision. Giving up on parole supervision is a perverse but simple solution to the alleged problem of too many parolees winding up back in prison for violating parole. In anticipation of the new realignment policies, Brown canceled $4.1 billion in previously authorized prison-construction bonds that would have added another 53,000 prison beds. That new construction was no longer needed, Brown said, since realignment would keep convicts out of prison in the first place.

AB 109 is nightmarishly complex and has produced a host of wholly foreseeable and potentially disastrous burdens on county sheriffs and city police departments. It did generate one intended effect: it greatly accelerated California's already-falling prison count. After realignment began in October 2011, the prison population dropped nearly 10 percent in the first three months alone, mostly because of the disappearance of parolees no longer getting punished for parole violations. From 2011 to the start of 2013, the prison count fell 24,000, to 120,000, the lowest level in 17 years and well below the 150,000-person "operational" capacity of the prison system. The majority opinion in *Brown* v. *Plata* had featured—quite unusually—two outdated photos of bunk beds in prison gymnasiums. By February 2012, such nontraditional beds were gone, as was evident on a visit in August 2013 to the California Institution for Men in Chino. A dayroom outside a high-security block, once filled with beds, now contained only a TV and a single inmate watching it.

California has also invested heavily in new medical facilities and staff. A prison hospital at Stockton with 1,722 beds—1,622 of them for longterm and intensive mental health care—opened in summer 2013, at a cost of $840 million. Hundreds of additional hospital beds have been added and treatment and office space constructed up and down the state. Most offenders get better medical care in prison, with greater access to specialists, than they would in their own neighborhoods, as reflected in part by a comparison of mortality rates in and out of prison. "How many of us ever have 18 people helping us get less depressed?" asks a correctional consultant who has sat in on lengthy discussions of an inmate's mental health treatment plan.

In early January 2013, Jerry Brown did the unthinkable: he asserted that California was capable of operating its prisons. The "prison crisis is over," Brown declared at a capitol news conference. "We spent billions of dollars" complying with the court orders; highly paid attorneys were "running around the prisons looking for problems" and trying to "gold plate" the system, he said. "At some point, the job's done." Brown backed up his words with actions. He asked Judge Karlton, who oversaw *Coleman*, the mental health–care litigation, to terminate the case on the ground that the level of care provided to mentally ill inmates far exceeded the minimal constitutional standard. And he asked the three-judge panel to vacate its 137.5 percent population cap. The outraged reaction from the judicial triumvirate and its agents showed how difficult it would be for the state to extricate itself from their control.

• • •

The state's motion to terminate *Coleman* presented two powerful expert reports about the current state of mental health care. "Few—if any—correctional systems have [California's] diligent provision and self-monitoring of mental health care," wrote one group of experts. That care places California "in the upper echelon of state prison mental health systems."

The report's lead author, clinical psychologist Joel Dvoskin, had testified against the state in *Coleman* in 1994, and in 2013 he was under contract with the Civil Rights Division of the U.S. Department of Justice to evaluate the Los Angeles County jails. The improvement in California's mental health service-delivery system since 1994 was "remarkable and dramatic," Dvoskin and his team wrote. The state was providing "types of care that do not exist elsewhere."

The Dvoskin report did note deficiencies, but they hardly rose to the level of cruel and unusual punishment: inmates at Salinas Valley State Prison sometimes had to choose between yard time and their mental health treatment groups, for example, and a recreational therapist at Pelican Bay was forced, owing to staff shortages, to stand outside the inmate exercise area, thus preventing meaningful recreation therapy. Both situations were being rectified.

The constant oversight by the court and the special master was by now vastly counterproductive, the review team noted. The California prisons are "subject to more micromanagement and detailed scrutiny than any correctional system in history," they wrote. Staff spend inordinate amounts of time preparing for the master's visits, instead of providing care. The master's grip depresses initiative and innovation, since staff believe that they need his approval for any change.

Another former critic of California's department of corrections authored the state's second expert report. Steve Martin, a use-of-force consultant for the Justice Department's Civil Rights Division, had testified against the state in three class-action lawsuits involving mentally ill inmates in the early 1990s. The difference in 2013, Martin told the *Coleman* court, was "striking." The state's "fully transparent, constantly evolving protocols" for controlling the use of force were "among the very best of any such systems with which I am familiar," Martin wrote.

Nevertheless, Judge Karlton threw out the state's expert reports, on the debatable ground that their authors had spoken to inmates outside the presence of plaintiffs' counsel. The state consultants had asked randomly selected inmates such allegedly incriminating questions as whether they knew the name of their primary-care doctor and psychiatrist and how to contact them, what psychotropic medication they were taking, and how to schedule an earlier appointment for care if they needed one. The inmates' affirmative answers were "very unusual," the experts concluded. If these interviews contributed in any way to the experts' conclusion that the care was now constitutional, Karlton held, they would be using the inmates' statements against them, without the benefit of counsel. In Karlton's universe, the prisoners' interests lay exclusively in the indefinite prolongation of the litigation, no matter the diversion of scarce resources from care that that litigation entailed.

Without the expert reports, Karlton noted triumphantly, he would have to deny California's motion because the rest of the state's evidence (hundreds of pages of affidavits and data) was insufficient to prove that the mental health care was now constitutional. Further, the fact that the state had not reached the 137.5 percent population cap ordered by the three-judge panel would also seem to dispose of its current motion, he said, since the panel had ruled that the state could provide constitutional care only by reaching that cap. (In one of the many Catch-22s now binding the state, the panel would announce six days later that it could not modify its population cap because, among other reasons, the *Coleman* court had just declared prison care still unconstitutional.)

As a consolation prize to the state, Karlton magnanimously volunteered to review its other evidence, anyway. His reasoning demonstrated the infinite regress that California now found itself in. Bear in mind the extremely high constitutional standard for finding an Eighth Amendment violation: the plaintiffs must show that the state is "deliberately indifferent" to "severe and unlawful mistreatment" of its inmates. What, according to Karlton and the special master, Matthew Lopes, was California's "severe and unlawful mistreatment" of its mentally ill inmates? One-third of the men's prisons did not "adequately" track patient referrals to higher levels of care (note: those deficient prisons actually *gave* inmates that higher level of care, and within the time frame prescribed by the special master), and over two-thirds of the men's prisons did not "timely complete" the accompanying paperwork. Equally shocking, the state had not yet refined and implemented its Internet-based mental health tracking system "to its fullest extent and benefit."

Karlton also found—relying, as usual, on old data—that the level of inmate suicides was too high, especially those that involved "at least some degree of inadequacy in assessment, treatment, or intervention" and that were therefore "most probably foreseeable or preventable." According to Karlton and the special master, the state should have foreseen the suicide of Inmate H, an illegal alien facing deportation. H had told his psychiatrist that he would be going home to Mexico and that his mother was there. Since H's mother was already dead, the psychiatrist should have divined that H was signaling his intention to return to Mexico as a corpse himself. Instead, the psychiatrist discharged him from suicide watch to a lower level of mental health care.

How could a judge equate such ministerial failings and good-faith errors of judgment with "deliberate indifference" and "cruel and unusual punishment"? The short answer: he didn't. The most powerful sleight of hand that the Prison Law Office, the special master, and the receiver accomplished, with the full acquiescence of the triumvirate, was to substitute a "best practices" standard of care for the *de minimis* constitutional standard.

Years earlier, the state signed on to a massive tome known as the "Revised Program Guide" for inmate mental health treatment. That guide, devised by the special master, sets out in excruciating detail ideal procedures for every aspect of mental health treatment and administration. And it is now the standard that the state must meet to get out from under court oversight. If the state doesn't comply with the guide's every last requirement—many concerning paperwork—it is now held to be a constitutional blackguard. Thus it is that the special master can argue that the state is still violating the Constitution (and therefore still in need of his costly oversight) because only a handful of prisons perform follow-up consultations with inmates discharged from crisis care within the five-day time limit that the guide prescribes. (Matthew Lopes's sky-high fees apparently don't come with a guarantee of timeliness on his own part. He routinely files his 600-page reports up to a year late, thus belying the purported urgency of their content.)

But this legerdemain is not the most galling aspect of the judicial regime under which California now labors. Every voluntary effort by prison administrators to improve inmate care may be seized upon as an admission that the care is constitutionally deficient. California requested additional funding for health-care infrastructure. You see? declared the three-judge panel—this proves that the existing treatment space is insufficient, and thus unconstitutional. The state's 2012 "Blueprint" for improving the prison system observed that some facilities were aging—another damning admission that solidified the judges' power. But according to that criterion, every prison system in the country should be under federal receivership. On its own initiative, California hired a nationally recognized expert in suicide prevention to advise it on how further to reduce inmate suicides. The state implemented several of his recommendations, but not all. Rather than giving it credit, Karlton blasted it for not contacting him again.

A prison system that contracts in good faith with a suicide-prevention specialist would not seem to be "deliberately indifferent" to "mistreatment" of its inmates. The evidence that the judges used to show the state's malfeasance actually demonstrates the opposite proposition.

• • •

Less than a week after Karlton dismissed the state's motion to terminate *Coleman*, the three-judge panel also denied California's motion to modify or lift the population cap. (Karlton was now wearing his three-judge-panel hat, of course, and primly citing the "*Coleman* court" as an independent authority on such matters as the constitutionality of care.) The state had argued that the size of the prison population no longer impeded the delivery of prison health care; indeed, it said, that care now far exceeded the minimal constitutional standard, thanks both to the huge investment in new treatment capacity and to the record-breaking drop in the prison census—nearly 42,000 fewer inmates since the plaintiffs filed their motion to convene the three-judge court. California had virtually eliminated preventable inmate deaths: in 2011, only two deaths occurred that were likely preventable, the lowest rate in the state's recorded history, and one was caused by an outside provider. In 2006, by contrast, there were 18 likely preventable deaths. The inmate suicide rate was equal to or lower than that of 20 other state prison systems and roughly equal to that of the male population at large. Medical positions were close to fully staffed. And the state could not meet the panel's mandate without releasing prisoners who posed an unacceptable risk of violence and other crime.

In asking the panel to reevaluate its order in light of current prison conditions, California was merely following the invitation of Justice Kennedy in *Brown* v. *Plata*. Kennedy had admonished the panel to be open to modifying its mandate if the state had made "significant progress . . . toward remedying the underlying constitutional violations." Kennedy even noted that any drop in preventable or possibly preventable deaths should be among the pieces of evidence that the panel should consider.

The panel refused to budge, asserting in an almost impossibly complicated and logic-chopping opinion that its 137.5 percent population cap was essentially unchallengeable. The figure represented a "legal conclusion," the court claimed, and parties to a lawsuit were not entitled to reopen judicial findings of law after a judgment was handed down. This doctrine, known as *res judicata*, is designed to prevent relitigation of already-decided cases. California is telling us, the panel said, that we "erred" in concluding that the 137.5 percent population figure was an essential prerequisite to providing constitutional care. But *res judicata* prevents the state from launching such an accusation, according to the court.

Well, yes, the state in effect was saying that the triumvirate erred. But if such a reevaluation violates *res judicata*, then the Supreme Court itself is guilty of advocating the violation. (There is, to be sure, a perhaps irresolvable conundrum in the dual jurisdiction of the single-judge and three-judge courts over the evaluation of care, but the panel did not rest its decision on that tension.) And California was not, *pace* the panel, seeking modification "based solely on a contention that some time has passed." It was arguing that the improvements in health care since the panel issued its 2009 order justified modification. Moreover, as the panel itself acknowledged, as if this were a defense of its intransigency, the population cap was a "predictive judgment . . . fraught with uncertainty." But it is precisely because the cap was a prediction, not a finding of law or even of fact, that the court should be willing to reconsider it in light of current conditions. In a case as complex as this one, involving such a monumental intrusion into the legitimate functions of state government, a court should be flexible in the exercise of its power.

The panel's distortion of California's position was of a piece with the rest of the opinion. In the early years of the litigation, the plaintiffs, the health-care receiver, and the judges had invoked the state inspector general's low ratings of prison care to buttress their arguments that the care was unconstitutional. Now that the inspector general had declared that overcrowding was no longer impeding care and had awarded high marks to the vast majority of facilities, those same parties rejected his findings, impugned his rating system (which was established by the receiver himself), and, in the case of the plaintiffs, questioned his independence.

After commending itself for its "exceptional restraint" in dealing with such an obstreperous defendant, the panel concluded by ordering California to submit to it every population-reduction measure that the state had ever considered, in the state's order of preference, and to identify which measures would require a waiver of California law. On May 2, 2013, California responded under protest, with a dizzying list of complicated mechanisms for getting felons out early—increasing "milestone-completion credits" for violent and second-strike offenders who had merely participated, however briefly, in a program, say—all matters outside the judiciary's institutional competence. The state refused to rank the measures according to preference, saying that it opposed them all, and again asserted that it was now running the best prison system in the country.

In this filing, the state more urgently raised the complex political situation that the panel was ignoring. Realignment had radically reduced the prison population by diverting newly sentenced and paroled offenders to county supervision; critics of that policy were seizing on the crimes committed by realigned felons to argue for the repeal of AB 109. Jails were releasing criminals early because of the crush of new offenders redirected their way. The state's Democratic Assembly and Senate leaders had announced that any new law requiring the early release of state prisoners would be dead on arrival. Asking the counties to shoulder a prisoner release on top of their existing burdens could obliterate realignment's already-tenuous political support and reverse the progress made to date.

• • •

One might think that any federal judge, conscious of the limits of his own knowledge and democratic legitimacy, would tread carefully in light of such large-scale, evolving, and poorly understood changes in the criminal-justice system. No such luck.

On June 20, 2013, in a breathtaking assertion of judicial power, the panel declared that it was "compelled to enforce the Constitution," since the state had purportedly guaranteed the perpetuation of constitutional violations into the indefinite future. It then proceeded to waive any California law that stood in the way of the release of 9,600 convicted felons. It ordered the state to expand the "good-time" credits available to violent and second-strike offenders (such credits reduce a sentence for time spent behind bars without incurring serious discipline). This retroactive award of credits to violent convicts paved the way for their immediate release without parole board approval or notification to their victims, as formerly required by now-superseded state law. Presumably to insulate itself from future recriminations, the panel added in a footnote that it would allow the state to write regulations requiring that no one deemed a *particularly* serious threat to public safety be prematurely released. The state was to submit a list of the offenders it intended to release and to report to the court every two weeks on its progress. The triumvirate viewed the political opposition to a prisoner release as all the more reason to enforce it, and set the end of the year as the deadline for the state to comply.

In the reams of documents that have poured forth from the triumvirate, the special master, and the receiver in 2013, it is their belief in their own crucial importance to prison operations that comes across most strongly. The panel's June 20 prisoner-release order quotes extensively from the receiver's May 2013 Twenty-Third Tri-Annual Report. Receiver J. Clark Kelso notes lachrymosely that "the substance and tone of leadership set by State officials has changed from acquiescence bordering on support for the Receiver's work, to opposition bordering on contempt for the Receiver's work and for implementation of court orders, including the orders of the Three Judge Court." If that tone had changed, it was because Kelso kept raising the bar on what it takes to achieve compliance. State leaders had the impertinence, Kelso complains, to observe that "reports from the Special Master are not worth reading or following"—in fact, those inevitably late reports are virtually impenetrable. But most outrageous, from Kelso's point of view, was the state's announcement that it "stands ready immediately to take over prison medical care from the Receiver notwithstanding the State's shortcomings." How dare it assert such independence?

It has been apparent for some time that the health-care issue is a pretext for a broader policy of deincarceration. High-stakes legislative maneuvering in late summer 2013 called the advocates' and the judges' bluff. Governor Brown submitted a bill in August to meet the panel's 9,600-inmate population-reduction order by leasing additional capacity, including out of state, and reopening previously shuttered facilities, rather than releasing offenders to the streets. Brown's proposal won backing from the speaker of the California State Assembly, John Pérez, a Democrat who had criticized the triumvirate for "running the prison system." Republicans in the legislature also supported it. If the advocates were motivated solely by concern about the burden that (alleged) overcrowding poses on prison health care, they should be indifferent to the means that the state uses to reduce it. Instead, the Prison Law Office's lead attorney, Don Spector, groused that leasing more space would be "an incredible waste" of money "for no benefit to public safety"—unlike, apparently, early releases.

Things got more interesting the day after Brown submitted his bill. The Senate president pro tem, Darrell Steinberg (also a Democrat), proposed seeking a three-year extension of the panel's population-reduction order in exchange for an extra $200 million in rehabilitation funding and the formation of a panel to reduce the state's sentencing laws. This proposal presented a new test: if overcrowding were, in fact, posing a dire risk of harm to the state's sick prisoners, the three-year extension should be unacceptable to the plaintiffs' bar. Instead, it welcomed Steinberg's plan. "Sen. Steinberg's substantive proposals are acceptable to us and we are open to an extension," the Prison Law Office announced. In other words, the urgency of meeting the triumvirate's 137.5 percent population figure was a sham.

Brown and Pérez reached a compromise with the Senate president, and on September 16, pursuant to a newly enacted law, the state asked the panel to extend its December 31 deadline by three years. If the panel agreed to an extension, California would deposit up to $225 million into a Recidivism Reduction Fund for community-based social programs. If the panel refused to lift the deadline, the state would go forward with Brown's plan to lease additional cell capacity to avoid early releases.

The panel responded on September 24 with yet another startling assertion of power. It banned California from entering into any contracts regarding out-of-state cells and ordered the state to discuss with the plaintiffs how "this Court can ensure a durable solution to the prison crowding problem." The panel suddenly expanded its purview to juvenile offenders, adding them for the first time to its preferred candidates for early release. The panel gave the state a one-month extension of its population deadline to confer with the plaintiffs.

Brown immediately filed a brief with the Supreme Court, supplementing his existing appeal of the panel's June 2013 release order. The panel had cited no authority in the Prison Litigation Reform Act or elsewhere that gave it the power to limit California's sovereign authority to enter into contracts, the brief noted, especially ones related to core police functions. The panel's orders were bald attempts to legislate criminal-justice policy, the state alleged, by releasing inmates whom the panel and the plaintiffs did not believe should be incarcerated. On October 15, the Supreme Court rejected all of the state's outstanding appeals with a single cryptic sentence, citing a "want of jurisdiction."

The three-judge panel unquestionably made a fetish of its population cap. "I never would have lopped on that 0.5 percent," says a corrections expert. "To establish such a precise figure? C'mon! All of us in the business know that that number is arbitrary. There are so many other variables than population to whether prison conditions spill over into harm."

But the state could be accused of making a fetish of its opposition to early releases as well. Early releases are obviously a political hot button, but they don't change the basic calculus of incarceration: most offenders come out at some point, anyway. True, early releases enable criminals to start reoffending a few months earlier, but they don't change the likelihood of their committing another offense. To avoid lessening prisons' powerful incapacitative effect, the incarcerated should never be let out at all, or should be let out long after prisoner menopause has set in.

But in California's present criminal-justice environment, an early release of 9,600 offenders would impose a significant additional burden on local law enforcement and could well have a greater-than-expected effect on crime. Realignment has produced an upheaval in California's criminal-justice system. "The United States has never experienced . . . what is going on in California" because of it, writes Joan Petersilia. An unprecedented 90,000 offenders were removed from correctional control and let loose through 2012 alone. County sheriffs and police departments have been struggling to oversee the new crop of offenders that AB 109 has sent their way; giving them thousands more in one stroke would be asking for trouble. The panel's refusal to take judicial notice of realignment's effects to date is a grave mistake.

• • •

James Mendez, 34, is typical of the new class of criminal that realignment has dumped on the county jails. Bald and goateed, with a slender face and soft brown eyes, the tattooed gun trafficker is in a high-security wing of the Theo Lacy jail in Orange County. Mendez began his criminal career as a juvenile and proceeded to rack up a complicated incarceration history in federal and state penitentiaries for various gun and drug charges. "I've never completed a sentence in one prison, but get bounced from one prison to another for disciplinary issues," he says, adding judiciously: "I've been a management problem, but I have my reasons." He also has a "reason" for his "bad luck" with weapons charges.

He is in Lacy, a squat jade and taupe postmodern edifice across from a shopping plaza, on a drug conviction and for absconding from parole. Both charges would have sent him to state prison in pre-realignment days. But since the drug offense is "nonviolent" and "nonserious," it falls into the large category of felonies (virtually all the drug and property crimes in the penal code, according to Hastings law professor Aaron Rappaport) that must now be served in county jail, not state prison. Mendez has brought his lifetime of prison habits with him. "I've been in trouble here since I've been sentenced," he says—"fighting, contraband, disrespect to staff."

Thanks to inmates like Mendez, the Orange County jail system saw a 35 percent increase in inmate-on-inmate assaults and a 200 percent increase in drug incidents in the year after AB 109 began. "The AB 109 offender is more criminally sophisticated," says Assistant Sheriff Lee Trujillo. "He has a longer record and is bringing prison politics into the jails." Asked if there are prison gangs in the jail, Mendez smiles beatifically and, like every jail inmate to whom I pose that question, says that he prefers not to answer. The realigned offenders are sucking up staff resources, since 50 percent need protective custody (meaning that they are from gangs or have committed offenses against children, which puts them at risk of retaliation). Everything that the AB 109 felon does in jail, including work, requires more supervision.

Offenders waiting in the lobby of the Orange County Probation Department attest to the changed jail population as well. "There's more violence in the jails because it takes so long for people to get picked up and sent to prison now," reports a 21-year-old pusher.

Despite Mendez's discipline problems, he will be released on schedule, having lost none of his automatic good-time credits on account of his fractious behavior. Most worrisome, he will still come out with no parole or probation supervision, as AB 109 allows. Of all the myriad changes wrought by realignment, this gutting of parole supervision may prove the most consequential.

California once put nearly all felons on parole when they left state prison and returned them there if they violated parole—a costly overreaction, according to conventional academic wisdom. Now, no felon sentenced to county jail under realignment comes out with any post-release supervision, unless the sentencing judge expressly orders it by splitting his sentence between jail and supervised time in the community. Mendez's attorney made sure that he would come out without supervision. And if a realigned felon does leave county jail with supervision (now provided by county probation departments, rather than the state parole agency), that period of oversight is much briefer than parole supervision was, and punishment for violating it is briefer still. Most crucially for the effort to decrease the prison population, punishment for violating parole (now called post-release community supervision) is served back in the county jail, rather than in prison. State parole officers now supervise only convicts whose most recent offense was violent, and only parolees who had been sentenced to life (but were nevertheless released) may be returned to prison for a parole violation.

Before AB 109, the California Institution for Men in Chino had three reception centers to accommodate parole violators; parole agents used to "just roll up to the gates and drop off vanloads of them," recalls a corrections officer there. Now two of those reception centers have been turned into housing units. But if the decimation of parole has provided a short-term benefit in eliminating prison overcrowding, that gain may prove a Pyrrhic victory if unsupervised ex-cons go on a crime spree. The academic doctrine behind realignment held that so-called technical parole violations—violating the conditions of parole by fraternizing with gang members, say, or missing an appointment or testing dirty for drugs—are largely innocuous. But a technical violation can signal a more serious problem. "Pressure to make me do something makes me not do it," Mendez says, explaining his history of parole violations. Now that he will be getting out of Lacy with no parole or probation supervision and "I don't have to run from nobody," he says, "I can just live." His neighbors, however, may not be so confident in his latent self-control and may wish that he had someone regularly checking up on him. His employment record is spotty, at best—he claims, unconvincingly, to have family connections to a cement finisher willing to hire him. Is his wife employed? (She shows up as a full-lipped seductress among a bevy of tattooed females on his left arm.) "She's an American Indian," he replies, as if that answer were self-explanatory.

For some criminals, especially neophytes, the reduction of the maximum punishment for a parole or probation violation from one year to six months may not diminish its deterrence value. Mark Kleiman, a professor of public policy at New York University, persuasively argues that for some subset of criminals, it is the swiftness and certainty of punishment that matters most, not its duration. (The following chapter examines this argument in more detail.) For this group, a night in jail is enough to get their attention and push them back into compliance with the law. But for a hardened offender, the shortened sentence for violating probation and parole means less deterrence. "People aren't as scared now," says a violent homeboy in the Orange County jail. "Hanging out with a gang member used to get you, like, one year. Now, it's three months, so screw it." (The maximum punishment for a parole violation is now six months, but this AB 109 expert reasonably assumes an automatic award of good-time credits, which would cut the sentence by half.)

You might think that AB 109 would be a hit with criminals. Not only does it radically reduce post-sentence supervision; it also keeps offenders in their home communities when they serve time, instead of sending them to a distant state prison. Moving incarceration to local county jails, nearer to family, was supposed to aid rehabilitation. In fact, criminals overwhelmingly prefer prison to jail. Robert, a 42-year-old member of Santa Ana's infamous F Troop gang, has served three prison terms, including for car theft. He is now waiting to see his drug counselor in the Orange County Probation Department after the husband of the woman he was "messing with" reported the three pipe bombs he had in his car trunk. "I loved prison. They give you more freedom," he says. "The way jails are now, they are far worse. The last time I checked, Lacy has a $200,000 budget for movies, but they don't give it to you."

"Being in jail sucks," says Bryant Islas, a rapping, meth-dealing member of Santa Ana's Alley Boys gang. Islas is currently in Lacy awaiting retrial for a 2011 attempted gang murder, committed while Islas was AWOL from an Orange County drug rehab program. His ubiquitous tattoos—So FUCKING SICK across his forehead ("It's a little saying amongst us guys," he chuckles) and the usual Aztec-Mayan Brown Power iconography—attest to his deep expertise in prison culture. "The guards are more respectful to prison inmates. Here they try to challenge us and we get in fights. There's substance abuse treatment in prison, and anger management and school. They offer a lot of stuff—parenting, you can get certified."

Ironically, several jail inmates tout the prison medical care. "In prison, the medical care is free. Here, they charge you," says Islas. He had been carrying around a bullet in his stomach from a gunshot to the back. The last time he was in prison, he decided, "Why not take it out?" He put in a medical slip and was seen in three days. (The surgeon gave him the bullet, which he has since lost.) "I thought the care was pretty good," he says. "The complaining comes from the older lifers. A lot of the dudes fake psychiatric problems."

A blond carjacker in hiking boots, shorts, and no shirt in the Chino men's prison did accost me to grouse that "the doctors aren't as good here compared to other institutions" that he has frequented. He only sees his cardiologist every four to five months, instead of every three months, and he is supposed to be on Coumadin but is taking aspirin instead. Neither failing would seem to rise to the level of a constitutional violation.

Some AB 109 convicts are even pushing to get back into prison. Islas recently came across one of the bizarre consequences of realignment: an AB 109 offender serving a whopping ten years in jail with half off for good time. Why didn't you go to prison? Islas asked him. "I tried to," he responded, "but my commitment offense was not violent."

• • •

Early releases from jails have shot up in California since AB 109, even for some violent offenders. Jails have much greater discretion to release inmates early than do state prisons, which were banned from doing so by statute and the California constitution until the triumvirate canceled those laws. By March 2012, just five months into realignment, county sheriffs across the state were granting early release to 11,000 offenders each month, thanks to AB 109–induced overcrowding. The Fresno and San Joaquin County jails are not taking in any more parole violators because they have no room. Sex offenders have been cutting off their electronic monitoring bracelets with impunity because they know that they won't be sent back to prison and there is little room in the county jails to lock them up. Arrest warrants for GPS tampering by fugitive sex offenders rose 65 percent from October 2011 through all of 2012, reported the *Los Angeles Times*. A sex offender in San Joaquin County who had violated parole 16 times without punishment, including cutting off his ankle bracelet, went on to rape and kill his grandmother, reported CNN in the summer of 2013.

In response to such incidents, Democratic state senator Ted Lieu introduced a bill to make a sex offender's tampering with his GPS device a felony punishable by up to three years in prison. The idea could not survive the triumvirate's grip on California's criminal-justice system. To avoid putting any pressure on the prison-population cap, Lieu's final bill—even then opposed by the Public Defenders Association and the ACLU of California—merely reconfirmed the realignment status quo. GPS-tampering sex offenders would serve 180 days (already the maximum allowed under realignment for any kind of parole violation) in county jail, not prison, for their first removal; subsequent tampering would land the offender in jail for up to a year. Other inmates will undoubtedly be bumped to make room.

County probation departments, now responsible for the vast majority of offenders given post-release supervision, are as overwhelmed by realignment as county jails. "This population was thrust on the counties without giving them the opportunity to build an infrastructure to monitor them," says Margarita Perez, assistant chief probation officer for Los Angeles County. "The administration has put a spin on this that these are low-level offenders. I had these guys on my caseload when I worked as a parole officer. The population that has been diverted—addicts, car thieves—is the most problematic. They violate the most often. And you're going to get cases that fall through the cracks."

Probation departments traditionally had supervised the most reclaimable misdemeanor offenders, and certainly not the felons now being channeled to probation. Few probation officers are trained to carry guns. To beef up their muscle, many probation departments are partnering with local police to do home compliance checks on AB 109 offenders, even though police agencies themselves have no manpower to spare. The Los Angeles Police Department planned to spend $18 million in 2013 sending about 160 officers to do home visits on 5,400 ex-cons. As of autumn that year, about 57 percent of those AB 109 felons had already been arrested for new crimes or a probation violation, according to the Los Angeles Times, and about a fifth were absconding at any given time.

In June 2013, an AB 109 offender hiding in his attic in South Central Los Angeles opened fire on a compliance check team, hitting an LAPD officer in the face and grazing the probation officer. At least there was no violence one day in July when a task force of police (and no probation officer) from across the San Gabriel Valley tried to track down a set of AB 109 probationers in Baldwin Park. Their first stop: a bungalow owned by Mexican drug lords and bristling with surveillance cameras, on a barren lot on an equally barren street. The FBI had been monitoring the compound and had asked the team to parade out the probationer in order to create the impression that he was the extent of the law-enforcement interest in the property. Two pit bulls lunged at the compliance team and barely escaped getting shot. But the probationer, "Darts," living in a trailer at the back of the lot, presumably guarding the drug stash, came out quietly.

Darts had a record including car theft, burglary, a long list of DUI convictions, and a $30,000 bail warrant issued for him on another offense; the team was arresting him this time for absconding from probation. Slender and compact, he complied like a professional during booking at the station house, while a gang detective cataloged his Mexican Mafia tattoos. His arrival at the Baldwin Park police station, however, required moving a fantastically reeking-high Irish Pride gang member into the next pen for his own safety.

No one was at home at several other locations, but the team did find Martha, a 42-going-on-62-year-old gang member with slurred speech, a shock of white through her pepper-gray hair, and minimal teeth. Two officers searched her slovenly bedroom for contraband while the rest of the team bantered with her and her pregnant daughter. The search turned up only a few empty meth bags, a gang scrapbook with an old newspaper clipping about a fatal shooting, and the meth-head's usual DVD porn collection. A veteran of drug-treatment programs, Martha supports her meth habit with her General Relief welfare check ("The check's not much," she says—$200 monthly, which really isn't a lot considering her gram-a-day habit) and by "clucking" (fencing stolen goods). Her daughter is also collecting welfare for her unborn child. Everyone parted amicably.

While this day went without incident, Margarita Perez's prediction that some AB 109 offenders would fall through the cracks has been borne out. In November 2012, a Filipino gang member, Ka Pasasouk, killed four people outside a boardinghouse in Northridge, northeast of Los Angeles. Though carrying a previous robbery conviction, he was on county probation supervision because his last offense was car theft. A judge had decided to let him go free after an arrest for meth possession two months before the quadruple murder. In March 2013, Tobias Dustin Summers kidnapped a ten-year-old girl from her bedroom in Northridge during a burglary and raped her; Summers was an AB 109 probationer, despite a record of kidnapping, robbery, explosives possession, and petty theft.

•   •   •

The Republican opponents of realignment have busily collected such cases to use against Brown, but these incidents, however horrific, do not in themselves prove that realignment is a failure or a misguided policy. Traditional parolees have committed heinous crimes in the past, sometimes after serving long sentences. And such miscarriages of justice could be counterbalanced over the long term by less visible positive effects from realignment, such as decreasing offenders' exposure to criminogenic prison culture. Nevertheless, the first full year of crime data after realignment was not reassuring: California's crime rate climbed considerably over the national average.

The state's recession-decimated policing budgets cannot be the explanation for the national crime disparity; police budgets have declined everywhere. A San Bernardino public defender has an explanation: "We were over-incarcerating before; now we are under-incarcerating." Still, one year of data does not make a trend, and there could be other reasons for California's outlier status. And even if the crime spike in 2012 *was* due to the surge of early releases from jails and the decline of post-release supervision, maybe the new regime simply needed time to work out the kinks.

If California's disproportionate crime rise persists, however, deincarceration advocates could just say that the state is still relying too heavily on incarceration and not spending enough on rehabilitation. AB 109 encourages counties to fund "evidence-based" treatment programs in lieu of law enforcement. It would be wonderful if such successful alternatives existed. Prison is a depressing affair that too often worsens a criminal's antisocial habits. It puts the taxpayer on the hook for a criminal's ever more expensive upkeep. But prison does one thing very well: it prevents crime on the streets while a criminal is locked up.

The proof that "evidence-based treatment" can have a similar effect on crime is not there, at least not yet. "We don't have the models, we can't replicate them, and if we can replicate them, we can't scale them up," said Joan Petersilia, herself an advocate of alternatives to incarceration, to the National Institute of Justice in 2012. And it is virtually impossible to find a previously incarcerated criminal who has not been offered programs or, almost as likely, participated in them numerous times. Here again, though, the anti-incarceration advocates can say that those weren't the right programs, at the right treatment intensity.

Meanwhile, the litigation onslaught accelerated. In July 2013, the Prison Law Office reopened a branch of *Coleman* that had long since been disposed of. It asked Judge Karlton to order the *Coleman* special master to hire his own use-of-force expert to conduct a "comprehensive review" of the use of force against mentally ill inmates—somewhat akin to "ordering" an ice cream addict to buy some Häagen Dazs. "The state is never going to be free of this case," a consultant close to the litigation says. In *Plata*, the plaintiffs and the receiver seized on the incidence of valley fever, an airborne bacterial infection, in two Central Valley prisons to argue that California still cannot run its prison system. (J. Clark Kelso had told the state that it should transfer out black prisoners, who are more susceptible to the infection; the state delayed while seeking confirmation from the Centers for Disease Control that such a race-based policy was needed, thus proving its managerial unfitness, per Kelso.)

In a long-anticipated, final pincer movement, the Prison Law Office began suing *jails* for overcrowding-induced health-care deficiencies. Fresno, Riverside, Monterey, and Alameda counties have all been hit; "every sheriff up and down the state is worried," says Orange County sheriff Sandra Hutchens. The jails are easy targets: designed for short-term stays, they cannot offer anywhere near the services, amenities, and medical specialists as state prisons, as the inmates themselves attest. Yet they will now have to spend millions of dollars that they don't have to bring their own medical care up to a state-of-the-art standard or face litigation and further population-reduction orders.

The activists' agenda is clear: to make incarceration so expensive that law-enforcement authorities will have to abandon it for all but the most heinous crimes. Both sides of the deincarceration debate can claim valid arguments. Mostly ignored in the discussion is proactive policing, which lowers the prison population by interrupting an offender's criminal behavior before it turns into a felony. One thing is certain, though: a federal judge has no institutional expertise to resolve the debate. It belongs in the political arena, not in the courtroom.

The Decriminalization Delusion

In July 2015, President Obama paid a press-saturated visit to a federal penitentiary in Oklahoma. The cell blocks that Obama toured had been evacuated in anticipation of his arrival, but after talking to six carefully prescreened inmates, he drew some conclusions about the path to prison. "These are young people who made mistakes that aren't that different than the mistakes I made and the mistakes that a lot of you guys made," the president told the waiting reporters. The *New York Times* seconded this observation in its front-page coverage of Obama's prison excursion. There is but a "fine line between president and prisoner," the paper noted. Anyone who "smoked marijuana and tried cocaine," as the president had done in his youth, could end up in the El Reno Federal Correctional Institution, according to the *Times*.

This conceit was preposterous. It takes a lot more than marijuana or cocaine use to end up in federal prison. But the truth didn't matter. Obama's prison tour came in the midst of the biggest delegitimation of law enforcement in recent memory. For the previous year, activists, politicians, and the media had been broadcasting a daily message that the criminal-justice system is biased against blacks and insanely draconian. The immediate trigger for the Black Lives Matter movement was a series of highly publicized deaths of black males at the hands of the police, but it also built on a long-standing discourse from the academic Left about "mass incarceration," policing, and race.

Now that discourse is going mainstream. As the press never tires of pointing out, some high-profile figures on the right are joining the chorus on the left for deincarceration and decriminalization. Newt Gingrich is pairing with left-wing activist Van Jones, and the Koch brothers have teamed up with the ACLU, for example, to call for lowered prison counts and less law enforcement. Republican leaders on Capitol Hill support reducing or eliminating mandatory sentences for federal drug-trafficking crimes, in the name of racial equity.

At the state and city levels, there is hardly a single criminal-justice practice that is not under fire for supposedly oppressing blacks. Traffic monitoring, antitheft statutes, drug patrols, public-order policing, trespass arrests, pedestrian stops, bail, warrant enforcement, fines for absconding from court, parole revocations, probation oversight, sentences for repeat felony offenders—all have been criticized as part of a de facto system for locking away black men and destroying black communities.

There may be good reasons for radically reducing the prison census and the enforcement of criminal laws. But so far, the arguments advanced in favor of that agenda have been as deceptive as the claim that prisons are filled with casual drug users. It is worth examining the gap between the reality of law enforcement and the current campaign against it, since policy based on fiction is unlikely to yield positive results.

Two days before his Oklahoma penitentiary visit, Obama addressed the NAACP national conference in Philadelphia and raised the same themes. The "real reason our prison population is so high," he said, is that we have "locked up more and more nonviolent drug offenders than ever before, for longer than ever before." This assertion, which drew applause from the audience, is the most ubiquitous fallacy of the deincarceration movement. It gained widespread currency in 2010 with Michelle Alexander's book *The New Jim Crow*. That a president would repeat the myth is a demonstration of the extent to which ideology has ruled the Obama White House.

Pace Obama, the state prison population (which accounts for 87 percent of the nation's prisoners) is dominated by violent criminals and serial thieves. In 2013, drug offenders made up less than 16 percent of the state prison population, whereas violent felons were 54 percent of the rolls; and property offenders, 19 percent. Reducing drug admissions to 15 large state penitentiaries by half would lower those states' prison count by only 7 percent, according to the Urban Institute.

True, drug traffickers make up a larger (though declining) portion of the federal prison population: half in 2014. But federal prisons hold only 13 percent of the nation's prison population. Moreover, it is hardly the case that "but for the grace of God," as Obama put it, he could have been incarcerated in Oklahoma's El Reno for getting stoned as a student. Less than 1 percent of sentenced drug offenders in federal court in 2014 were convicted for simple drug possession, according to the U.S. Sentencing Commission, and most of those convictions were plea-bargained down from trafficking charges. Contrary to the claims of the deincarceration movement, blacks do not dominate federal drug prosecutions. Hispanics were 48 percent of drug offenders sentenced in federal court in 2013, blacks were 27 percent, and whites 22 percent.

Even on the state level, drug-possession convicts are relatively rare. In 2013, only 3.6 percent of state prisoners were serving time for drug possession, often the result of a plea bargain, compared with 12 percent of prisoners convicted for trafficking. Virtually all the possession offenders had long prior arrest and conviction records. The meth users encountered by Officer Mark Turner of Tustin, California, in his undercover narcotics days were sentenced to drug classes. "Then they would skip out of the classes and always reoffend," he says.

Nor is it true that rising drug prosecutions drove the increase in the prison population from the late 1970s to the present. From 1980 to 2009, drug offenses accounted for only 21 percent of state prison growth, while violent and property offenders accounted for more than two-thirds of the growth, according to John Pfaff, a professor of law at Fordham. (Chapter 19 has more data on these proportions.)

Obama and other incarceration critics have targeted mandatory minimum sentences for federal drug crimes. The current penalty struc-ture is hardly sacrosanct, but mandatory sentences are an important prosecutorial tool for inducing cooperation from defendants. The federal minimums are also not lightly levied. A ten-year sentence for heroin trafficking, for example, requires possession of a kilogram of heroin, enough for 10,000 individual doses, with a typical street value of at least $70,000. Traffickers without a serious criminal history can avoid application of a mandatory sentence by cooperating with investigators. It is their choice not to do so.

• • •

The critics of "mass incarceration" love to compare American incarceration rates unfavorably with European ones. Crime is invariably left out of the analysis. Jeremy Travis and Nicholas Turner, head of the John Jay College of Criminal Justice and the Vera Institute, respectively, penned a classic treatment of this theme in the *New York Times* in August 2015. Germany's incarceration rate is one-tenth that of the United States, they fumed. "To be sure," they acknowledged, "there are significant differences between the two countries." And might those "significant differences" have anything to do with crime, perhaps with the fact that the U.S. rate of gun homicide is about 17 times that of Germany? Of course not. No, for Travis and Turner, the key difference is that "America's criminal-justice system was constructed in slavery's long shadow and is sustained today by the persistent forces of racism."

The same people who denounce American gun violence and call for gun control in a domestic context go silent about gun violence when using Europe as a club to cudgel the American prison system. The U.S. homicide rate is seven times the combined rate of 21 Western developed nations plus Japan, according to a 2011 study by researchers of the Harvard School of Public Health and the UCLA School of Public Health. This disparity is largely a function of the American firearm homicide rate: 19.5 times higher than in the comparison high-income countries, according to 2003 data. Among 15- to 24-year-olds, Americans kill with guns at nearly 43 times the rate of their counterparts in those same industrialized nations. Since the American prison system is driven by violent crime, it is not surprising that America's incarceration rate is higher than Europe's.

Contrary to the advocates' claim that the U.S. criminal-justice system is mindlessly draconian, most crime goes unpunished, certainly by a prison term (as we saw in Chapter 19). For every 31 people convicted of a violent felony, another 69 people arrested for violence are released back to the streets, according to a 2007 Bureau of Justice Statistics analysis of state courts. That low arrest-to-conviction rate reflects, among other reasons, prosecutors' decisions not to go forward with a case for lack of cooperative witnesses or technical errors in police paperwork.

Far from being prison-happy, the criminal-justice system tries to divert as many people as possible from long-term confinement. "Most cases are triaged with deferred judgments, deferred sentences, probation, workender jail sentences, [and] weekender jail sentences," writes Matt DeLisi, an Iowa State University sociologist, in the *Journal of Criminal Justice*. Offenders given community alternatives "are afforded multiple opportunities to violate these sanctions only to receive additional conditions, additional months on their sentence, or often, no additional punishments at all," DeLisi adds. In 2009, 27 percent of convicted felons in the 75 largest counties received a community sentence of probation or treatment, and 37 percent were sentenced to jail, where sentences top out at one year but are usually completed in a few weeks or months. Only 36 percent of convicted felons in 2009 got a prison term. Among convicted violent felons in 2009, 17 percent received community supervision and 27 percent were sentenced to jail, leaving 57 percent on their way to prison. (The numbers have been rounded by the Bureau of Justice Statistics.)

A 17-year-old gang member in Tustin, who has just been arrested for stealing a bike and leading the police on a chase through residential backyards, tells of a friend who stole a car and took off on the freeway with the police in hot pursuit. His friend had a gun at the time. Though this car thief already had a serious felony on his record, he was given a ten-month jail sentence and was out in five months, hardly an overly harsh sentence for the public danger he caused. The bike thief himself has a long record of burglaries, assault, and absconding but has never gone to jail.

The vast majority of felony defendants whom a district attorney decides to prosecute rather than divert out of the system have an extensive criminal history, yet were still in the community committing crime. Half of the defendants charged with a felony in 2009 in the 75 largest counties had five or more prior arrests, and 36 percent had ten or more. About three in five had at least one prior conviction, and 30 percent had multiple felony convictions, with 11 percent of felony defendants having five or more previous felony convictions. Yet the majority of those offenders will still not get a prison term. Among those who wind up sentenced to prison, the prior records are even longer. The average number of prior convictions for inmates released from state prison in 2005 was five; the average number of prior arrests was more than ten.

The Los Angeles County Probation Department has supervised a "frequent flier" whose extensive arrest record includes multiple charges of assault with a deadly weapon, grand theft auto, taking a vehicle without the owner's consent, threatening a crime with intent to terrorize, robbery, escape from custody, failure to appear, driving without a license, possession of a controlled substance, possession of drug paraphernalia, false imprisonment, exhibiting a deadly weapon, and murder. He has twice been sentenced to prison for those crimes, but he is out on the streets as often as not. In August 2015, he was in jail after getting arrested for another violent crime.

Steve, a 49-year-old convict in Santa Ana, is a typical career criminal who is unconfined and still offending. He has a long rap sheet for burglary and firearms charges. His last prison stint ended in 2013, with a three-year term of supervision. A more recent case implicating him in 12 burglaries in nearby Irvine was thrown out by the district attorney because of technical flaws in the police report. In August 2015, he sat with his brother, son, and a friend on the cement back porch of his classic California bungalow, surrounded by a Mercedes 300 SL, a pickup truck, and a jumble of household detritus, as probation officers searched the bungalow's dark interior for contraband and other occupants. The probation team found a semiautomatic handgun in a backpack and a 30-year-old female probationer hiding in a bathroom. She was absconding from her probation officer and high on meth. Steve claimed that he had found the backpack on the front porch a few days earlier and put it in the front hall closet but that he had no idea that it was still there and that it contained a gun. "If it was my pack, I wouldn't keep it in the hall closet," he told the officers. The syringes for his diabetes medicine that were also in the backpack seemed to belie his claim that the pack was not his.

• • •

The biggest myth about the criminal-justice system is not that it mindlessly metes out overlong sentences, but that the disproportionate number of blacks in prison reflects bias by police, prosecutors, and judges. "The bottom line is that in too many places, black boys and black men, Latino boys and Latino men experience being treated differently under the law," President Obama told the NAACP conference in July

2015, echoing a claim he has made frequently. (We have already seen him deploying the line in a speech shortly after the Baltimore riots of April that year.) Incarceration "disproportionately impacts communities of color," Obama said. "African Americans and Latinos make up 30 percent of our population; they make up 60 percent of our inmates."

Naturally, Obama said nothing about crime rates. It is not marijuana-smoking that lands a skewed number of black men in prison; it is their disproportionate rates of violent and property crime. Nevertheless, the racial disparity in incarceration rates has shrunk by nearly a quarter since 2000, with the black incarceration rate down 22 percent and the white incarceration rate up 4 percent. A 2011 study of California and New York arrest data led by Darrell Steffensmeier, a criminologist at Pennsylvania State University, found that blacks commit homicide at 11 times the rate of whites and robbery at 12 times the rate of whites. Such disparities are repeated in city-level data. In the 75 largest county jurisdictions in 2009 (as noted in Chapter 13), blacks were 62 percent of robbery defendants, 61 percent of weapons offenders, 57 percent of murder defendants, and 50 percent of forgery cases, even though blacks are less than 13 percent of the national population. They dominated the drug-trafficking cases more than possession cases. Blacks made up 53 percent of all state trafficking defendants in 2009, whites made up 22 percent, and Hispanics 23 percent, whereas in possession prosecutions, blacks were 39 percent of defendants, whites 34 percent, and Hispanics 26 percent.

Repeated efforts by criminologists to find a racial smoking gun in the criminal-justice system have come up short. If the prison population were not a reminder of a reality that the political and academic establishment would rather cover up—the black crime rate—it is unlikely that the deincarceration movement would have generated the same momentum. After all, the nearly fourfold rise in the prison population since the early 1980s played a major role in the record-breaking crime drop since the early 1990s. That prison buildup represented a backlash against the anti-confinement ideology of the 1960s and 1970s that had lowered the incarceration rate, as crime was exploding in cities across America. Many of the same alternatives to penal custody that are now being proposed had been put into place in the late 1960s and early 1970s to keep criminals out of prison. But these alternatives lost support as crime spun out of control.

Legislators started lengthening sentences, especially for repeat felony offenders, and pressing for a greater confinement rate. During the 1980s, crime rates fluctuated as the prison population steadily grew; it was only in the early 1990s that crime began a steady downward trajectory, ultimately to be cut in half by the mid-2000s. Anti-incarceration advocates point to the divergent paths of crime and imprisonment in the 1980s to argue against the role of prison in the 1990s crime drop. But Franklin Zimring, a law professor at the University of California at Berkeley, has argued that it was not until the 1990s that the prison buildup reached its most effective incapacitative strength and kicked in as a sustained antidote to lawlessness.

Statistical war continues to be waged over the role of incarceration in the last two decades' crime decline, with all activists and many academics still denying that incarceration contributed to the crime drop. Given the nonstop pressure from the Black Lives Matter movement, we may be embarking on another real-world experiment testing the relationship between incapacitation and crime. If the country is really serious about lowering the prison count, however, it is going to have to put aside the fictions about the prison population. The legendary pot-smoker clogging up the rolls is long gone, if he was ever there. Cutting the prison population would require slashing the sentences of violent criminals and property offenders (many of whom have violent histories) and keeping more of them in the community after their convictions. The problem is not "the Michelle Alexander story that we have too many harmless people in prison," says Mark Kleiman of New York University. "Most of the problem is that we have too many murderers in prison."

Compared with the rhetoric around "mass incarceration," current sentences do not seem outrageously high. In 2009, the median sentence length for all felony convictions was 30 months. For violent felonies, the median was 48 months, and for nonviolent felonies it was 24 months. In 2011, according to the Bureau of Justice Statistics, 43 percent of new admissions to state prisons had sentences of two to four years; 57 percent of all prisoners had sentences of four years or less. About 42 percent of incoming prisoners had sentences of five years or more. Whether you find those numbers shocking depends on your view of retribution and incapacitation. To be sure, some very long sentences are meted out.

California, for example, has one of the strictest sentencing-enhancement laws in the nation for the use of guns during felonies. Rob someone with a knife, and you may get two years in prison. Threaten your victim with a gun, however, and you may, depending on your criminal history and plea bargaining, face an additional ten years. In Iowa, class B felonies like armed robbery have a 25-year prison sentence, of which at least 70 percent must be served.

Still, it will take a lot of sentence cutting and diversion to the community to make a difference in the prison population. Cutting the time served by violent felons in New Jersey state prisons by 15 percent, for example, would lower the prison population there only 7 percent by 2021. Cutting violent felons' time served by half would still yield only a 25 percent reduction, according to Erik Eckholm of the *New York Times*, who used an Urban Institute estimation tool. Such measures would hardly end the era of "mass incarceration." To get back to our historical level of incarceration, we would need to reduce the prisoner headcount by 80 percent.

· · ·

Some deincarceration advocates argue that more social programs for criminals can significantly reduce the risks of letting offenders out early or not confining them in the first place. They tout "evidence-based practices," or EBP, meaning social services and therapeutic programs, delivered to the "at-risk" population, that have purportedly been scientifically shown to reduce offending. The EBP movement represents an "embrace of scientific data and expertise" and a "rejection of penal populism and of ill-informed common sense," writes Joan Petersilia, a Stanford law professor. Of course, it was the "expert"-run corrections regime of the 1960s and 1970s that eventually ushered in "penal populism" and "ill-informed common sense" in response to the ensuing crime wave.

The problem with the EBP movement is that there is not much E for the P. As Petersilia herself acknowledges, few programs have been shown to work. And if a program produces an effect in its initial iteration, that result may not be replicable, especially at a larger scale. None of the six programs evaluated by the Justice Department for prisoner reentry was rated as effective. Two had no positive results, while the efficacy of the others had not been established. The federal government funded a large "collaborative" reentry program for serious and violent offenders. Though "collaborative" is almost as favored a term as "evidence-based," the program had no impact on employment or the rearrest and reincarceration rates of the ex-cons.

Even programs concentrating on work may not have lasting effects. An evaluation by MDRC, a social-policy research organization, found that 55 percent of ex-offenders placed in government-subsidized jobs in Chicago, Detroit, Milwaukee, and St. Paul had been rearrested two years after the program ended, compared with 52 percent of ex-offenders in a control group who were not placed in jobs. Of the subsidized jobs recipients, 29 percent had been reconvicted two years out, compared with 27 percent of the control group.

Moreover, it is hard to find an offender who has not already been given programs galore, whether "evidence-based" or not. "These guys have been through so many programs," says an Orange County probation officer. The officer is checking up on a heroin dealer and user in Santa Ana. "I've offered this guy programs, but he's declined. I've forced him into residential programs. We tell them to get counseling, they don't show up. I offer people resources, but they don't follow through because they're addicts." The dealer is not home, but his sister complains that nearby Saddle View Park is a favorite hangout for druggies and an easy place for her brother to get high.

The female meth user hiding in Steve the burglar's house during the Santa Ana probation check had previously been given a government-subsidized job at a Marshalls department store as a "women's associate" in the handbags section. She has also received residential treatment for drugs and alcohol use and been placed in a maternity home. When the job subsidy ended, the store cut back on her hours, and the probationer, who falsely gave her name as "Yvette" during the probation check, stopped showing up. She was fired. Six months later, she returned to a practice that she had begun at age 15: stealing cars, this time from an auto dealership when she noticed a bunch of keys left unattended.

• • •

Other deincarceration advocates are frankly skeptical about programs as a means of reducing the prison population; instead, they focus on sentence length. "To lower the prison population we need to change the penal code," says James Austin, president of the JFA Institute. "Don't talk to me about programs. We need to bring sentences back to a rational level." The advocates even admit that letting prisoners out after a shorter time in prison will lead to more crime, though such acknowledgments rarely make it into the public discourse. But under a cost-benefit analysis, a crime increase may be an acceptable result if the incarceration savings are put to better uses, they argue—though here, deincarceration advocates seemingly reimport a belief in programs. "If we let everyone out six months earlier, some guy will throw a little old lady off the roof," says Michael Jacobson, executive director of the Institute for State and Local Governance at the City University of New York. "The substantive argument to be made is that reinvesting the enormous savings from reduced prison populations into programs that we know effectively reduce crime will make us all safer in the end." Fordham professor John Pfaff says: "If we are experiencing more $30 thefts because we aren't spending $6,000 or $7,000 per year to lock someone up, that could be an efficient reallocation of costs," especially if the savings are put toward more treatment options.

In defense of this bracingly honest argument for shorter sentences, one has to recognize that all sentences are arbitrary to begin with. Though there is political risk in reducing sentences once they have been established at a certain length, if the sentence had always been set at the lower level, no one would notice or complain that it was too short. Even deincarceration advocates ignore the inherent arbitrariness of sentences. In the American Society of Criminology newsletter, Jeremy Travis and Bruce Western recently called for sentences to be "proportionate" to the crime, echoing a 2014 National Academy of Sciences panel that they chaired. This is a meaningless principle, since no objective, "proportional" relationship between a crime and its punishment exists.

But though we have no ideal, Platonic length for sentences, we have arguably arrived at our current sentences through trial and error. During the halcyon days of "expert"-driven corrections in the 1960s and 1970s, crime was raging. Sentences got longer until, in conjunction with a policing revolution that began in New York City, they finally put a lid on crime, ushering in the biggest national crime drop in recorded history.

Further, the costs of prison are comparatively modest, contrary to dein-carceration advocates on both the right and the left. The states spent $48.5 billion on corrections in 2010, the last year for which a full breakdown of corrections expenditures was available at this writing. Never acknowledged is the fact that more than one-fifth of that amount goes to noninstitutional oversight, such as probation and parole, as well as to training. The amount spent on operating prisons and jails was about $37 billion in 2010. The 2010 budget for the federal Bureau of Prisons was $6.1 billion, bringing total federal and state expenditures on institutional confinement that year to $43 billion. (Groups such as the Koch brothers–supported Coalition for Public Safety regularly claim $80 billion in annual prison spending.) That $43 billion is a small fraction of the $1.9 trillion that the states alone spent in 2010, an outlay dominated by education and welfare payments. In 2011, the states contributed $283 billion to federal means-tested welfare programs like Medicaid and Temporary Assistance to Needy Families cash aid. Los Angeles has proposed a $5.8 billion budget to host the 2024 Summer Olympics, an amount lowballed by several billion. Americans spend $7.4 billion on Halloween, according to the National Retail Federation. By comparison, $43 billion nationally to incapacitate serious offenders seems a bargain.

The costs of uncontrolled crime dwarf $43 billion—and $80 billion, for that matter. Estimates of those costs are necessarily incomplete. Immeasurable is the psychological toll of feeling unsafe in your own neighborhood. It is conventional in anti-incarceration circles to dis-miss property crime as "nonserious" and an acceptable consequence of lowered law enforcement. But a street experiencing home or car break-ins is under siege, its residents restricted in their freedoms and well-being. Add violence, and the inhibition on lawful civic and com-mercial activity intensifies. The loss of business-generated wealth and tax revenue in crime-plagued inner-city areas across the country has spurred usually useless government spending to try to jumpstart those crime-strangled economies. That spending eclipses prison outlays. The federal Housing and Urban Development agency alone spent $88 billion in 2014 on Community Planning and Development grants to troubled communities.

Just as total prison spending is exaggerated, so too is the cost of incar-ceration per prisoner. A widely quoted figure is $2,600 a month, but that is an average including fixed capital costs and wages. According to John Pfaff, the marginal cost of each new prisoner is closer to $500 a month, at least until a threshold is crossed that either allows the shutting down of a wing or facility or requires the addition of a new one.

• • •

The current case against incarceration may have been built on multiple fictions, but prison unquestionably is, on average, a squalid, spirit-killing enterprise that can turn borderline offenders into more hardened criminals. (Research is divided on whether incarceration in the aggregate increases recidivism: some studies find increased lawbreaking among ex-prisoners, some studies find no effect, and some find a decrease in recidivism. The impact on future employment and earnings is also contested, with some studies finding no negative effects and others even finding a short-term bounce in employment upon release.) If there are alternatives to arresting and confining criminals that provide the same anticrime benefits, they should be implemented

California provides a test case for how not to go about deincarceration and decriminalization. In November 2014, as the shockwaves from AB 109 were still reverberating, voters passed Proposition 47, a ballot measure to reclassify retroactively many drug and property felonies as misdemeanors. All thefts under $950—including theft of a car or a gun, or yanking a handbag or laptop from someone's hands—would now be a misdemeanor, which can be punished, at most, only by time in jail, not prison. In fact, misdemeanor convictions only infrequently yield jail time. Misdemeanor offenders are not put under probation or parole supervision in the community, which means that they are not subject to search by probation officers; they cannot be ordered into drug treatment. DNA cannot be collected from misdemeanor suspects, which diminishes law enforcement's ability to solve past and future crimes. Many officers have stopped making arrests for a range of drug and property offenses, since the "juice is not worth the squeeze," as a Santa Ana gang detective put it: the time spent processing a case exceeds the consequences to the offender. Prosecutors previously could file a shoplifting incident as a felony commercial burglary if the facts warranted it and the thief had a serious criminal history. They have lost that tool when the goods stolen are worth less than $950. "Now many so-called misdemeanor offenders are hard-core criminals," says Jennifer Contini, an assistant district attorney in Orange County.

Prop. 47 was sold to voters as a way to remove from offenders the stigma of a felony record and to further lower the prison and jail populations, with their attendant racial disparities. Someone arrested for a misdemeanor, if he has identification and no outstanding warrants, is cited in the field and asked to come back to court on another day, rather than being taken into a police station or jail for booking. The measure also promised to reroute the money saved on incarceration into truancy, treatment, and mental health programs, starting in 2016.

The state's jail population dropped after Prop. 47 passed, though it subsequently began rising again, thanks to an immediate increase in crime. "People are no longer incarcerated, they're not in treatment, they're out reoffending on the street," said Jim McDonnell, the Los Angeles County sheriff, to the Associated Press in August 2015. In the city of Los Angeles, violent crime for the year through August 22 was nearly 20 percent higher than for the same period in 2014. Property crime was up 11 percent. Shooting victims were up 27 percent. Arrests were down 9 percent. In Santa Ana, felony crime was up 33 percent in May 2015, compared with May 2014. Violent crime was up 28 percent, property crime up 43 percent, and robbery up 89 percent. In nearby Costa Mesa, violent crime increased 47 percent and theft was up 44 percent through late July, compared with the same period in 2014. In San Francisco, violent crime was up 13 percent and property crime up 22 percent through June 2015 over the previous year. Granted, cities across the United States experienced a sharp crime increase after the summer of 2014, as officers backed off of proactive policing in response to the anti-cop calumnies of the Black Lives Matter movement. But the addition of Prop. 47 in California appears to be compounding the challenges to law enforcement.

The criminal world is well versed in the new regime. "Sure, I know about Prop. 47," says Mitchell, a 62-year-old vagrant hanging out in Santa Ana's perennial Civic Center homeless encampment. Mitchell, who sports sunglasses, cargo shorts, and a ponytail, has spent 22 years in prison for 24 felony convictions, including for burglary and meth trafficking. "I've seen 47 in action," he says. "If someone is busted, the police cite and release them right there. People [i.e., criminals] are getting a little sloppier. If it's a felony and I'm sitting there with the cops, I'm going to be a little nervous. Now it's just a ticket." Mitchell winces: "I think that's a little lax." Theft *should* be serious, he says. Even when theft was a felony, the system used discretion in prosecuting: "If you're caught at Kmart, you're not going to do time for your first offense. If it's your second, *maybe* you'll do 30 days in jail." Now there's more dope flowing and the drug trade is picking up, Mitchell says. "There's more people on the streets. It's fast living and a fast life."

Skid Row in Los Angeles is the most anarchic and fetid homeless colony in the nation, compared with which the tormented figures of a Boschian hellscape might as well be in a *fête galante*. Through August 22, 2015, violent crime in the area was up more than 57 percent over the previous year, shots fired were up 350 percent, and property crime had increased more than 25 percent. In July, a man was nearly decapitated with a machete. "I see the effects of 47 every day. People are emboldened," says Wendell Blassingame, the self-described mayor of San Julian Park (known as "marijuana park"), in the heart of Skid Row. Blassingame is seated at a cardboard table with flyers for social programs, as mentally ill addicts stumble past, headed for the park's picnic tables. Prop. 47 has made it harder to keep order, he says, because police can't ask the gang members who prey on the local population if they are on parole or probation. It has led to the "WDNC phenomenon: 'We do not care,'" says Blassingame. "People say: 'What can they do to me?' Everyone knows they're not going to prison. Even if they commit a violent crime, the D.A. may let them plea out. And they're back on the streets."

The proponents of Prop. 47 say: not to worry. By 2016, the promised savings from prison and jail diversion will have materialized and been redirected to treatment programs. This reassurance overlooks the fate of another California prison-diversion program, Proposition 36, which has fallen out of official memory. That ballot initiative, passed in 2000, gave nonviolent drug offenders the option of free treatment in lieu of incarceration. One-quarter of defendants who chose treatment never showed up; less than a third who did start treatment completed it. Arrests increased, even among those who completed treatment, according to Angela Hawken, a public-policy professor at Pepperdine University. Prop. 36 has quietly been shelved, but 47 seems to be treading the same path by removing the threat of confinement as a means of getting people to change their behavior. The number of offenders enrolled in California's drug courts has dropped sharply after Prop. 47, since they no longer face the threat of prison time for most drug and property crimes.

Deincarceration advocates still applaud Prop. 47 anyway. The fact that prosecutors have lost discretion to charge a felony for most theft and drug offenses is a good thing, says John Pfaff, because prosecutors needed reining in. Their excessive zeal to prosecute was a significant cause of "mass incarceration," Pfaff and others argue.

• • •

California's experience with Prop. 47 to date suggests that a wholesale downgrading of offenses is a reckless solution to "mass incarceration." There might be another way to keep people out of prison while also constraining crime, however: tight supervision in the community, accompanied by modest but guaranteed sanctions for slipping up. A movement known as Swift and Certain (SAC) argues that what changes criminal behavior is not the severity (i.e. the length) of a punishment, but its certainty and the swiftness with which it is imposed. Most criminals have short time horizons, as SAC proponents point out, so telling them that they *may* face a prison sentence of five years after six arrests is not as much of a deterrent as telling them that they *will* go to jail, if only for a day or two, as soon as they offend.

The crown jewel of the SAC movement is the HOPE (Hawaii's Opportunity Probation with Enforcement) program, developed by Steve Alm, a superior court judge in Hawaii. Alm noticed that probation officers would regularly come into his court seeking to revoke probation for their clients in punishment for repeated meth use, which violated the conditions of their probation. But the probation officer would show up to Alm's chambers only after the offender had accumulated his sixth or so dirty urine test—at which point the exasperated officer would announce, in essence: "That's it, no more Mr. Nice Guy. I'm sending you to prison on your original felony sentence" (which could be five or ten years for such offenses as sexual assault or burglary). This pattern was the opposite of how best to modify behavior, Alm concluded. It sent the message that the offender could expect to get away with drug violations almost indefinitely, until some arbitrary and unpredictable moment when the system would come down hard by reimposing the original long prison term. By contrast, we train teenagers by meting out punishment exactly as promised after, say, a weekend curfew violation. The longer that punishment is deferred, the less relationship it seems to have to the underlying behavior and the less deterrent and retributive effect it possesses.

Alm devised HOPE as a fundamentally different probation regime. Probationers would be randomly tested for drug use six times a month— a more frequent testing regime than usual. At their very first dirty urine, they would immediately be sent to jail for a few days. Other probation violations, such as missing an appointment with a probation officer or skipping out on mandated treatment, would also immediately be sanctioned with a short jail stay. Subsequent violations would bring lengthening jail commitments, culminating in a probation revocation to prison. Alm called every probationer entering the HOPE program into his court and explained the system, so that the probationer would know exactly how to avoid sanctions and what to expect if he violated the rules.

The results were startling. Half of the probationers in Alm's experimental program never tested dirty for meth again. Another quarter of the experimental population stopped using meth after one trip to jail. Those who continued to use after repeated short stays were ordered into treatment. Arrests for new crimes also dropped in the HOPE population. One-fifth of probationers in the HOPE program were rearrested after a one-year follow-up, compared with nearly half of the probationers in a control group given traditional probation without swift and certain sanctions.

HOPE revealed a previously unrecognized fact: many drug users can stop on their own, without treatment, if the right incentives are in place. Placing all drug offenders in treatment is a waste of resources; a sanctioning regime like HOPE acts as a sorting mechanism to distinguish the drug users who can control themselves from those who can't—about 9 percent in the original HOPE sample. In that respect, HOPE is crucially different from drug courts, which place every enrolled offender in mandated treatment without seeing if he can stop on his own. Drug court should be something you fail into, says Mark Kleiman.

HOPE also validated the principle that lengthy punishment is not necessary to change behavior, at least regarding substance abuse; short sanctions can work so long as their application is certain and immediate. The question is how far the SAC principle can go in transforming the criminal-justice system. As of July 2015, there were SAC programs operating in 28 states, with interest in the concept growing daily. The largest jurisdiction so far is the entirety of Washington State, where the statewide probation department has retooled itself for immediate, no-discretion sanctions for probation violations. An evaluation of the Washington State program will be out shortly. South Dakota created a SAC program for DUI offenders that requires twice-daily alcohol testing, while otherwise allowing convicted offenders to drive so long as they blow clean. Half of the participants never skip or fail a test. Jurisdictions are experimenting with how minimal sanctions can be and still change behavior; some are assigning offenders to community service instead of sending them to jail. Others are using carrots in addition to sticks: in Washington State, for example, if a probationer complies with all the conditions of his probation for 18 months, he can free himself from further oversight. Preliminary results show that those released probationers are not rearrested.

Could the Swift and Certain principle provide the key to unlocking prisons, by so closely regulating offenders' behavior in the community that they can remain there without needing long-term confinement in prison or jail? Perhaps, but the implementation challenges are great. Swift and certain sanctioning sounds intuitively obvious, but it takes an enormous amount of institutional buy-in and coordination. Everyone in a local criminal-justice system—including police and probation officers, prosecutors, defense attorneys, and judges—must be committed to making sure that offenders are immediately punished. If the sanctioning is not consistent, the credibility and legitimacy of the threat are undermined.

Some jurisdictions have been unable to ensure uniformity of response. Sometimes this lack of uniformity represents lack of manpower and management capacity; at other times, it reflects disagreement with the program. Many probation officers take satisfaction in the exercise of discretion regarding punishment; they see an individualized response to each probationer's situation as a mark of justice. "I give people chances. I am fair," says an Orange County probation officer proudly. SAC removes that discretion to give an offender a second, third, or fifth chance; every offender who violates the conditions of his freedom must face immediate and preset consequences. (The tension between uniformity and discretion pervades the criminal-justice system. Do we want police officers to arrest everyone for drinking in public, or should they make an ad hoc judgment about whether simply to pour out the liquor and warn the drinker, at the risk of unequal treatment? Judicial discretion in sentencing, once the norm, was curtailed during the 1980s and 1990s because of the perception that judges were being too lenient with criminals. Now the pendulum is swinging back.)

Taking SAC to scale in large urban jurisdictions would require a revolution in management. In 2015, New York City had more than a million open arrest warrants for failure to appear in court or pay a fine for a low-level offense. No one was going after those absconders. In Los Angeles, 2,000 felon absconders were still at large, having never checked in with authorities after AB 109 changed their confinement status in 2011, according to Michel Moore, an assistant L.A. police chief. Under such conditions, it is almost unthinkable that someone who skips out of a Breathalyzer or drug test would be immediately picked up and brought to court. SAC advocates suggest starting small in urban areas. Probation departments would need to be enlarged. But once the deterrent effect of immediate sanctioning kicks in, the caseload requiring sanctions would drop precipitously, SAC advocates maintain.

More foundational questions arise about Swift and Certain's potential to lower crime and the prison population. The trigger for SAC sanctions at present is substance abuse, as well as violations of other easily monitored probation conditions, such as showing up for appointments. There is not a technology now available for immediately detecting property and violent crimes, though GPS monitoring holds out some promise. Yes, a huge proportion of criminals abuse drugs and alcohol and are thus candidates for SAC monitoring and sanctioning: a 2009 study by the Office of National Drug Control Policy found that 87 percent of arrestees test positive for drug use. The theory is that reducing a criminal's substance abuse and rigorously enforcing key probation conditions will leave less opportunity and inclination to commit crimes, so that the person can be kept safely in the community. The theory seems plausible, but more data are needed on changes in reoffending rates among SAC enrollees.

A final question is whether short but certain punishments are always as effective as long but uncertain ones. Offenders facing their first institutional confinement will likely be traumatized by a weekend in jail. But for seasoned offenders, short-term sentences are less of a deterrent. California has a flabby version of SAC called "flash incarceration," which allows probation officers, at their discretion, to summarily send a client to jail for ten days. "A career criminal can do ten days standing on his head," says Steve Martin, the Justice Department consultant on prison and jail management. Another Steve, the burglar on probation in Santa Ana, had recently done a ten-day flash for associating with his felon girlfriend, in violation of his probation terms. He seemed to regard it as the equivalent of a trip to a spa: "I just wasted the time, it was a chance to catch my breath and get some exercise with push-ups," he said. "When you're locked up, at least you're working out inside your cell."

The response to Prop. 47 would also seem to suggest that length of sentence matters, since criminals are scoffing at the lowered sanctions associated with misdemeanor offenses. A SAC proponent would respond that those shortened misdemeanor sanctions lack the swiftness and certainty of application essential to behavior modification. A persistent offender may brush off a short jail sentence to be imposed at some indefinite day in the future, but if you tell him that he's going to jail now and losing his Saturday night out with his homies, you've got his attention, claims Kleiman.

Many criminologists and prisoner advocates resist SAC because they think that it is too punitive and because it de-emphasizes services and treatment. "Deterrence-oriented programs [should be] subsidiary to the delivery of therapy aimed at fixing the deficits (or criminogenic needs) leading to reoffending," argued three criminologists from the University of Cincinnati in the 2014 *Federal Probation Reporter*. But it is precisely its simple, behaviorist approach to criminal offending that makes it so appealing. We don't need more services—we need more immediate consequences, says Kleiman.

For all the challenges of bringing SAC principles to scale, the concept is the most promising alternative to the carceral status quo. At the end

of 2013, there were twice as many criminals in the community on probation and parole as there were confined in prison or jail. Those 4.7 million
probationers and parolees have not been particularly well supervised. If
the institutional population—2.3 million at the end of 2013—is greatly
reduced, many more offenders will be in the community needing supervision. The more that probation and parole departments can embrace the
idea of SAC sanctioning, the better the chances for keeping offenders
out of trouble.

Kleiman has proposed the most radical application of SAC yet, as part
of a reentry program for violent offenders. Violent felons would serve the
final part of their sentence in small scatter-site apartments, where they
would initially be under something close to house arrest, permitted to go
out only to work or to look for work, to make necessary purchases, and to
meet with their correctional supervisor. Employment attendance would
be monitored. A GPS ankle bracelet and camera in their apartment would
track their movements. Every day that they comply with every condition
of release would gradually gain them more freedoms. Violations of those
conditions would be immediately sanctioned. The costs would be offset
with savings on incarceration.

The idea of early release for violent felons, however, strikes even some
SAC advocates as a step too far. "Let them serve their time if they're violent offenders," Judge Alm told me. "It's not that easy to get into prison."
Alm predicted that well-organized victims' rights groups would penalize
any legislator who contemplated Kleiman's reentry program.

• • •

The other major alternative to incarceration is policing—above
all, pedestrian stops and Broken Windows policing. New York's prison
population dropped 17 percent between 2000 and 2009, while the number of prisoners in the rest of the country continued to rise. The decrease
in the New York prison population was all the more surprising given
that the average sentence meted out to convicted felons over that period
increased considerably, contrary to the deincarceration platform. The
different trajectories of the New York and national prison counts reflect
the onset, in 1994, of the New York Police Department's practice of
aggressively enforcing quality-of-life laws and stopping and questioning

people engaged in suspicious behavior. Misdemeanor arrests in New York City doubled from 1990 to 2009, while felony arrests (and thus, felony convictions) plummeted, as documented by Michael Jacobson and James Austin in a 2013 study for the Brennan Center for Justice. Even though convicted felons in New York were being sentenced to longer terms, there were far fewer such convicts, so the overall incarcerated population fell. And the reason for that drop in felony crime is that the NYPD was apprehending potential felons for lower-level quality-of-life offenses and getting them off the street before they had the opportunity to commit more serious crimes.

Reasonable-suspicion stops represent an even earlier intervention in potentially serious criminal behavior: questioning someone who looks to be casing a jewelry store in an area plagued by burglaries may prevent a subsequent break-in. And the possibility of getting stopped deters crime in the first place. An NYPD detective who used to work the club scene in midtown Manhattan during the Rudolph Giuliani mayoralty recalls talking to someone who had come into Manhattan from the outer boroughs to party. "We don't carry guns into Manhattan," the club goer said. "I've been stopped three times since I got off the train." But under Mayor Bill de Blasio, according to the detective, "no one is getting stopped and everyone's carrying." Of course, the political opposition to policing, especially to misdemeanor enforcement and pedestrian stops, is even more pointed now than the opposition to incarceration.

●　●　●

No matter how effective the police are at deterring crime, there will always be criminals who should be incarcerated. It is a truism that prisons should be safe, orderly, and conducive to self-reform. But that is easier said than done, or it would have happened long ago. Ideally, all prisoners would work, because there is no better rehab program than the discipline and self-esteem that come from regular labor. The larger the prison, however, the harder it is to get the entire incarcerated population productively engaged, since the logistics of moving large numbers of prisoners from cells to a workplace without a violent incident are complex and labor-intensive. Unions fight prison labor as unfair competition. Prisoner advocates complain if prison work is not paid the minimum wage. Most prisoners, however, if given the choice between earning minimum wage and earning significant time off from their sentence for a flawless work record, will unhesitatingly choose the latter option. High-quality vocational training should also be available for the off hours when prisoners are not working. Such a universal work and training regime would be expensive but may pay off in lower recidivism costs.

In the final analysis, America does not have an incarceration problem; it has a crime problem. And the only answer to that crime problem is to rebuild the family—above all, the black family. The media troll incessantly for an outlier case of a hapless bourgeois who got slammed in prison for a one-shot mistake. In fact, the core criminal-justice population is the black underclass. "Young black males between the ages of 17 and 26 drive the system," says corrections expert Steve Martin. "Family is the solution—and the work ethic. You show me people with intact families and those folks work—their chances of ending up in prison are zero."

The demonization of the police and the criminal-justice system must end. As the Black Lives Matter movement marches forward with no apparent diminution of strength, there are signs that the very legitimacy of law and order is breaking down in urban areas. Resistance to lawful police action is becoming routine. Officers are reluctant to engage, given the nonstop campaign against them. Homicides in the 50 largest U.S. cities—as noted at the beginning of this book—were up by nearly 17 percent in 2015 over the previous year. Liberal elites have successfully kept attention focused exclusively on phantom police and criminal-justice racism while squelching even the most tentative discussion of the crime-breeding chaos of inner-city underclass culture. We are playing with fire.

INDEX